DOING VISUAL ANALYSIS

Sara Miller McCune founded SAGE Publishing in 1965 to support the dissemination of usable knowledge and educate a global community. SAGE publishes more than 1000 journals and over 800 new books each year, spanning a wide range of subject areas. Our growing selection of library products includes archives, data, case studies and video. SAGE remains majority owned by our founder and after her lifetime will become owned by a charitable trust that secures the company's continued independence.

Los Angeles | London | New Delhi | Singapore | Washington DC | Melbourne

PER LEDIN AND DAVID MACHIN

DOING VISUAL ANALYSIS

FROM THEORY TO PRACTICE

Los Angeles | London | New Delhi
Singapore | Washington DC | Melbourne

Los Angeles | London | New Delhi
Singapore | Washington DC | Melbourne

SAGE Publications Ltd
1 Oliver's Yard
55 City Road
London EC1Y 1SP

SAGE Publications Inc.
2455 Teller Road
Thousand Oaks, California 91320

SAGE Publications India Pvt Ltd
B 1/I 1 Mohan Cooperative Industrial Area
Mathura Road
New Delhi 110 044

SAGE Publications Asia-Pacific Pte Ltd
3 Church Street
#10-04 Samsung Hub
Singapore 049483

Editor: Michael Ainsley
Editorial assistant: John Nightingale
Production editor: Imogen Roome
Copyeditor: Neil Dowden
Proofreader: Christine Bitten
Indexer: Silvia Benvenuto
Marketing manager: Lucia Sweet
Cover design: Jennifer Crisp
Typeset by: C&M Digitals (P) Ltd, Chennai, India
Printed in the UK

Library of Congress Control Number: 2017945679

British Library Cataloguing in Publication data

A catalogue record for this book is available from the British
Library

ISBN 978-1-4739-7298-8
ISBN 978-1-4739-7299-5 (pbk)

At SAGE we take sustainability seriously. Most of our products are printed in the UK using FSC papers and boards.
When we print overseas we ensure sustainable papers are used as measured by the PREPS grading system.
We undertake an annual audit to monitor our sustainability.

CONTENTS

1

WHAT IS VISUAL COMMUNICATION?

Introduction

We often hear that society is becoming more visual, that we are becoming dominated by 'the image'. It is certainly true that technology has made it much easier for us to produce and distribute images. It is also the case that the development of consumerism has led to new levels of visual sophistication in the production and dissemination of advertisements, through social media, the Internet and on our mobile devices. If we just compare the technical standard of commercials and promotional material that we find now to that of 30 years ago, the changes are staggering. But in fact this idea of the visual is rather restricted. Those who research the visual have argued that this is problematic (Smith, 2008), that the visual involves so much more than photographs, commercials and film clips. This book agrees with this position offering a very specific kind of tool kit for analysing a much wider range of visual communication. We say more about the book and how it sits alongside others which provide introductions or methods of visual analysis shortly. But first we want to say what we mean by visual communication. What does this book take as the visual? This has huge importance as regards how we approach and carry out visual analysis.

This idea of the increasing impact of images is not as clear as we might think. Images can be pictures, but we also have mirror images, images in our minds and dreams. Even writing on a page presents an image including the kinds of typeface used and the texture of the paper upon which it is printed that may bring certain kinds of associations to the reader. If we look at the two menus in Figure 1.1, they are a kind of image or visual wholes used to communicate. The menu on the left for a gluten-free burger kitchen is printed on a rougher type of paper than that for the fast-food restaurant to the right where everything looks shiny and smooth. The gluten-free menu has no pictures, whereas we see photographs of almost shining burgers in the fast-food case. But why is this so? Why might it be inappropriate for the gluten-free menu to also carry these? Also the two use colour, fonts and spacing in very different ways. Visual communication in this sense comprises objects and things that we experience as wholes, which are part of everyday life activities and which are built up of observable qualities.

At a superficial level a casual observer might say that the gourmet-kitchen menu looks more 'up-market' than the fast-food menu. They may say it looks more 'serious' than the more 'lively' fast food. In this book such menus are the kinds of data for which we provide tools for analysis. Both of these are instances of visual communication that are intended to communicate ideas and values about burgers. In marketing terms one of these must communicate ideas of a consumer experience of something more 'natural', 'unprocessed', perhaps 'authentic', while the other must communicate 'lively', 'quantity', 'immediate'. What we want to show in this book is that these forms of visual communication can be broken down and analysed in details. While the viewer may experience the menu or other forms of visual communication as a whole, as a physical thing, it is at this level of detail that we can begin to understand how they work. We will be highly specific as to how these ideas of 'natural' or 'lively' can be communicated. And the tools that we present that allow us to do so can allow us to

Figure 1.1 A gluten-free burger menu (left) and a fast-food Burger King menu (right)

ask and answer all kinds of research questions. For example, a research project may take an interest in the marketing of 'healthy' food, in other words in how food stuffs that are quite ordinary are dressed up to appear 'natural', 'traditional' or 'honest'.

The materials of visual communication

When analysing visual communication in this book we do not use the notion of 'images' which is fact very vague and not useful for analytical purposes, but the idea of 'semiotic materials'. This has the advantage that it captures the 'stuff' of which all kinds of visual communication is made. Semiotic materials can be photographs, office spaces, commercials or food containers. All these artefacts have materiality, a physical presence and a design that make them into the wholes that we experience, like the menus, or like the room or place where you are sitting. This idea of semiotic materials is fundamental for how we approach such artefacts, such instances of visual communication. It captures how we experience them in everyday life, how we use them, and how we can explore them as researchers. It also helps us to think about how these materials are manufactured and designed in our societies for specific reasons and how they shape what we can do with and through them.

To help us to think about materiality and wholes, we can use the example of a shampoo bottle. This is a semiotic material that we take to be a whole. A shampoo bottle has, of course, a physical shape. If manufactured for a female consumer group, they are often tall, slender and slightly rounded, suggesting elegance and smoothness. The texture may also be very glossy to indicate the results once used to wash the hair. You would not want a jagged and uneven surface. This surface is used to brand the product, using letter forms, colours, an icon that resembles an item of fruit and a small scientific-type diagram. We immediately recognize such a bottle on the shelf in a grocery store and relate to it as being a form of visual communication. We take it to be an artefact that sets up and codes social meanings. In this case the meaning relates to 'elegance', 'natural', 'ingredients', 'smoothness' and of course 'femininity'.

But other shampoo bottles may use shape, texture, colours and fonts to tell us that the product is for men, where we find a matt black finish, a squat-shaped bottle and more angularity in both shape and the use of fonts. These material objects are experienced by people as whole things that are interrelated with ideas about 'naturalness', 'beauty', 'masculinity', 'technology', and so on, as well as simply regarding the nature of personal hygiene. And fundamentally, on another but interrelated level, such objects are part of a longer history of the growth of the commodification, standardization and commercialization of goods in society and the technologies that are used in these processes. These objects are therefore part of wider forms of social meanings, ideas and types of social interaction. A person from 150 years ago would not really understand what they were looking at. They would not really know what kinds of visual communication these bottles were, nor would they grasp the meanings that would come so naturally to us regarding things like nature and gender.

The notion of visual communication we are getting at here is one that encompasses the design of a menu or a bottle that holds shampoo. It is also related to the clothes we wear, children's toys, how we design our office and home spaces, and the way a school building is constructed to suggest things like 'conformity' or 'creativity'. Visual communication is done and shaped through computer software, the look of weapons, the construction of your bicycle, or the meaning given to the configurations of stars in the night sky or the scientific models used to show how it works. And it is not so much that we simply look at this communication. It is a part of our world into which we are infused. It is how we express ourselves and forms the realms through how we can do this as prescribed by the available tools, technologies and shared understandings. This visual world is not just pictures that we look at but is the very world of meanings in which we live. And crucially, for all forms of communication this is not necessarily a consensual world, but one where different interests compete to define how things are and how they look.

Semiotic materials and social behaviour

In Figure 1.2 we find three pictures of IKEA kitchens from IKEA catalogues. A simple observation would be that the former ones, from 1975 and 1985, look 'old fashioned' as compared with 2016. But the word 'fashion' can conceal the way that objects can communicate very specific kinds of ideas. As with the menus and the juice carton we can think about the way that a different fashion in kitchen design involves different social meanings.

If we look at the photographs we see that the kitchen from the 1970s was personalized and by present standards fairly randomly organized. It is a practical place inhabited by an everyday family eating but not interacting. In the 1980s this has changed as all parts of the kitchen have become fixed and integrated as a whole. There is an emphasis on everything being the same kind of shape. Here interior design began to become normalized. In this image we also see a single place set to eat, with a glass of white wine. So unlike the earlier kitchen which was a place to get things done, the 1980s kitchen begins to say something about you as a person. At this point we begin to sense the rise of what came to be named 'lifestyle marketing' where products become more aligned with issues of taste and the ideas people have about themselves.

In the 2016 kitchen we see something different again. Here, on one level, there has been a reduction of order and integration. The units are now designed for flexibility, to be multipurpose. This is part of the marketing approach where it is emphasized that furniture can be moved and adapted to a range of needs. In the catalogues the kitchen is no longer an isolated space but open-plan, linked to other living spaces. We find a shift to more natural materials and textures. And the activities depicted in the kitchens tend to be social or creative. These activities often foreground 'solutions' and point to the way that the kitchen can help manage typical life challenges. Here the design as it is presented not only hints at taste but lays out very clear scripts for how the kitchens meet the needs of contemporary family life, where for example, as in the 2016 kitchen, dad and son enjoy 'quality time'.

What we can see in these examples of kitchen designs are not only changes in fashion but the coding of domestic space with different social meanings. We see how semiotic materials can structure how we behave and interact. The kitchen designs, as a form of visual communication, are semiotic materials shaped into a whole. We can then ask what kinds of ideas about domestic life are communicated? What kinds of identities are valued or devalued? While the 1985 kitchen is ordered, modern, uncluttered and aligned with taste, the contemporary kitchen is rich with organic textures and full of earth-tone colours, yet also incredibly designed. Looking at the image, colours are carefully matched to create a kind of coherence amongst plants, surfaces, object and clothing. These kitchens are sold for people who need solutions, who need to manage their lives better. We might ask why it is so. Why was it simply not important in 1975 to seek out solutions or to think about your selection of kitchens as part of a life-management project? And why has there been a rise in this kind of

Figure 1.2 Kitchens in the IKEA catalogue from 1975 (left), 1985 (middle) and 2016 (right)

coordination of semiotic materials, where the colour and texture of children's clothing may match with that of work surfaces and cooking utensils? As we show in this book semiotic materials tend to have certain social meanings built into them. But how they are used in contexts relates to ideas and values present in a particular time and place.

In Figure 1.3 we see another semiotic material designed as a whole, which also shapes behaviour and social interaction but in a very different way. This is a PowerPoint slide containing a diagram. It is taken from a presentation at a 'leadership' meeting attended by one of the authors. The diagram was used as part of a workshop where management explained how collaboration amongst colleagues and quality on teaching and research could be improved if everyone more carefully described their roles and what they do. Yet the diagram, while on the one hand 'explaining' things, also conceals other things. It uses semiotic materials to carry out a form of symbolism to hide a number of things that in fact make the proposed idea both pointless and also highly problematic.

If we look at the diagram we can see that the three stages presented by the management sit on an arrow that grows in width from left to right and that also moves in an upward direction. From left to right we have 'role clarification', which leads to 'cooperation and coordination', and then to better quality of work and work environment. The diagram does not explain how one stage leads to the next but symbolizes this sequence of causality through the arrow. The slide also carries a

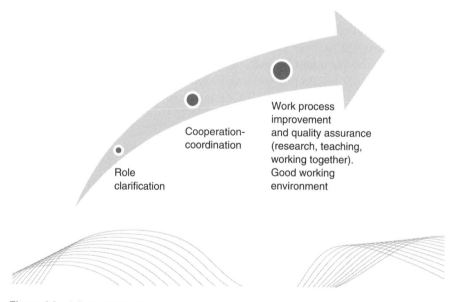

Figure 1.3 A PowerPoint slide from a university meeting on 'leadership'

'wave' at the bottom comprising fine lines (and is part of the graphic profile of the university). This symbolizes a kind of light, easy, constant movement. At no point are these ideas communicated in language, yet this becomes part of how the process is presented.

One present characteristic of public institutions is a growing bureaucratization as part of processes of marketization, where outputs must improve and increase. If you work in such an institution you will be constantly showing how you are doing things better, improving qualities. Management must demonstrate that they are steering work processes in ways that will lead to such improvements, and the PowerPoint slide is part of such a performance management. But researchers have shown that these bureaucratic processes often do nothing to actually change the work environment but rather create extra work and distract from actual institutional priorities (Power, 1999).

In fact there are many concrete and practical obstacles to improving quality at the university. The majority of staff at the university simply have no research time factored into their contracts. Describing their role will not change the quality of research. And there had been problems with heavy teaching loads where many staff had become stressed and overworked. Many staff also work on temporary contracts which does not lead to the kinds of settled work environment that fosters quality. Of course, the solutions to such things are costly and relate to deeper budgetary problems in the institution and factors within the Swedish educational system. But nevertheless management are required to show what they are doing to improve outputs. So these often happen in ways that exist at a bureaucratic level only. The above PowerPoint is one such example. If we all define our roles better at different levels of management then we will all work together better and the quality of everything will improve. The causal process is communicated visually through the arrow that rises, meaning higher quality, and that gets thicker, somehow suggesting 'more'. The wavy lines at the bottom help to communicate that it will be light and easy and part of a 'dynamic' process. Like the menus, shampoo bottles and kitchens the PowerPoint slide deploys semiotic materials to communicate social meanings. And this also communicates about actions and social relations. If you like, the ideas and values of marketization, of quality assurance, are built into the diagram.

This diagram also points to one important way that visual communication has changed. While society may not have necessarily become 'more visual', a new design culture has evolved. We saw this in the details in the burger menus where ideas about the food are communicated by fonts and colour, the 2016 kitchen with its 'rhyming' between different kinds of semiotic materials. And we see it in the PowerPoint diagram. It has been argued that in society we now tend to rely less on writing to communicate (Kress and van Leeuwen, 2001). The menu designs could be thought about as part of such a change. But such a shift means that things like process, causalities and identities may no longer be so much explained as symbolized. The naturalness of the burger is not explained but symbolized through fonts and textures. On the PowerPoint slide, causality is communicated by an arrow and a wavy line. In such a case writing, as in the words 'role clarification', is not linked to 'cooperation and coordination' by language but by a graphic shape. In the new IKEA kitchen design there is much greater use of a variety of semiotic materials to tell us about naturalness, to communicate 'creativity', 'flexibility' and 'solutions'. The way that writing has become more integrated with other semiotic materials has been called the 'New Writing' (van Leeuwen, 2008a). But throughout this book we show in fact that this shift is more of a 'integrated design' of which language is one semiotic material.

To ask and answer research questions

In this book we show how this way of viewing visual communication, as the deployment of semiotic materials to communicate specific social meanings, can provide the basis for posing and answering concrete research questions. Each chapter provides a set of tools for carrying out research on different kinds of visual domains. The examples we have used so far begin to explain what we mean by visual communication and point to what such research questions might look like.

As regards the menus in Figure 1.1, this could relate simply to asking what different kinds of designs are used to sell foods in different ways. The gluten-free menu is interesting as there is now a huge boom in different kinds of 'healthy' foods. Many of these claim to be 'wholefood', have 'natural ingredients', be 'simple' or 'honest'. Such ideas may be communicated directly in language through slogans, such as a fruit juice called 'innocent'. But they will also, and mostly, be communicated through packaging designs, through semiotic materials such as shape, colour and texture.

As regards the kitchens in Figure 1.2, a research question could relate to how space is represented and organized and what ideas and values this communicates about how we should behave and what kinds of social interactions can take place there. For example, the local library where one of the authors lives has been redesigned. Whereas it used to have rigid rows of book shelves and a row of reading tables at the side with hard upright chairs, shelves are now different shapes and sit at different angles, created by flexible interlocking units. They are arranged in a more 'creative' way, more integrated into relaxation areas and play-reading areas. One reading corner with comfortable chairs gives the impression of sitting in a nineteenth-century book room. There is a café where there is great fresh coffee and cakes. Overall the meaning of the library space has changed. The meaning of reading here has shifted from something austere, silent and individual to something more engaging, related to comfort, pleasure and fun. The layout itself suggests 'exploration' and 'discovery'. A research question could relate to the changing designs of specific kinds of public spaces and what kinds of social meanings these communicate. The aim in the case of the library would be to show what kinds of ideas about literacy are communicated by the design. Here we will need tools that allow us to describe and analyse the semiotic materials that are used in designed space.

The PowerPoint diagram in Figure 1.3 could form part of the data for a research question that asked how work processes in a particular organization are represented. The study might make a collection of all documents used to represent increasing quality of work in that organization and then ask what semiotic resources are used to accomplish this. From this the analysis might show, as we indicated above, what kinds of processes, causalities, things and persons are included and that are either absent or that are symbolized. Such analysis could have the practical consequence of pointing simply to why such a management plan was failing.

We have also begun to hint at some of the things we would need to analyse in order to answer these kinds of research questions. In the case of the menus it was things like typeface, borders and texture. In the kitchens, which could be applied to our library example, it was about partitions, making the room more or less closed and open, and about the way that this positions people and gives different possibilities for interaction. In the diagram, graphic features such as arrows and wavy lines become important. We need to understand visual communication, therefore, as regards the semiotic materials that are used to carry social meanings.

In each chapter of this book we explain in depth what kinds of tools we need to carry out systematic analysis of semiotic materials such as film clips, packaging, photographs and interior spaces. In each case we show how semiotic materials have social meanings built into them. To some extent semiotic materials may always be used in fresh and creative ways. But to a larger extent they are deployed in ways that have become historically established and that are routinely employed for specific purposes. In this sense when each of us encounters an instance of visual communication, such as food packaging, the design of a room, a graphic representation of data, we know what it is doing, what kind of typical, what we call 'canonical', use it is. And this too, as we show, is an important part of visual communication.

What we have begun to suggest in this introduction is that it may be possible to look more closely at specific instances of visual communication to ask *what* exactly is being communicated and also *how* it is communicated. Or, to put it another way, what kinds of semiotic materials have been harnessed by a designer, or team of designers, to do a particular job, to communicate a specific message? Of course visual designs should be to some extent functional. A menu must serve the function of allowing a customer to choose what they want to eat. A kitchen must be designed so that you can cook in it. A carton of orange juice must be designed to transport and store its contents and later allow them to be consumed. But in each case the functionality is achieved through design choices. And it is the idea of visual communication as being about design choices done for specific ends that is the basis of this book. This allows us to construct research projects that ask questions about which choices are used for which end.

Guides to doing visual analysis: what is unique and special about this book?

A number of commentators have pointed to a growing popularity in the analysis of visual communication (Pauwels, 2012; Rose, 2012). This has taken place across a wide range of academic disciplines. This can be seen by the growth of academic journals that deal with the visual more broadly such *Visual Communication, Journal of Visual Culture* and *Visual Communication Quarterly,* and those that deal with the visual in specific fields such as *Journal of Visual Communication in Medicine, Journal of Visual Literacy* and *Visual Art Practice.* All of these journals provide a wealth of material that can form a valuable resource for visual research projects that have a specific focus.

For those looking for an introduction to doing research on visual communication a number of handbooks and introductory texts have also appeared, each offering a unique and important contribution. One of the first of these was van Leeuwen and Jewitt's (2001) *Handbook of Visual Communication,* which brought together a number of scholars from different fields to show how they would deal with the visual. More recent have been Spencer's (2010) *Visual Research Methods in the Social Sciences,* Rose's (2012) highly successful *Visual Methodologies,* which offers a range of visual methods from the humanities, including semiotics, art history and discourse analysis, and Margolis and Pauwels's (2011) *Handbook of Visual Research Methods,* which brings together systematic approaches to analysis from the social sciences. There is also Machin's (2015) *Visual Communication,* which presents a collection of unique methodological approaches to visual analysis where researchers each illustrate these using data.

There have also been textbooks that are more field specific such as Reavey's (2011) *Visual Methods in Psychology* which presents the diverse ways of dealing with visual data in psychology.

Doing Visual Analysis is different from each of these for a number of important reasons. It became clear that there was a need for a textbook that dealt with the visual in a way that was designed for carrying out detailed empirical analysis of the visual for the purpose of answering research questions. The above volumes do their own unique jobs very well. But *Doing Visual Analysis*, as we have indicated in this introduction, is designed to provide students and more advanced visual researchers with a practical tool kit that allows them to analyse many different kinds of visual communication.

Doing Visual Analysis is inspired specifically by several books dealing with visual communication that are influenced by linguistics, semiotics and also by Marxist theories. The most important of these is Kress and van Leeuwen's (1996) classic *Reading Images: The grammar of visual design*, along with other excellent books by these authors such as *Multimodal Discourse* (2001), *Introducing Social Semiotics* (2005) and *Multimodality* (2010). One core idea in these books, which was the great innovation of *Reading Images*, was to demonstrate that we could develop a more systematic way to break down and analyse visual communication. Much analyses of the visual until this time had tended to be more interpretive or theory driven. There was great potential in the idea that we could break images down into components and show how they work. This would be even better if such an approach could be to some extent predictive. In other words if it could provide tool kits for making meaning in different visual domains.

The work of Kress and van Leeuwen was also highly influenced by critical linguistics. Here the aim had been to show how closer analysis of language use could reveal less obvious ways that particular kinds of political or other motivated and self-interested views were being communicated (Fairclough, 1992). So the idea was that it is also possible to carry out a close analysis of visual communication to show how it can carry ideologies. An example may be the way we talked about the kitchen designs above communicating certain views about the family and domestic life. These combined influences allowed the authors to present a set of models and notions that indicated that a more systemic approach could contribute to existing ways of dealing with the visual. This new approach offered something that was more predictive and something that could help us to understand more about the strategic ways that visual communication was used.

The work of Kress and van Leeuwen has inspired what can almost be thought of as an academic field in its own right, called 'multimodality', which has attracted mainly linguists. This field has been characterized by a number of different kinds of sub-threads. The linguistic model that greatly influenced Kress and van Leeuwen was that of Halliday (1978) called Systemic Functional Linguistics. This model had what can be thought of as two parts. One, the systemic part, was to show how language functions as a set of systems of choices. The second, the functional part, was about how language is used to do things and what parts of language are used to accomplish this. In the field of multimodality some work can be characterized more by the systemic part of the model. In, for example, Bauldry and Thibault (2006) the aim is to show how Halliday's model for language can be used to look at all forms of communication. Other work, and this is where we place *Doing Visual Analysis*, is characterized more by the desire to look at what communication is used to accomplish. In our view it is this approach that best serves the task of answering concrete research questions. In fact the more systemic approach has been criticized for being more of a process of imposing concepts onto the visual than actually showing how it works (Ledin and Machin, 2017d) and that in the end it runs the risk of treating all forms of visual communication as being of the same order, subsumed under its own concepts and terms. This process can suffer from producing lots of descriptive tools but fall short on showing how these reveal what added insights are produced (Reynolds, 2012). The labelling of phenomena, as Antaki et al. (2003) point out, is not the same as actually doing analysis and showing what the pay-off of that analysis actually is.

Doing Visual Analysis comes out as part of the need for a visual communication introductory book that is more oriented to answering research questions as well as providing a predictive type of tool kit. In this book we provide tools for carrying out research in different visual domains. We present our own model for thinking about how visual communication works, which is designed in the first place for understanding how the visual is used to accomplish things. This is a book designed for students and researchers who want to carry out research projects where they ask concrete research questions.

Outline of the chapters

Doing Visual Analysis is different from many methods books in that we present the chapters in terms of how to analyse specific domains of visual communication rather than by using each chapter to present a different method. The domains we have chosen overlap to some degree. But these have been selected as they are those domains students and researchers often want very much to research but are less sure what model to use. Many other areas could have been included such as art, computer games or graphics software. But we felt that our choices reflect more closely areas where there is a lack of clear analytical guidance. And the chapters we have chosen offer many possibilities to be combined to adapt to a range of forms of multimedia visual communication.

2 Approaches to visual communication

This chapter accounts for the social semiotic approach that the book is based on, also comparing it to other approaches to visual communication. We depart from what we call semiotic materials as a whole when researching visual communication, be it photographs, commercials, packaging or space design. Ways we think and act are largely dependent on such materials shaped as wholes, and they have evolved historically in social contexts by the use of technologies available to certain social groups. This also means that they have affordances that makes them apt for some but not other uses.

3 Photographs

This chapter provides our first tool kit for a semiotic material, which here is the photograph. The chapter begins by looking at the importance of considering different 'canons of use' of the photograph and exemplifies photojournalism, photograph as art and symbolic images. This helps us first to address what is being done with a photograph, what is its communicative purpose. The tool kit then follows with analytical categories for settings, participants, objects, actions, colour and the position of the viewer. Throughout the chapter we show what 'doing' analysis looks like, but at the end we relate this to specific possible research questions.

4 Document design

In this chapter we look at document designs. We give examples of three different types of document design that are related to different specific social practices. These are movie posters, mobile-phone screen interfaces and magazines. This allows us to show what kinds of tools are needed for such an analysis and also to show that we need to always understand visual communication as regards specific communicative aims and purposes. The tool kit then follows and accounts for the semiotic resources of typography, line spacing and alignment, colour and borders, and possible research questions round off the chapter.

5 Packaging

Here we are interested in the packaging of commercial goods. We begin by looking at some of the ways that packaging communicates different discourses, ideas and values. We show how packaging is related to ideas of gendering, innocence and value for money. The tool kit comprises categories for looking at materials, textures, shape, colour, writing and typography, and iconography. Throughout the chapter it is clear what doing this kind of analysis involves, but in the final section we explain how such tools can be used for concrete research questions.

6 Space design

Here we are interested in space as a form of visual communication. Space shapes and controls the positioning of bodies and communicates how and why we should behave in certain ways. This involves providing ideas and values about what should take place in that space, which we show relates to wider ideas in a society at any time. We use the examples of classrooms, restaurants and office design to draw out such social meanings and regulations. The tool kit focuses on partitions, interactional affordances, materials and texture, and colour and the chapter ends with research questions.

7 Film clips

Many students want to analyse the kinds of short promotional films and commercials which we now commonly find on the internet and social media. These short film clips tend to have a smaller number of narrative structures, or genres, that communicate different ideas, values and identities. We focus on the genres of entertaining narrative, projection narrative and recount. The tool kit comprises categories for analysing narrative genres and states, scenes, settings, characters, rhythm and sound in scenes, and language and evaluations and research questions round off the chapter.

8 Data presentation

Here we are interested in the way that data is visually communicated, which has been made much easier by cheaply available software. But while on one level such data appears to make things easier to understand or at least more visually interesting, it can also shape and transform the reality it claims to represent. In this chapter we look at different types of data presentation, which include lists and bullet points, tables, line graphs and bar charts, and flow charts. The tool kit comprises the resources of paradigms, spatialization, vertical and horizontal orientation, graphic shapes and icons, temporality and causality and research questions follow.

9 Conclusion

Here we discuss how to combine chapters or use them in different combinations for the needs of answering different research questions.

2

APPROACHES TO VISUAL COMMUNICATION

Introduction

This chapter explains the social semiotic approach upon which this book is based. *Doing Visual Analysis* provides tools for breaking down different kinds of visual communication into parts. This is done in order to allow us to show 1) *how* they create social meaning and 2) *what* social meanings they create. Each chapter shows how this can be done for different kinds of visual communication in order to carry out systematic analysis that is required to answer concrete research questions. In this chapter we explain what such a form of analysis involves, what concepts we use overall and what is our view of visual communication.

In the first part of the chapter we place *Doing Visual Analysis* as part of, and in relation to, a number of traditions of communications analysis. From these we draw concepts and characterizations regarding the nature of visual communication and its motivated nature. In the second part of the chapter we provide our own framework that provides the basis of the tool kits provided in the chapters that follow. Overall, we show that analysing visual communication involves grasping how humans come to give meaning to things in the world in ways that are shaped by dominant ideas and through fairly well-trodden forms.

Social semiotics

Our account of visual communication as the use of semiotic materials to achieve a particular end is inspired by one particular model or theory of communication called social semiotics. You may have come across the term 'semiotics' in regard to theorists such as Barthes (1977) who looked at things like the symbolism in advertisements. So, for example, a packet of dry pasta may carry images of fresh tomatoes and a small illustration of an Italian rural-type village. For Barthes what is interesting is the associations that such images and sketches can carry. In this case they allow a dry pasta to communicate that it is related to a form of 'traditional Italianness'.

Social semiotics is also interested in the meanings that can be carried by elements in visual communication. But whereas this Barthesian form of semiotics attends more to the meaning of individual elements, social semiotics is interested in making inventories of the kinds of things available for making meaning which are called *semiotic resources*. It asks what are the available choices of such resources and what kinds of meanings can these be used to produce. This offers the possibility of producing an account of communication that is much more detailed and systematic. It also helps to clarify the process of showing and understanding how specific semiotic resources create meaning.

A more detailed and descriptive approach would mean that we consider all the design details that comprise any form of visual communication. In the case of Barthes's pasta packaging a social semiotic approach would carefully describe the qualities of the fonts, colours, uses of borders, texture of the packaging, and so on. For example, it would ask whether the font was curved, angular, narrow or wide. This is important since in each case such design choices can communicate quite specific ideas. To communicate that a food product was more filling we may want to use a heavier rather than lighter font. The lighter font might be better for a 'diet' low-carb pasta. The same level of detailed description analysis would take place for all other design choices since they all play a role in telling us about the kind of food product we are getting. In the case of the two menus in Figure 1.1, such choices in fonts, colour, composition and texture were used to communicate very different meanings about very similar products. One was healthy and natural, the other lively and filling. A social semiotic approach would want to understand what choices are available to a designer and what these are able to communicate. This could be applied to a pasta packaging or a menu or an office design, an advertisement or the interface on your mobile phone.

Social semiotics, while used to analyse all kinds of communication, such as photographs, spaces, sounds and textures, is inspired by a theory of language called Systemic Functional Linguistics (SFL) pioneered by Halliday (1978). This was an approach to language based not on trying to describe grammar as a rigid system, which is how it has often been studied, but by looking at its social use in accomplishing different communicate needs. This social semiotic approach saw language as a system of choices, or alternatives, which can be used in contexts by speakers depending on what they want to achieve (Halliday and Hasan, 1989). Language here is thought of as a system of interrelated choices which users tap into.

According to this model of language, when we want to describe a person, thing, place or idea, we have a range of options we can use depending on social context. For example, if we describe a person there are choices relating to size and shape, but also to things like religion and ethnicity. Such words, in one sense, do not really 'describe' that person in any neutral sense but allow us to use culturally evolved terms to 'evoke' things about them from a particular point of view.

These different choices in language are loaded with particular meanings, or *meaning potentials*, which can be brought out in particular instances of use. The idea of meaning potential here points to the way that meanings are not so much fixed as activated in use in specific contexts. For example, we can consider the following hypothetical news headline: 'Youths arrested for attack on local family homes'. Here the choice to use the word 'youths' over 'young people' allows the newspaper to create a simple and more dramatic story. The word 'youths', unlike 'young people', has more negative associations. We find the same as regards the choice 'local family homes'. It could have read 'properties'. But the use of 'family homes' suggests something safe, respectable and in contrast to the unlawfulness of the youth. In fact a closer look at the contexts where the events described in the headline took place could reveal an area of social depravation and marginalization. But choices here have been made that background such complexity and frame the events in a way that is meaningful for the reader as a typical news story. Clearly the words 'youth' and 'family' could be used in many other ways but have the *meaning potential* to be used in a way to create these particular meanings. These notions of choice and of meaning potential are a fundamental part of the way we view visual communication in this book.

Returning to our pasta packaging we can also think about the way that different qualities of fonts, colour or textures represent choices on behalf of the designer. Like the writer of the headline above the designer makes choices from different semiotic resources to achieve a specific communicative aim. This may involve choosing the meaning potentials of thicker typefaces or of rich saturated colours to tell the shopper this is a filling foodstuff aligned with the emotional vibrancy of Italy. On the two menus in Figure 1.1 designers have chosen different semiotic resources to communicate different things about burgers in each case.

Important in this social semiotic approach is that language is *functional* (cf. Halliday and Hasan, 1989: Chapter 2). Language and its grammatical forms and rules have evolved through the requirement to fulfil very specific functions for humans in specific settings and circumstances. Language emerged through the need to make meaning of our world and experiences. But since social relations have been such a central part of human societies it has also developed through the need to manage these relations. Halliday (1978) argued that language therefore has three functions, or necessarily accomplishes three tasks.

He called these 'metafunctions' and applied them to linguistic clauses. First, language allows us to communicate ideas about the world, such as the word 'youth' being able to communicate an idea about unruly and problematic young people. This is called the *ideational metafunction*. Second, language allows us to say what kind of relationship we have to the ideas we communicate about so that people know where we stand. This is called the *interpersonal metafunction*. This can relate to how certain we sound about something or whether we are inviting someone to do a thing or commanding them. Third, language allows these things to be assembled into a coherent clause structure, so ideas and attitudes can be communicated as understandable language. This is called the *textual metafunction*.

These metafunctions have been applied not only to language but to all forms of communication (Kress and van Leeuwen, 1996; Bauldry and Thibault, 2006). In this view we can think about things like photographs, fonts or colour as semiotic systems that can fulfil these metafunctions, albeit with more or less different choices attached to them (cf. Machin, 2007: Chapter 8; Ledin and Machin, 2017d). For example, a photograph of a scruffy teenager can represent the idea of 'unruly youth'. A close-up shot of the teenager could create a greater interpersonal connection with them, which in this case may amplify revulsion. The photograph itself may be placed on a page where it has coherence with the text and other graphic elements due to the way a colour has been taken from the image to use for the fonts and box shadows as part of the design.

While these three metafunctions are important for understanding a social semiotic approach to language, they are, however, not so useful for analysing visual communication. While we give an example for the photograph above, such a process is not really so much analysis, but rather labelling things as 'ideational' or 'interpersonal'. And it has been commented that using these concepts for visual analysis is little use for carrying out empirical research (Bateman, 2013). It is absolutely crucial for our purposes to use the notion of choices and meaning potentials, but in a way that grasps how different forms of visual communication, what we call *semiotic materials*, simply are used to accomplish very different kinds of communicate acts. This possibility for uses is to some extent built in these materials. This is what we look at in our next section. We show how semiotic resources must be thought of as regards the way they comprise semiotic materials, which are the actual things we experience in the world.

Semiotic materials and affordances

We have so far been looking at language and visual communication as regards choices in semiotic resources. So in language and design we know what choices are available to accomplish different communicative aims, whether it is to show that a burger is 'natural' or that some young people in a deprived area should be thought of as vile criminals. But social semiotics is also interested in the choice of the form of communication that we call *semiotic materials*.

In the cases of Barthes's pasta the material used is food packaging. This is a form of communication that has evolved to do specific things as processes of commodification, standardization and consumerism have progressed since the end of the nineteenth century. While people like us, who were born when such processes have become well established, know what is intended by this instance of communication, a person from the early nineteenth century transported to the present would not.

For the pasta we could ask why use packaging and not a book, a song or a monument? On one level this may seem a very odd thing to say, or at least 'obvious' to point out. Of course food packaging is the logical semiotic material used to sell pasta in a supermarket. These other kinds of materials have evolved to do very different kinds of things. But when we start to investigate concrete examples of the way that we use visual communication to represent, understand and relate to the world and the people in it, this becomes an important part of description and analysis. This is because semiotic materials themselves also come loaded with ideas and assumptions, what we call *affordances*, and shape communication and social behaviour.

Our approach to affordances is greatly influenced by the linguist Voloshinov (1973) who stressed that communication has a material basis. This would mean a material like language, food packaging, menus or monuments. It is through such semiotic materials that we interact with, experience and understand the world. Semiotic materials should not be seen, therefore, as something only physical, but also as designed for making meaning. When we use and experience semiotic materials such as language or food packaging this is as whole forms that have qualities and features that facilitate and shape certain types of communication. They have affordances that make them apt for some uses but not for others.

Semiotic materials also shape social organization and social interactions. We can illustrate this if we think about how different materials fulfil different communicative aims, for example as regards how we might represent a female acquaintance to others. If we wanted someone who had not previously met her to later recognize her it might serve our needs better to make a drawing or take a photograph of her rather than try to describe her to them in language. Another kind of aim, such as to express our feelings of loss since she moved away and broke our heart, may be better met by composing a song about her. If we wanted to communicate that she was a national hero since she discovered a drug that changed the face of the world, we may build a monument. In this case a rough sketch may be less appropriate. But if we wanted to conceal something about her, such as ethnicity, or her body piercing, we may want to use language rather than a photograph, where such information can simply be omitted. In each of these cases the material has different affordances, established over time. Such communication is necessarily part of social processes and often conflicts, where competing interests might well condition the meaning-making. And social ideas and values are very much related to these semiotic materials which give them a material reality (cf. Hodge and Kress, 1988).

Facebook is certainly an example of a semiotic material designed as a whole that affords certain types of communication (cf. Bezemer and Kress, 2016: Chapter 6). Specifically, it is designed as a page, which codes the contextual configuration, the bonds within which communication can unfold. The top section states who is the owner of the page and contains a photograph. There is a left column that specifies more about the page owner and that displays photos of friends, and a right column with adverts. The middle section is designed for posts ordered in reverse chronology, which points to a culture where 'the latest' is valued. Here a communicative infrastructure is set up enabling some, but not other, types of social interaction, where, for example, boxes for posts and comments are prefabricated, as is the button 'like', affording an immediate and positive response to posts and making comparisons possible in the sense of 'most likes wins'. So a basic affordance of Facebook is that we can interact with many friends. The design affords a personal and multimodal communication, so that photos and videos might well carry the messages. It is not built for long texts, so writers of novels or essays have little use for the platform and it does not allow longer forms of explanations or accounts of things. The author of a book could use Facebook to publish a picture from the book in order to market it, but not offer the actual book.

The kind of social relations Facebook fosters are praised by some. For example, a person with disabilities who seldom gets out of her apartment can keep in contact with friends and acquaintances. Others have seen Facebook as typical of an exhibitionistic culture where self-branding is everything (Miller and Shepherd, 2004; Thurlow, 2013). It presents 'everything about me' with lots of likes and positive comments and with a particular usage of images. We meet people's more intimate lifestyle issues, where they went, what they are eating, cuddling their dog, training, on holiday, and all this drawing on current trends. There is constant ranking and evaluation and a constant flow of adverts. This, it has been argued, undermines rational argumentation, also because fake news can be spread and wreak havoc, which was an issue debated during US President Trump's election campaign. And, of course, another criticism concerns the way that huge global corporations use such platforms to gather data which can then be used for more tailored forms of advertising, marketing and even to provide us with more personalized news.

The notion of affordance was coined by the psychologist Gibson (1979) as part of his theory about how animals and humans relate to and make use of their environment. This is hugely important for thinking about the 'stuff' we use to produce visual communication and how it can be meaningful to a viewer. Gibson's idea is that the environment contains possibilities to enhance and help support different actions. An easy way to picture what he means here is if we picture a blind man with a stick. This is an object that affords a new perception of the environment and can guide his walking. This is one way we can think about all ways that we are part of the environment.

Gibson discusses different substances, including the human use of water, which does not, contrary to some animals, afford breathing. But it affords drinking, which is a prerequisite for human life, and also washing and bathing. Furthermore it gives optical information since it fluctuates by rippling, which can be gentle or more dramatic. As regards surfaces and spaces, Gibson notes that a horizontal and stable surface has important affordances. It gives an equilibrium that helps us to maintain balance and posture in relation to gravity (ibid.: 131). If we are to use an object as a ladder to climb to another surface, this stability is certainly helpful. In other words the environment becomes meaningful to us and its qualities carry certain associations.

Gibson also notes that people manipulate and transform the environment. For example, an 'elongated elastic object, such as a fiber, thread, thong, or rope, affords knotting, binding, lashing, knitting, and weaving. These are kinds of behaviour where manipulation leads to manufacture' (ibid.: p. 133). So humans take what is at hand and manufacture objects, which gives new possibilities to understand and act in the world. So we end up with things like monuments, menus and Facebook, which draw on existing affordances, which have then been manufactured to create new meanings. This idea is very useful for thinking about semiotic ones shaped as wholes and used for the purposes of visual communication.

This approach is 'anthropological' in the sense that it is about the study of humans who make meaning in societies. The basic argument here is that human thinking and possibilities for action are largely dependent on semiotic materials and their affordances and that such materials are deployed in the interest of certain individuals or groups. Facebook is, for example, shaped to gather data that afford advertising to exact consumer groups.

The anthropologist Geertz talks, in a similar fashion, about 'significant symbols', which are 'words for the most part but also gestures, drawings, musical sounds, mechanical devices like clocks – anything, in fact, that is disengaged from its mere actuality and used to impose meaning upon experience. From the point of view of any particular individual, such symbols are largely given' (1973: 45). And this idea of largely given means that such semiotic materials become simply the natural way to get things done.

A simple example of affordances in a social semiotic perspective would be that writing affords setting up a meeting with someone the following day (cf. Kress, 2010). You could draw a picture, although if they were not expecting you to invite them they may not fully understand. On the other hand, writing might be less efficient if you want to explain exactly where to meet, especially if it is a place your friend has not visited. Here drawing a map (or emailing a screen shot from or link to Google Maps) affords us to be precise about the place. If you were cycling along the road and wanted someone to get out of the way, neither writing nor pictures would afford the fast communication needed. Here sound is suitable, such as shouting or using a horn. We can also think of the example of the monuments where large permanent objects placed in city squares are felt more appropriate for communicating a sense of commemoration than pictures, for example – although pictures, in the form of photographs, can be more compelling as evidence, since they are credited with being factual.

While Halliday's three metafunctions may be helpful to characterize language they are not so helpful if we want to understand why food packaging is used as a semiotic material and why we perceive semiotic materials as wholes (cf. Berge, 2012, for a similar discussion of SFL). It does not help us to understand why a particular type of photograph was used on a document; for example, whether it is used to document an event or to symbolize a set of values such as 'fun' and 'freedom'. Each use of materials must be understood as a kind of 'canon of use'.

There is one final point to make about this social semiotic approach as regards the nature of choice. Simply this is not something unlimited and unrestricted. Choices are related to what has become established for doing different kinds of communicative acts. This is also regulated in any society by those who have the power and interest to do so. Because of these two factors, making a choice that is not part of, or usually included in, a certain domain or context will likely be found to be odd or provoking.

To give an example: a designer is asked to create a commemoration for soldiers from a war. The designer is told to give a sense of a gentle, yet solid, heroism. To begin with a particular kind of semiotic material has become established for such communicative acts in the form of the monument. So the designer would not be expected to suggest a food package or a style of kitchen. They would lose the commission immediately. We then come to the semiotic resources that will comprise the monument. As regards the kind of substance to be used for the monuments in most European societies this has become established as stone or bronze. These suggest timelessness, durability, 'forged by hand'. In this case were the designer to suggest yellow plastic, which of course would be highly durable and almost indestructible, those commissioning it would not be happy. Plastic has associations of cheapness and lightness. Heroes need something that looks heavy, since lightness here could have associations of trivialness, impermanence, and so on. Also the colour yellow is associated with brighter energetic moods. This would not be appropriate where in most European societies death and respect are considered to be more measured types of emotions and therefore requiring a more muted use of colour.

The designer might go further and suggest that the plastic statue should be hollow so that you can see through it. It should be filled with holes of different sizes so that it looks almost skeletal. Again here the choice is wrong. Statues of heroes should appear solid to point to certainty. In fact those statues that are hollow or transparent tend to suggest some kind of vulnerability. One example is the Oscar Wilde monument in central London, seen in Figure 2.1. If we look

Figure 2.1   Oscar Wilde monument in London (Photograph by author)

at the form of this monument it is clear it would not be suitable to represent a heroic soldier. The fact that we can see through the monument, see into the inner parts, that its form is not solid, not heavy, gives a sense of uncertainty, of inward contemplation, of fragility. For a genius and somewhat tragic poet and writer this may work. But we can imagine the outrage if the same design was used to commemorate soldiers who fought in Afghanistan, for example (Abousnnouga and Machin, 2013).

Social semiotics therefore is a form of analysis that emphasizes the idea of choices that come with associations built up over time. It sees these as functional in that they have evolved due to the needs of humans to communicate specific things in specific settings using certain materials and technologies. The analysis it carries out involves identifying the affordances of different semiotic materials and making inventories of the semiotic resources that lie in their design. The aim is to show, then, what exactly is communicated, what are the kinds of social meanings. In the sections that follow we go on to think about important shifting patterns in the nature of visual communication and show how we can connect social semiotics to a very clear idea of power and social relations.

Multimodality

Multimodality is a term that often has been used in place of social semiotics and that emerged from the mid-1990s. The term itself must be understood as coming from linguistics to emphasize that meaning is created in texts not only by language but also visually. This was no surprise to scholars from other fields such as media and cultural studies or film. But this work had something important to offer not only to linguists but to the wider field of visual analysis. While not using the notion of multimodality, Hodge and Kress (1988) pioneered a social semiotic approach to visual communication. Here the material basis of communication was stressed and objects such as family photos, comics and art were analysed in their social contexts to point to how they shape experience and action as part of different ideologies. Then a few years later Kress and van Leeuwen (1996) published what has been the main inspiration for the whole new field of multimodality, *Reading Images*. This book suggested that Halliday's metafunctions, devised for language, may apply to visual communication generally. It also pioneered the idea of looking for choices and making inventories for instances of visual communications. The kinds of analysis we have been suggesting so far in this book are very much inspired by this work, as well as by Hodge and Kress (1988).

Multimodality has developed over the past few decades into a field of its own, with a number of sub-fields (cf. Jewitt et al., 2016). One problem with some of the work done, however, from a research project point of view, is that it can tend to appear rather relentless in its drive to apply concepts from the study of language. The aim, rather than to investigate uses of the visual, has been to model visual communication somewhat in the fashion that linguists model grammar in language. So such analysis tends to seek to show how instances of communication can be described through Hallidayan terminology. And it seeks to create maps of choices linked to each metafunction in order to construct a 'visual grammar' just as they might do with the grammar of language. One result of this is that the qualities and affordances of different semiotic materials become lost, where all semiotics resources are described as departing from the same metafunctions and using the same concepts. There is a risk of a 'tunnel vision', of seeing all research matters through one single theory of language and missing robust forms of analysis in other academic fields (Forceville, 2010; Machin, 2013).

Kress and van Leeuwen (2001) went on to give more insights into visual communication which are of central importance to what we do in this book. They argued that communication in our societies has not so much become more image-based but that it has become more multimodal. What this means simply is that roles formerly occupied by language are now taken by other kinds of semiotic materials. A simple example is that there was formerly a very clear division as regards what images communicated and what language communicated. If you look at school books from the 1970s you will find an illustrative picture at the top and the explanation in the text below. In a contemporary textbook, in contrast, we would find bullet lists and short chunks of text integrated with diagrams, images and illustrations all performing interlocking roles. Or it could be completely digital with links to click on to view videos and connect to different multimodal exercises. To give another example an energy bill may have formerly used language and numbers to explain that you need to pay. A more contemporary bill may use gentler rounder fonts and soft colours to communicate softer moods, so the bill appears less of a threatening document.

One major change, resulting from these changes in how these modes are used over the past 20 years, has been that documents have become both highly *functional* and also more *affective*. By this we mean that semiotic materials are used both to communicate more precisely for a purpose (function) but also to communicate wider ideas and moods that are used to engage us in different ways (affect). As we explain more about our own model in this book we show that this simple observation is one important key to understanding all kinds of contemporary visual communication, of which even language itself has become much more integrated.

Kress and van Leeuwen (2001) argue that more elaborated uses of semiotic materials have become much easier as software has appeared making it an everyday possibility. However, we also argue that it is important that people felt that it was desirable or required to carry out more sophisticated designs both for functional and affective reasons. This takes us to our next point where we suggest that such cultural changes can be understood in part using Fairclough's (1992) term 'technologization' of discourse. This term can be used to capture what we can think of as the creeping codification of all semiotic discourses for purposes of more systematic control over communication.

Fairclough (1992) wrote that he was seeing a shift in the use and control of language. What he saw was an increase in the 'level of conscious intervention to control and shape language practices in accordance with economic, political and institutional objectives' (Fairclough and Wodak, 1997: 260). An example of this could be the way that politicians talk has become more managed and is often 'engineered' by professional writers who have tested different versions out on focus groups. Marketing language also goes through more stages of careful management and testing. At a call centre language is carefully scripted for specific purposes. The work of teachers becomes 'technologized' where quality becomes codified into increasingly detailed categories of learning objectives and outcomes created by management and policymakers (Hopmann, 2008; Ledin and Machin, 2016b). And we argue that in visual communication too we find increasing attention to the codification of semiotic resources and materials.

For Fairclough these processes of increased codification and technologization were related to other process of 'commodification' or 'marketization' that were taking place in society at the time. Here parts of social life not formerly concerned with producing goods become 'organized in terms of production, distribution and consumption' (1992: 207). So in terms of language and visual communication it became more important to target specific consumer groups. But it also meant that parts of life like schools must act in the fashion of a company, increasing and improving products and outputs in forms that could be codified and measured. And such organizations must compete with other schools to demonstrate excellence.

This idea of technologization is highly useful for the approach to visual communication we take in all of the chapters in this book. Across areas like interior design, web-page layout, product packaging, and so on, we show that we are looking at an increased codification of semiotic resources and materials, used in interlocking ways. Technologization, at least during the last decades, is clearly linked to the drive for marketization, the need to sell products and to carry out promotional activities. And in turn it has transformed our relationship to visual communication and our expectations. If we look at magazine or newspaper designs from the 1980s they appear dull and old-fashioned. But what we are actually seeing are forms of visual communication that were pre-technologization, and before viewers had the expectation of the levels of codification that allow much more control over visually addressing very specific markets that we find today. This also means that semiotic materials are reshaped and that new semiotic forms appear. A global social media platform like Facebook simply did not exist 30 years ago, and very few people could then have imagined contemporary social media. In all of the chapters in this book we look at examples of these kinds of new semiotic forms.

Discourse and social practice

One strand of multimodality called multimodal critical discourse analysis (MCDA) has pointed to the need to think more about the social part of communication. This draws attention to how choices are deployed in actual contexts such as menus, monuments and school designs, with the primary aim of identifying the underlying ideas, values and identities that are communicated. MCDA has used a number of other concepts that allow it to describe the relationship between the use of semiotic materials and the ideas and values that they communicate (Machin, 2013). These concepts come from critical discourse analysis (CDA).

In the late 1970s a number of critical linguists drawing on the work of Halliday (1978) and on the Marxist linguist Voloshinov (1973) began to look at language as a system of choices that were both ideologically loaded and that were always used to promote specific interests through the use of semiotic materials (Fowler, 1990; Fowler et al., 1979; Hodge and Kress, 1979). Here the term 'ideology' means the ideas and value systems held by particular groups in society. The kind of analysis done by these critical linguists might, for example, involve looking at the language found in school books or in a newspaper. Such analysis would reveal the use of certain kinds of loaded words, certain kinds of persons and actions being either foregrounded or absent. The way we looked at the newspaper headline regarding youth attacking family homes resembles this kind of critical approach. The point in such a case would be to reveal what was missing, such as the impoverished social context, and to ask why this should serve particular ideological interests. In this case problems in society become the responsibility of individuals and not of society as a whole, distracting from the way crime is connected to social inequalities.

Later in the 1980s and 1990s this approach was developed by scholars such as Fairclough (1989, 1995) and Van Dijk (1985). Here a way of doing analysis called critical discourse analysis emerged. Details of language were analysed to draw out what were called, using a concept from Foucault (1977), 'discourses'.

Discourses here are accepted understandings of how things work. For example, in many societies we have a discourse of national identity. In this discourse people are proud of their belonging to a nation that has existed for eternity. There will be a national anthem, myths and national symbolism that help to make it real. This discourse is present when footballers talk about their proud nation or when we are taught history in schools (Billig, 1995). Yet historians and sociologists show that nations were a quite recent invention. Even the oldest nations were only established a few hundred years ago and were only more widely experienced as such by regular people after the propaganda of the First World War. Yet many of us share a discourse that there is such a thing as timeless national identity. In fact in critical discourse analysis, through the analysis of newspapers and political speeches, it has been shown that national discourse has often been used to legitimize things such as why we must go to war (Graham et al., 2004), to discriminate against migrant populations (Krzyżanowski and Wodak, 2008) and to conceal social inequalities (Abousnnouga and Machin, 2013). In other words such discourses serve very specific power interests.

In CDA language is therefore about power and can be seen as a site of social struggle – a struggle for the definition of reality (Richardson, 2006). Language is not simply a transparent vehicle for communication but constructs social reality. It is not that ideologies ever come to dominate completely. We can also be critical of them, but those who generally are able to hold sway over how we commonly talk about things are said, using a concept from Gramsci (1971), to have 'hegemony'. In such cases we will find, for example, that the main institutions such as journalism and schools will tend to take the hegemonic ideas and values for granted.

Two concepts from CDA are important for us: *discourse* and *social practice*. For CDA these two things are entirely interrelated. How we represent the world in language is related to social practices. So language about national identity, about who is foreign or an immigrant, is related to how people act and the kinds of institutional processes and rules that we set up. Discourses are not only ideas about the world, but become the basis for what we do, how we plan and organize. It can be noted that CDA as a field of research today has become institutionalized as critical discourse studies (CDS). (Wodak and Meyer, 2016, for example, give an overview of methods in CDS.)

Other scholars work in a sub-field of multimodality called multimodal critical discourse analysis (MCDA) (Machin and Mayr, 2012; Machin, 2013). Here it is argued that these concepts of discourse and social practice are highly useful for looking at visual choices in communication. Not only language but other semiotic materials can carry discourses. A packet of pasta can communicate discourses as can a menu or a kitchen. Menus can, for example, through use of semiotic choices communicate discourses about what is 'healthy' as regards food. This may never be clearly articulated, and is in fact a highly complex and contested matter and deeply related to and colonized by food marketing. But the use of colours, textures and styles of font help to point to the personal and unprocessed which we associate with healthy food. As we suggested in the introduction to this book, the design of a kitchen can also communicate discourses about the meaning of domestic space. Each relates to social practices of shopping, eating and how we behave in such spaces.

MCDA can be thought of as a social semiotics which is aligned with the project of revealing discourses, the kinds of social practices that they involve and the ideologies that they serve. The idea of choices in semiotic resources must be thought about as far as this is related to ideology. Semiotic materials must be considered as regards how canons of use themselves have become established in social and political contexts in order to serve specific interests. As a whole visual communication is also part of social practices and how we live.

New writing and integrated design

It may seem odd to use a notion such as 'new writing' in a book about visual communication. But as we have already indicated so far in this chapter, writing and visual communication have become much more interrelated and now take on communicative roles formerly accomplished by the other. What we mean here by new writing is the way that language and visuals now often operate in highly integrated ways (van Leeuwen, 2008a; Ledin and Machin, 2016b). Understanding this process is also key to grasping the nature of what we call *integrated design*, through which we intend to capture the way that there have been fundamental changes in the nature of all visual communication. We will be looking at this throughout the chapters in the book, on documents, the use of images, interior design and data presentation, and so on.

Van Leeuwen (2008a) argues that while communication in documents, books, brochures and other media has become more multimodal, as we described in the previous section, it has also involved a fundamental shift in the use of language including the demise of the use of running text, what he refers to as *new writing*. New writing is therefore related to the way that to some extent language becomes much more a part of visual communication. But it is also related to how language and visuals come to operate as coherent wholes. And throughout the chapters in this book we will be emphasizing this new type of multimodal communication. It is one where visual materials and language are increasingly codified and used in interrelated ways.

We can see new writing in contemporary documents and media design which are highly visually stimulating as compared to those of 30 years ago. For example, an internal management document in a company may have formerly used mainly written text. But now we find bulleted lists, flow charts, images and graphics (Ledin and Machin, 2015a). A plan of work may be represented in a bulleted list, while a flow chart is used to represent the relationships between different jobs and the overall output. We see a photograph of a small group of business people chatting and smiling. We find the same kinds of changes in school textbooks or lifestyle magazines where rather than larger dense sections of written texts and single images we find information communicated across more interrelated configurations of different components. Such visual engagement is now created not only in such documents but in all kinds of visual communication.

This integration of text, images and graphic elements has led to a shift in how basic things like causalities and categorizations are communicated. Full running text, as we are using at the moment, is very good for showing clear causalities, for showing who does what, for explaining the relationships between groups. But chunks of text like bullet points or language integrated into flow charts does not do this. The overall coherence no longer comes from what linguists call 'cohesion', for example by 'conjunction' that codes the relations between sentences and ideas with devices such as 'because', 'on the other hand', 'consequently' or 'thus'. Nor does the new writing rely on an overall structure and reading order where different sections are placed after each other. Instead the overall coherence comes from a visual design where different semiotic materials are deployed such as alignment, spacing, colour coordination, iconographic representations and graphic shapes. The reading order does not have to be top-down and left-right but might well be bottom-up or centre-outwards.

What happens through this new writing, what we now want to call *integrated design*, is that things like cohesion, causalities and coherence can now be communicated by symbolism. For example, as we see in Figure 2.2, arrows might connect similar boxes. The things contained by the boxes are classified as the same in this instance since they are the same shape and size and they use the same colour for fonts. There are acronyms, a feature typical of new writing, with short explanations in parentheses, for example ILOs (Intended Learning Outcomes), ATs (Assessment Tasks) and LAs (Learning Activities). Such acronyms are typical of what we have previously discussed regarding technologization, where we are given the impression of coding of the parts of process, so that they can be dealt with and managed in such technical and systematic ways. We see that the four boxes to the right are classified as slightly different to the box to the left since they are also placed within a box created by a dotted line which seems to suggest some kind of more permeable kind of boundary.

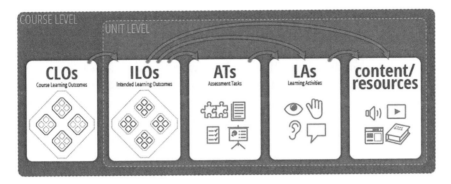

Figure 2.2 A diagram explaining the teaching ideology 'constructive alignment'

Importantly these things are put in boxes with rounded edges (where the rounded edges might suggest something that fit un-problematically into social practices whereas angular edges would suggest something more definitive and closed) and connected by unevenly distributed rounded arrows. We also see that in each box four icons are used that symbolize different activities such as 'looking' and 'listening', or the jigsaw pieces suggest putting ideas together. What such icons mean is not always made clear, but it communicates simplicity, breaking things down into basic components. And each has four icons as if all such things comprised the same number of basic elements.

The diagram in Figure 2.2 represents a globally used model for teaching called 'constructive alignment'. This is a general method for teaching in schools and university regardless of the subject. It is very much a part of the technologization of education in society driven by the ideology of marketization. This method is supposed to guarantee that every pupil achieves both the course learning outcomes (on the 'course level') and the intended learning outcomes (on the 'unit level'). This is done through matching specific assessment tasks and learning activities, all of which are coded and broken down into components. The term 'constructive alignment' stresses that objectives and assessment should be aligned.

Many teachers who have to use these kinds of plans find them awkward and believe they misrepresent the processes of teaching and learning by trying to codify and categorize everything. Research shows that such processes are counter to actual learning theories (Hopmann, 2008). And teachers say that such a model can stifle creative and critical thinking as all things are prescribed and planned out. What this tells us is that this integrated design here carries a particular discourse about teaching and learning, that it can be coded, measured and carefully regulated to ensure better outcomes. And this can be understood as part of an ideology of marketization.

What interests us here specifically is that the design appears to be systematic and draw out the core principles. It makes a proposed model look easy and logical. Yet how things are alike or different and how causalities take place are only communicated at a symbolic level. If we look closer many things are in fact not clear. Why is the box containing resources to the right when the directionality of causality in the diagram suggests left to right? We might assume that all of these processes depend on available resources in which case it should be placed to the left. It is hard to understand what kinds of processes the arrows actually mean. And certainly it is not clear what the items in the boxes represent.

This integrated design has its advantages. We find livelier, more engaging forms of documents. The diagram in Figure 2.2 could be used in place of a long descriptive document. Viewers now expect whole new levels of visual appeal and interest. But we must ask what it means if causalities are now more often represented through arrows and not specified, if things like order and precision are communicated as much symbolically as through clear explanation. We now see these changes in the pages and designs we look at each day, even weather and sports reports, news on election results and events in conflict and disaster zones (which we look at in Chapter 8). From the point of view of doing visual analysis, research projects can ask what kinds of ideas, values and identities are therefore communicated and what elements, processes and causalities are hidden. In the case of the diagram, critics of the system point out that it hides all kinds of different challenges in teaching and learning such as regarding socio-economic differences in school catchment areas and ethnicity of children (Hopmann, 2008).

We can, in the spirit of new writing, condense these observations into five features:

1. *It is visually designed.* This design is what creates the overall coherence, which comes through the use of graphics, colour, icons, form, alignment and so on to shape a structured whole. The parts of a document, of a web page, food packaging, a café become an integrated whole.

2. *It intertwines semiotic resources.* The idea of multimodality is about combining semiotic resources. So we might combine lists, graphics, numbers, spacing and writing. But the integrated design, avoiding running texts, takes this a step further. Tables might be coloured and designed to request information interactively, enforcing a certain reading. 3D representations might well be used to show parts of the process. In an organic café, the textures of the tables, the look of the menus and the plates will be designed to intertwine. But how these parts interrelate is not communicated in running text.

3. *It is highly symbolic.* Hodge and Kress (1988) made a distinction between transparent and opaque texts, where running text would be an example of the former. It has been argued that visually we were shifting from an era of documentation to one of symbolization (Machin, 2004). This can be realized in different semiotic materials, through graphics, like arrows and iconic-shaped bullet points. And here language too is used symbolically. Words like 'concept', 'innovation', 'communication' and 'growth' appear as buzz words, but also as symbolic components of design.

4. *It is decontextualized.* This can be thought of at two levels. First it relies on sets of interrelated documents rather than self-standing texts. An institutional document will tend not to be stand-alone but will constantly cross-reference other documents, often through symbolism or through words that are used in a symbolic fashion. It may contain bullet points that signal concepts and processes that are on other documents, where they are only represented symbolically. But a restaurant or gym might use old premises where signs of former labour are used to suggest something 'traditional' or 'authentic'.

5. *It is digital.* Much of what we now see in communication has risen partly due to software. Affordances are built in to different software such as PowerPoint, Excel, InDesign, Photoshop (Djonov and van Leeuwen, 2014). This means that these come pre-loaded with templates that favour certain kinds of representations. When we look at institutional documents, web pages, football sports reports or news graphics these are all produced easily from the templates and choices provided within the software. A graphic representation of data has been produced through software which offers a range of possibilities. Of course, as with language and other semiotic materials, a system of choices is never completely neutral. It favours certain kinds of ways of representation and suppresses others.

Materiality and consciousness: A model of communication

We have now presented most of the concepts and ideas that we use in this book. In this last section we show how all this fits together using a model of communication by the semiotician Hjelmslev (1961). This is especially useful as it is a model that encourages us to see instances of visual communication, like a school room, a commercial or a menu, not as something separate from us in the world but as based on a materiality that is interrelated with our consciousness. It is simply part of how we perceive the world. This is also a model that explains why meaning-making in visual communication is both flexible yet at the very same time regulated and loaded with ideology.

Hjelmslev was interested in relationships between materiality in the world and human consciousness of that world. This relationship is based on what he called 'complex signs'. To explain this we begin with a hypothetical person who is the first ever human to just appear alive on earth. At this point the environment is not meaningful to this person. The environment has no affordances, since no interactions have yet taken place with it. For this person, the world is simply therefore a meaningless amorphous mass. The consciousness, that is the thinking of this person, too is unordered and amorphous, since, unlike us, they do not have the accumulated repertoire of meanings that we use to think about the world. Put simply, the way the environment becomes meaningful is the same as the way we are conscious of it.

Hjelmslev was interested in the way that we build complex signs to understand the world – complex signs would be things like Facebook or a menu for healthy burgers. To understand what he means, we first look at simple signs, which comprise the relationship between a signifier (expression) and signified (content). A particular sound, say the horn of a car, is a signifier with the signified being the presence of the vehicle. The horn is the expression and the vehicle the content. The colour orange can be an expression for warmth. This conception of the sign draws on the classic work of Saussure (1974), considered as one of the founding fathers of linguistics and semiotics (cf. Hodge and Kress, 1988: Chapter 2). Saussure argued that signs have two faces: a signifier and a signified. In the case of language the signifier would be a sound (of a word, for example *horse*) and the signified our mental image of the sound (here of this animal). Saussure's conception of the sign was psychological, it was something occurring in our brains. He also viewed signs as arbitrary. An actual horse has no relation to the English sound *horse* or the equivalents *pferd* and *cheval* in German and French.

Hjelmslev has a more social than psychological view of the sign, which very much fits with the model we have in mind for visual communication. He suggests that the sign is more complex than this and that 'expression' (signifiers) and 'content' (signifieds) are coded on several levels (cf. Eco, 1979: Chapter 2). This helps to introduce the social aspect and get away from the idea that signs are arbitrary. As we have been arguing throughout this chapter, signs, or semiotic materials and resources, carry very specific kinds of ideas and values that relate to social practices.

For Hjelmslev the complex sign comprises on the one hand expression that relies on materiality, or on things in the environment, either that exist there naturally, or that humans have fashioned from it, and on the other hand content that relies on consciousness. Here the sign has a role in giving order and meaning to our environment (which would remain an amorphous mass without it). We must understand the sign as regards how the content shapes our consciousness about the environment. Put simply, it is from materiality and consciousness that meaning-making arises. The sign is at the same time the stuff of consciousness itself and the form of the world as we perceive it.

Hjelmslev's view also leads us to see the sign as fundamentally motivated, not arbitrary. This is akin to Kress's idea of the motivated sign where 'signs are made – not used – by a sign-maker who brings meaning into an apt conjunction with a form, a selection/choice shaped by the sign-maker's interest' (2010: 62). From such a perspective, signs become part of social processes and conflicts. They become part of the marketing that tries to tell us that their food is healthy, that a war is about heroes and protecting the nation, that a model of teaching can make everyone achieve better grades.

Besides materiality and consciousness Hjelmslev argues that we must think about the sign comprising what he calls 'substance' and 'form' for both expression and content. We represent this as a diagram in Figure 2.3 to show his three coding levels for the complex sign (cf. Eco, 1979: Chapter 2; Taverniers, 2011). At first glance the diagram looks complex. But it contains a few very basic and simple ideas. It shows in the first place how the complex sign (a monument, Facebook, teaching model) can be viewed as the connection between human consciousness and the material world. Then it lays out the basic way that the sign works. We must remember that everything in the table is mutually dependent, something we perceive as a whole. Consciousness and materiality, the substance and form of expression and content all interact and come together as a complex sign. But showing the 'parts' in this way helps us to grasp how it works.

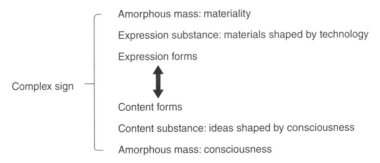

Figure 2.3 A model of communication based on Hjelmslev (1961), showing how the complex sign is determined by the coding levels amorphous mass, substance and form

If we look at the middle coding level, that of 'substances', this captures the possibilities of making signs from substances from the environment. Such substances exist since materiality and consciousness here have been shaped or moulded and become part of culture. Substance at the level of expression presupposes that some kind of technology is involved to make material distinctions. In spoken language the substance would mean the sounds that we use, the phonology, as grammarians call it, and these are formed by using our larynx together with our mouth and tongue. In writing we have produced the alphabet which is a technology for coding sounds. Colour is another substance. At the highest coding level, that of the amorphous mass, colour is a continuous spectrum and part of the electromagnetic spectrum of the universe. Here what is visible light for humans comprises a very limited range of wavelengths. For making meaning, this visible spectrum must somehow be divided into parts and become a substance, which involves what we can call technology. This can be achieved in many ways. Naming colours in language imposes categories, and different languages have very different numbers of colour words and do this slightly differently. Or a diagram can be used to divide the visible spectrum and show what colours 'exist' in a certain culture.

In the case of graphic design, a prime example would be the way that Microsoft Word provides the substance for expression where it provides ready-made geometric and graphic forms to use, when we build a diagram or flow chart. In Figure 2.4 we see a screen shot from part of the drop-down menu for 'shapes' where all sorts of graphic devices are sorted into groups. These therefore become an expression substance which are easy to use. Just as we divide colour up in language for particular purposes to make it possible to talk about colour, so this software provides pre-set choices to create diagrams or flow charts and to represent things like teaching and learning.

Turning to content substance we here mean the ideas and discourses that structure our thinking. These too can be thought of as substance. And these are always in relation to the material world. These can be the ideas and discourses associated with words like 'youth' and 'families' we saw in the case of the news headline earlier. They can be associated with colours and graphic elements or with monuments. They can be the different meanings that have emerged for the use of the photograph, whether it documents, symbolizes or is art. Thus, our model predicts that 'canons of use', or what Miller calls 'genres', will emerge and both restrict and facilitate communication. Substance and form on different levels will be 'fused' and become part of how we experience and act in the world in actual contexts (1984: 160).

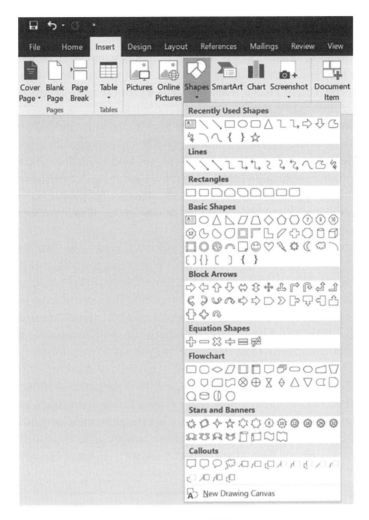

Figure 2.4   The menu Shapes from Microsoft Word 2013

Creating analytical tool kits

In our following chapters on different semiotic materials we begin by looking at canons of use, which capture the typical work that semiotic materials, as complex signs, carry out in our visual culture. This could be photographs, documents, food packages, study and work spaces, promotional films. Each of these uses are tied to a certain expression substance, to certain technologies that have evolved for communication. And they are linked to social practices and infused with ideas, identities, values and purposes – in the terms of our model they draw on a certain content substance. In other words, uses of semiotic materials are ideological and have affordances that have evolved in specific socio-political moments that came to shape them. Yet, of course, such uses tend to appear more or less natural and neutral to members of a society.

So materiality and consciousness have been shaped or moulded and become what we know as our everyday culture, expressed in and through visual communication. Such canons of use structure how things tend to get done and what kinds of materials we choose to do so. So here we are interested in questions like what kinds of photographs do we use to do specific things, what kinds of documents do we use in different settings? What are the canons of use of food packaging and of interior design?

This first step of analysis is important since it allows us to then present tools that capture exact forms of expression and content that form the material whole. In each chapter we present inventories of those forms of expression and content used in different domains of visual communication. Here in each case how we can analyse the semiotic resources that have been deployed to form the material whole in order to answer concrete research questions. So we present tools for analysing how photographs represent the world, people and events, for how typefaces, colours and other elements are used in different kinds of documents, how shapes and materials are deployed in food packaging, how promotional films set up and organize sequences of scenes, how space shapes social interactions and informs about the meanings of the activities that are to take place there, and how data and quantitative information are presented to shape how we understand them. The aim is to allow a systematic form of analysis that allows us to make concrete observations about the kinds of ideas, values and identities that are communicated.

3

THE PHOTOGRAPH

Introduction

The aim of carrying out research on photographs, in social semiotic terms, is to find out what ideas, values and identities they represent, and therefore ultimately how they represent the world and for what purpose. We present a tool kit for describing and analysing the contents of photographs in order to answer such research questions. We show how we can best analyse things like the settings, people, objects, activities and perspectives employed. Such tools allow us to reveal how the world is being shaped for us in any particular image or set of images.

We also take account of the kind of photograph and the canons of use we are dealing with. In other words we need to understand a little of the history and traditions of how images are used in specific contexts and also what discourses, ideas and values they are usually used to communicate in such cases. As with all forms of visual communication we deal with in this book each individual instance of a photograph must be understood as part of established and accepted patterns of uses of semiotic materials, which, as we have explained in Chapter 2, have affordances. All semiotic materials and their canons of use are ideological in their nature and have evolved to accomplish things that serve particular social interests. A clear affordance of the photograph is that it can capture scenes and people in great detail, as if we had direct access to reality (Barthes, 1977). It produces an all-seeing spectator yet removes the means of its production, which, Tagg (1984) argues, makes photographs ideologically potent.

The photograph and its uses

The photograph accomplishes a range of communicative tasks. These have been established over time as canons of use that we easily recognize. And each, visual theorists have argued, represents a particular way we have come to look at the world which is very much driven by ideology and power. Here we give examples of three types of photographs: photojournalism, photograph as art and the symbolic image. The aim is to point to how these must be thought of as canons of use, which tend to be characterized by more or less typical patterns of semiotic features.

Photojournalism

In Figure 3.1 we see a photograph in a Swedish newspaper. We may not be able to read the text, but our experience tells us that the photograph plays a very specific role here. We see a smallish group of soldiers and assume it documents a specific event involving these soldiers. The story here is in fact about the

Figure 3.1 A photograph of soldiers on the front page of the Swedish newspaper *Dagens Nyheter*

presence of the Swedish army on the Swedish island of Gotland and whether this is now a necessity given the present foreign policy of Russia. Here we would assume that the photograph shows us a scene where soldiers are either arriving at or departing for Gotland, since we see a boat and water in the background. The history and traditions of photojournalism have built up a sense here of the role of the photograph as bearing witness, and being a reliable document, or recording, of reality.

The photograph, in this case, carries what has been called a 'burden of truth' (Newton, 2000). The photograph appears to provide an unmediated view of a scene as it happened, as if we had been there. But for authors like Barthes (1977) this is the trick of the photograph. It seems to provide a window on the world by concealing how and why it has been made. A photograph is not simply a neutrally recorded moment. Each photograph is a result of a number of decisions as regards things like angle, proximity, exposure, cropping, later editing and then the editorial decision to choose this particular image over another. But all this tends to be invisible to the viewer due to the compelling nature of having a visual document in front of our eyes (Goldman and Beeker, 1985).

In the image we see only a small number of soldiers. Visually, therefore, we are not given a sense of a massive military occupation, but rather 'keeping guard' or 'assembling'. There may in fact have been more soldiers than were depicted. In Sweden issues of military activity are contentious and at the time there was some concern as to what message this would send to Russia. But what is of relevance here is that all photographs involve such choices. Images in the press of a 'humanitarian intervention' by the UN in a particular country may show only a handful of soldiers to help to soften the idea of it being an invasion (Bouvier, 2014).

Huxford (2004) argues that since the conventions of photography go unnoticed by the viewer they will tend not to see how their understanding of a moment is being shaped. An image that appears uneven can suggest frank and immediate reporting where in fact there is none. A close shot can create a sense of intimacy or threat where this is none. The point here is that we may therefore mistake proximity with association and an uneven, candid shot with frank and immediate reporting. An accused person may come across as evil simply because the picture of them frowning has been chosen over one with a neutral expression. We may find an image of a politician where they happened to scratch their head, also cropped to make them appear not only confused but alone and isolated. One of the authors interviewed the designer of *Dagens Nyheter* who said the kind of photograph in Figure 3.1 was used as part of the overall page design. There had been a recent redesign that emphasized space. New fonts had been used along with a new look oriented also to reading on mobile devices. Photographs were to appear more engaging in an era where older authoritative style newspapers were on the wane. Formerly photographs may have shown such a scene side-on and sought to represent the scene more literally (Machin and Polzer, 2015). At the time of writing a number of researchers were taking an interest in such changes in new photographs (Caple and Knox, 2015, 2017).

While such photographs therefore, to some extent shape a moment for us, canons of use also bring other kinds of demands, relating what they should contain. Photographs are, of course, snapshots of events. They are, as Sontag (2004) puts it, 'reality interrupted'. But they are used in news media and for information purposes precisely as they do appear to capture or represent more complex events. The danger here, Sontag (1973) argues, is that the tradition of news photography has encouraged us to think about the world in terms of memorable moments rather than more complex ongoing processes. For example, a news photograph of a child in a famine will tell us little about the many decades of complex political and colonial processes that lead to a breakdown of the social order and mass population movements. The role of the researcher here, therefore, is to understand the semiotic choices being made and also how these shape the way actual events are represented for us. What kinds of ideas, values and processes are being foregrounded or backgrounded, for example?

Another crucial criticism of news photographs is that they tend to be a key part of meeting what media studies scholars call 'news frames' and 'news values'. As regards news values, scholars have shown that news tends to be produced around a very specific set of criteria. It tends to involve those defined as the elite such as politicians, celebrities, and so on. It tends to rely on official sources, so stories must come from those in authority positions such as the police, a leading doctor, and so on, meaning that news is a very official view of the world (Fishman, 1980). Other values are that news should be 'dramatic' and also that it needs to be 'simple'. In other words we will tend to see photographs that resonate with the beliefs already held by the viewer.

News frames are basic themes that have become established within news culture. They signal to a journalist that an event is newsworthy and how this event should be covered, who the key actors are and how they should be treated. It is thought within journalism that such frames are necessary for the public to recognize an event as news. These frames, therefore, are routinely used to structure how events are represented. For example, a complex war, involving more than two parties and also very specific interests from global powers in how subsequent oil deals will be organized, will tend to be presented visually as a 'people's uprising'. Images will focus on the 'human toll' of the conflict where we see children or women suffering. We will see images of 'militia' or 'rebels'.

Yet, as a number of scholars point out, this may provide very little sense of the actual, complex, ambiguous and shifting nature of the conflict (Bouvier, 2014). As researchers we must also understand these representations as part of pre-existing processes of how certain kinds of events tend to get represented. These are part of the history and traditions of the news photograph and the discourses they tend to carry.

Photography as art

A different use of the photograph is for artistic purposes. Here we do not mean those kinds of photographs used to create glamour or taste in advertising but the kind we find in galleries, magazines and news supplements. As with news photographs, these tend to have certain markers, certain kinds of semiotic choices, and also must be understood as a certain kind of canon.

A photo exhibition may show striking black-and-white images of a particularly harrowing context. In Figure 3.2 we see a photograph by Tom Stoddart, whose images are widely celebrated for their artistic merit. We see a girl in Sarajevo during the terrible civil conflict in the 1990s. Stoddart has photographed a range of wars and other disasters and his collections tour international galleries. While

Figure 3.2 Tom Stoddart photograph titled 'Bosnia, Sarajevo, Girl (4–5) standing near US soldiers in street' (Getty Images)

his images deal with topics that are newsworthy, they tend not to appear in newspapers. These beautiful and moving images are not so much intended to document, but, as the photographer himself said, to help to provide insights into everyday lives. Such images, he said, need to have around eight things to give them visual interest. In Figure 3.2 we have the compositional form provided by the two soldiers, the juxtaposition of the girl wearing her comfortable shoes, the bullet holes in the wall behind her, which gives a level of depth, the cropping of the soldiers' heads, and the battered, dirty, window.

Again here in Figure 3.2 we see the use of typical devices to make the images resonate with the viewer. We find the child. In Western cultures children are associated with innocence and purity and are often used in images of conflict, upheaval and disasters (a dirty-faced child in a war zone, a child's toy seen floating in a pool of water after flooding). Here we peer down at the girl which emphasizes her vulnerability. She appears to wear shoes suitable for indoors and a brightly patterned pair of shorts. Yet behind her, which may be her home, we see the marks of war in the bullet holes and chipped concrete.

But what is also of high importance here is that the photographs in Figure 3.1 and 3.2 indicate different kinds of looking. We look at them in different ways. In part this is found in the semiotic choices within the image, which we can describe and analyse. But it is also found at the level of canons of use and the discourses these are used to carry. Lutz and Collins (1993), for example, were interested in the kinds of images found in *National Geographic* magazine. They argued that these images reveal a highly romanticized view of cultures around the world. The images in these photographs relate to ideas of innocence and they represent fundamental human values about universal values such as motherhood, the family, the wisdom of older people and the purity of childhood. All these are based on highly Western cultural assumptions yet are used to frame the entire world.

The point here is that the meaning of an image is never present in the object itself. This does not mean the image itself cannot be analysed, but this should be done in the context of these wider discourses. The photographs found in galleries, in up-market newspaper supplements or the travel magazines for elite holidays must to some extent fulfil the semiotic requirements of the higher-status gaze. And such conventions can be drawn on by advertisers and in marketing to communicate certain kinds of discourses such as an intelligent way of viewing the world or greater authenticity to a product. And images taken for documentary purposes can be reused as art. For example, the black-and-white wall print of an Italian village found across the wall of a coffee shop in Los Angeles connotes something classical and tasteful.

The symbolic image

In Figure 3.3 we find a photograph that has a very different use. Such photographs have become highly ubiquitous from the beginning of the twenty-first century. This image sits on a website called Earth911 and is a kind of commercial hub where advertisers can place environmentally friendly products and services. This can be everyday domestic ecological products or services whereby companies are able to use consultants for environment-related matters of recycling or carbon offsetting. The website states: 'We've created a community that helps consumers find their own shade of green, match their values to their purchase behaviors.' To some extent the website can be understood as part of broader trends whereby environmental issues become intertwined with and colonized by consumer behaviour and marketing. We save the environment not through major international political law-making but by buying a set of products that claim some kind of eco-friendliness. This is clear not least in the case of packaging as we will see in Chapter 5.

The photograph here shows children in a classroom all smiling. The teacher stands at the back of the room and the girl at the front holds a recycling bin. This is not the same kind of use of the photograph in the case of the newspaper. This is clearly a staged photograph purchased from a commercial image archive. This is not a real classroom but a space that has been designed with a few props to connote 'classroom' – an old-fashioned blackboard and the

Figure 3.3   The website Earth911 with photograph on recycling

children sit in rows as in a typical schoolroom. Looking through international image banks, as we have, it is striking that these kinds of stock images focus on pupils sitting in rows facing a board of some kind, smiling or looking amused, often with raised hands. Once again we see how traditions historically take shape: this is simply how 'classroom' is signified in contemporary visual culture, as is also clear from the dynamic classroom filled with light that we see in Figure 6.3 in the chapter on space design.

The photograph feels optimistic partly because of the bright and soft light. The space is uncluttered by everyday objects and the colours are muted and coordinated apart from the saturated red and blue. The smiling suggests that recycling is a feel-good activity, and the image resembles the genre of an advertising image, although here it is not used in a traditional advertising role. What it shares with the advertising photograph is that it is idealized and is intended to symbolize a set of ideas and moods. Advertising photographs simplify and beautify the world as part of the process of loading a set of ideas and values onto products – see Chapter 7 on film clips for more examples of this kind of rhetoric. This website uses these kinds of images to help give a sense of recycling and green issues being 'feel-good', 'simple' and more easily aligned with consumer behaviour. What would be avoided are images of the more unpleasant, complex, expensive and time-consuming experiences of recycling that many people encounter; for example where bags of stinking tin cans, bottles and packaging have to be stored for the fortnightly collection, whether we are really prepared to scrub greasy pizza boxes to make them recyclable, and so on. We might argue that in this case these kinds of images serve to place saving the environment at the level of personal choice and consumer behaviour rather than something instituted on a large scale by governments. And what these images seek to do is brand products and services and certainly not in the first place to bring about solutions to actual environmental problems.

Such photographs can be purchased from commercial image archives such as Getty Images which has a collection of many millions of images and film stock. These images are created precisely to be used in this symbolic way. Professional photographers are guided by the companies as to what kinds of images sell best. The archives can be searched with key words such as 'women and confidence' which may throw up thousands of photographs of attractive women talking on mobile phones, striking confident poses or shown instructing men in an office setting. Such archives are driven by the need to understand what kinds of images are required at any time. In the case of recycling a search of the word 'recycling' throws up many images like we see in Figure 3.3, where children and their innocence symbolize recycling.

Analysing photographs

What we have shown so far is that researching photographs requires that we also place them within canons of use. While we can analyse the semiotic contents of an image, this alone will not help us to understand how they are communicating. It will not help us to understand how canons of use and semiotic materials are in a sense already ideological. In this section we present tool kits, drawing on Barthes (1977), Kress and van Leeuwen (1996) and Machin (2007). We use these to help us to describe and investigate more accurately what we see in photographs as regards the different ways that people, places, objects and actions are represented, how we are positioned as viewers and how semiotic resources such as colour and lightning are used. We begin with some basic concepts typically used in semiotics.

Denotation and connotation

Barthes (1977) provided a set of observations which provide some basic tools for the kinds of questions we can ask of a photograph. These are useful for thinking about what meanings are created for viewers by the kinds of things they see. For example, what meaning does the children create for us in Figures 3.2 and 3.3? What Barthes emphasized was the great importance in the act of description when carrying out any such analysis. We tend to be less used to describing the visual and have learned rather to give our first impressions of what we see, using adjectives. So a photograph might be described as 'tragic', 'beautiful' or 'striking'. But such terms have little use if you want to describe systemically. Barthes used the concepts of denotation and connotation and was influenced by Hjelmslev's (1961) idea of a connotative semiotics, where signs refer to each other and meaning, and therefore associations, occur on different levels. We will follow Barthes when accounting for denotation and connotation.

Denotation

This is Barthes's first level of analysis, where the analyst must ask what an image depicts. This is, in Barthes's terms, the denotation, the persons, places and things we see. In fact this act of description is less easy than it sounds. But getting used to the tools for description that we present in the following sections will help us to go on to produce more detailed and informed interpretations. Looking at the immediate level of denotation, in Figure 3.2 we find a black-and-white photograph of a girl standing behind two soldiers. She is wearing slippers and looks perhaps confused. There are bullet holes in the wall, and it is sunny. Figure 3.3 denotes three smiling children and a teacher in a room where there is a blackboard and a recycling box. And it denotes a scene saturated in soft high key light, where there are muted colours and two brighter saturated colours.

So here we are not interpreting these photographs. When we ask what a photograph denotes we are asking who and/or what is depicted. We are identifying the form of expression used, the meaning potentials chosen, for this particular instance of communication. In the following sections of this chapter what we present are a series of tools that can be used to greatly expand what we can describe in photographs.

As our Hjelmslev-inspired model of communication in Chapter 2 makes clear, semiotic materials never simply denote something. They are always loaded with ideas and values and shaped by technology for certain interest. They are in short ideological. Because of this, it can be a challenge for us to simply describe what we see. For example, the presence of a child in a news photograph is a choice laden with ideology. And the objects in the classroom in Figure 3.3 carry ideas and values about education and can in this sense never be simply described. But for Barthes (1977) carrying out this step of analysis is important. And the tools we provide here help to systematize the process.

Connotation

Once we have carried out the process of description, once we have identified some of the meaning potentials that have been deployed we can ask what they mean. Here we are interested in the ideas, values and wider discourses communicated. This means both as regards individual elements and as regards the wider meanings created by the combination of the semiotic resources. The children seen in Figure 3.3 may signify 'innocence' as does the child in Figure 3.2. But they are combined with other very different elements and features that allow them to communicate different kinds of ideas. Here we have in mind the term 'discourse' used by Foucault (1977) to describe the taken for granted models of the world that tend to be shared, or dominate, in a society to explain how things work. For example, we have already discussed the discourse where we see disasters such as famines as a humanitarian matter, signalled by images of vulnerable children, rather than political and economic matters. Such a discourse, we could argue, is deeply ideological and reflects the interests of the powerful.

In Figure 3.3 we could ask therefore what discourses about saving the environment are communicated by these clean, smiling children in this old-fashioned classroom. We say more about this throughout the chapter as we show how to describe the different features of the photograph. Barthes listed a number of key carriers of connotation that provide a highly useful starting point. Three of these are objects, colour and settings that we now look at in turn. We then turn to the matter of the people depicted in the photographs and what they do.

Objects

In Figure 3.3 we find a number of objects used to signify a kind of archetypal classroom, even though in such staged images the setting will be a photographer's studio. We see a blackboard – an object not now often found in classrooms – with numbers chalked in columns. And the blackboard is positioned oddly at the back of the classroom with the children facing away from it. At the bottom-right we see what appears to be several books in a shelving unit. Then we have the recycling bin. But there are a lack of other objects that we might usually find in an everyday classroom. There are no personal belongings and no learning materials. This order creates a feeling of space and airiness. We also find that colours in these images are coordinated. On the one hand, this serves to create links between the elements. So we find in Figure 3.3 that the recycling symbol on one box coordinates with the colour of the other box itself. It is unlikely that this would be the case before editing as these symbols would be white stencilled on each. And this colour also coordinates with the blue of the globe, which creates links in meaning and coherence.

In Figure 3.3 we of course do not see an actual classroom but the photograph sets up a happy learning environment into which recycling can be integrated in a simple way. In fact recycling is in many ways contentious. Governments tend not to make policies to control manufacturers as regards the amount of packaging they use. Much packaging is tough and expensive to recycle. Much of world's contamination of the environment is done through larger scale industrial and agricultural processes. Yet this website seeks to put responsibility for solutions in the hands of the consumer. One argument could be that it is consumerism that is the problem. We often hear that businesses must be brought in to help solve problems, that consumers must be given choice, even where there are good arguments that things like economic growth and healthy markets are the very antithesis of saving the environment.

Colour

Colour is a semiotic resource that become more and more important in visual communication (Kress and van Leeuwen, 2002; Machin, 2007). It can be used to link elements that would otherwise be of different kinds, create bonds or contrasts, evoke moods and associations. Its impact has to do with new and widespread technologies and software that make it possible for almost anyone to use and in different ways modify or manipulate colour. It is consequently a major design resource for all kinds of semiotic materials, and we present tool kits for colour also in Chapter 4, 5 and 6, where Chapter 5 on packaging has the most extensive account. Below we make comments on the use of colour in photographs specifically, following an inventory based on different ways that colours can be modified.

Modulation

The colours in photographs can be changed to make them appear flattened. This is called 'reduced modulation' and it is where the play of light and dark on a surface has been removed to some degree. If you look at your clothing or skin you will see the contours made by light and shadow. These can be reduced to make a cleaner-looking image. It has the effect of making something appear less blemished or more idealized. We can see this in Figure 3.3, where clothing and objects appear simplified in this way. We can also see this on the photographs of the burgers in Figure 1.1 in Chapter 1.

Saturation

Colours can be made to look more saturated or more muted. Colours that are highly saturated tend to connote increased emotions and exuberance. These can be used to communicate fun, energy and vibrancy. These are typical for children's products and we see saturated colours used in Figure 3.3, contributing to the message that recycling has a fun and emotional quality. Colours that are more diluted or muted tend to communicate more mellow or reserved moods. A photograph used for a film poster for a high-quality drama may use more muted colours to suggest a mellow mood.

Purity

Pure colours tend to be used to communicate simplicity and truth. Impure colours tend to be associated with complexity, ambiguity and hybridity. In Figure 3.3 we find pure red used for the recycling bin. The photographs of the burgers in Figure 1.1 use pure yellows and reds. A photograph for fusion food may in contrast carry more hybrid colours in order to communicate complexity.

Range

If a photograph contains a large range of colours it will tend to communicate fun and playfulness. Figure 3.3 uses the blue and red to create greater liveliness. Yet it combines these with more muted colours as found on the clothing of the other children, to bring a more measured feel to the image. In Figure 3.5 the photograph of the three lecturers to the left shows them being fun and intimate. But the colour palette is limited. Were the colour palette high they may appear more as children's television presenters. The more restrained use of colour here helps to moderate the poses. Many pop musicians use monochrome in publicity shots. The photograph in Figure 3.2 gains some of its effect from it being monochrome.

Coordination

We can also look for the way that colour qualities are used across an image or across a design. In Figure 3.2 the colours in the photograph link objects. We see the same in the IKEA catalogue image for 2016 in Figure 1.2 in the first chapter. White and green create rhyming and links across the setting. Clothing too can be part of the coding, linking with products and with work surfaces. The photograph in Figure 3.3 is linked to elements on the web page. The blue and red in the image link with the other primary colours on the page which are also pure and saturated. But the red and blue are also used in other elements on the page such as the buttons for Facebook and Google. What this does is code the objects and settings in the photographs into a whole of which these other elements are also a part, making them a coherent whole.

Settings

Barthes (1977) pointed to the important connotations carried by the settings we see in images. Again description, or denotation, is highly important in looking at the 'where' things are depicted as taking place. In Figure 3.2, the setting with bullet holes in the wall is important for the contrast with the girl wearing her slippers. The black and white helps to communicate something gritty and compelling. In Figure 3.3, the classroom setting is uncluttered. Objects are missing such as files, pens, papers and personal belongings. It is a room that shows no wear from everyday use and a place saturated with bright lighting. It is a setting typical of these kind of photographs created to be used in these kind of page design. They are stripped back of much artifice so that a number of objects can better serve their symbolic role, enhanced by the bright saturated lighting. In the case of Figure 3.5, with photographs from a Swedish university magazine, we see how settings are reduced so that actual contexts more or less disappear. To the left three people are shot against a white background, and in the middle photograph the background is blurred. To the right a lecturer sits on a staircase. We can ask what ideas these choices connote.

In Figure 3.4 we find a very different kind of setting. This is a photograph used on a website where companies can buy carbon offsetting. Carbon offsetting is where companies or institutions like universities can reduce their carbon footprint, not by actually making any changes in how things get done, but by buying into some kind of eco-developmental programme, such as building a windfarm for a village in India. For companies, it can simply be economically difficult to make such changes locally, or impractical, for example if their business involves many international flights. There are some criticisms of this system since the development of offsetting projects can in the longer term lead to further carbon emissions, for example as the village begins to change due to having electricity.

On the web page we find the top image shows a man in a field of grass and a horizon with a bright blue sunny sky containing a few bright white clouds. In this case, of course, we are not dealing with an image being used to document, but to symbolize something. Here the bright green of the grass connotes nature. And showing the grass in this fashion, running to the horizon and with the open sky, we get a sense of open space. It would be different if the grass were only a small section, or if we saw buildings in the background. And nature here is not dangerous, rugged or ugly. It is a little like an extended lawn. This image connotes clean open space where the man can raise his arms unrestricted and of course free from the constraints of worry. Compare the analysis of settings in Chapter 7 on film clips (see p.152), where the role of nature is discussed at length.

Figure 3.4 The web page Carbon Footprint

The image to the bottom right of the web page shows another nature scene, where wind turbines sit in farmland. Again we have the bright sky where a few white clouds float. Here we also find sunflowers. Of note is that were the figure of the man pasted onto this image, the setting would give it a different meaning. Rather than simply celebrating the space, freedom from worry, it would appear that he was celebrating the objects, the wind turbines. And this would not work for the message of the website, where in a sense the solution being offered is not one whereby the clients want to care about the environment, but where they need to be able to relieve themselves of the concern for meeting guidelines and regulations.

There is one other kind of setting that we often find in the photographs that we see. This is the setting seen in the left-hand image in Figure 3.5. Here we see three lecturers shown in a university promotional brochure. We do not see them in their offices, nor teaching students. And unlike the image to the right, we do not see them in a public setting. Here the background is simply a white space. There is no concrete indicator as to where they are. We might describe such settings as 'decontextualized'. In such images a greater symbolic role is played by the objects and people we find. Were these lecturers standing in an office, cluttered with administrative documents, or in a teaching environment with a large number of students, their close proximity to each other and their playfulness may appear out of place. Such decontextualized images are generally used to symbolize an idea or concept. And here it is that staff at the university are fun and

Figure 3.5 Photographs of staff from a Swedish university magazine

53

approachable. This can be seen as part of the shift where public institutions must market themselves, address students and customers who will be pleased, and to show they contribute in easily graspable ways to society (Machin, 2004; Ledin and Machin, 2015b). Such images attempt to shift away from ideas of academics as elite and distant.

Participants

So far in this chapter we have already begun to point to some of the ways that the people we see in photographs are important (cf. van Leeuwen, 1999a and 2008b, for an extensive analysis of the representation of social actors). For example, we considered the representation of the child in Figure 3.2 who was used to represent innocence. We find a disproportionate number of children represented in the case of war and disaster. The point is that there are a number of photographic choices here that we can document as part of building up a sense of what is taking place. Below we present an inventory.

Individuals and groups

To begin with we can ask the question as to whether the participants are shown as individuals or *en groupe*. 'Individualization' is realized where we see a shot of a single person, or where one person is made salient in an image, such as through the setting and other people being out of focus. This has the effect of drawing the viewer closer to the person. The child in Figure 3.2 above is shown as an individual. The viewer is invited to consider her thoughts. The shot would have worked differently had it been a group of ten children. But visual individualization can be to different degrees. It can be reduced where the person is seen further into the distance and can be increased by extreme close-ups.

'Collectivization' is found in photographs where we see groups or crowds. This can have a much more depersonalizing effect. In Figure 3.1 we see the soldiers who will occupy Gotland. We do not see a massive army but enough soldiers for them to appear much more depersonalized. A close-up of say three of the soldiers would have a very different effect and suggest that the viewer considers their experiences of the event, rather than the event itself.

Larger groups of people can also be further 'homogenized' to different degrees. This can be by things such as clothing, actions and poses. The two soldiers in Figure 3.2 strike the same pose decreasing individualization. The soldiers in Figure 3.1 wear the same clothing but, if we look closer, do not strike the same poses, as we might find in a photograph for military propaganda where they would all stand rigidly in the same way indicating their subjection to the regime.

Again this may be important here to show a more relaxed approach to occupying Gotland. In Figure 3.5, the right-hand photograph shows a more individualized image where the lecturer sits on the stairs. In the university brochure 'individualism' tends to be represented through a stock range of poses and settings such as sitting on the stairs, jumping in the air or standing in a playful pose.

Collectivization can also be found where there has been a focus on the generic features of a group turning them into types. So a group of militia are shown who all wear the same head gear and have a beard. A news photograph of a Muslim neighbourhood in London could foreground women with traditional clothing with a sense that these represent all Muslims. Of course where people become routinely represented as types, complexities of real and diverse experiences become supressed by the generic type. News media begin to represent a thing called 'Muslims in Britain' as if it were a singular entity, which scholars have argued suits extreme views from different ideological interests, the political right and more extreme Islamic stances.

Categorization

People can also be represented in photographs in ways that *categorize* them. This will be independent of the extent to which they are 'individualized' or 'collectivized'. Visual categorization can be 'cultural' and/or 'biological'. 'Cultural categorization' can be found through kinds of dress, hairstyle, body adornment, and so on. In Figure 3.4 we assume the man in the grassy field is a businessmen due to his clothing. Such commercial images often use selected items of clothing to signal cultural categorization. Militia shown in news photography are often shown scruffily dressed and brandishing weapons above their heads. Such images fit news frames of unruliness and lack of professionalism. But they also rely on kinds of cultural categorization, for example relating to the chaos of the Middle East.

'Biological categorization' is found through an emphasis on stereotyped physical characteristics. These can be both positive and negative. Photographs of soldiers who represent 'our boys' may be muscular with square jaws, to represent strength and heroism. Soldiers shown writing home may be slimmer built and appear more youthful to point to vulnerability and humanity. Commercial image banks often contain biological types as well as culturally categorizing through items of clothing. Chinese women are often used to connote some kind of spirituality for example. But even the children we find in Figure 3.3 are generic attractive children – not in any striking way, but enough to help give the image a feel-good look.

Generic and specific

While people can be represented as individuals, as collectives or as generic types, levels of genericity can also be increased through reduction of the articulation of details. Many of the photographs we now see in news media or on social media have been digitally manipulated in order to remove blemishes or wrinkles on skin or to whiten the colour of teeth and eyes. In this case we see less of the articulation of detail than we would have seen had we been there. We can also find reduction in the modulation of light and darkness so that surfaces appear flat and idealized as we often find in advertising. Of course if we know the person in the photograph on social media we may see it as simply an edited photograph of that person. But otherwise such changes can make a person appear more generic. This can also be done by slightly increasing exposure or lowering focus, again as we often find in advertising and fashion photography. We see this in Figure 3.3 on the faces and clothing of the children. This helps to make them more generic.

None representation

Finally it is important to ask if people are absent from photographs. For example, a news headline might read '50 killed in airstrike', but the accompanying image shows only one soldier patrolling an otherwise peaceful area. Here the victims of the airstrike, the families, and the agents of the attack are missing. Of course we could argue that the photographer had no access to either. But nevertheless we might note over a series of photographs that such details are always absent. And we can ask what they are replaced with. Where there are such consistent absences we should always identify the ideological motivations for this. If we look across photographs of recycling on educational resource sites we do not find images of heavily packaged photographs on supermarket shelves, nor of the companies who invest millions in marketing them. But we see children. In the photographs of learning and research in the university documents we never see students collectivized in larger groups. Rather, we see individual generic students. As a customer, of course, you should always be given a sense that you are an individual.

Actions and indexical links

While photographs depict persons and settings, they also depict actions and behaviours. Of course in photographs, since they are, as Sontag (2004) suggests, captured selected moments, we can only get a sense of what is actually going on. Actions in photographs are to a large extent read through 'indexical signs' (Peirce, 1984). In semiotics indexes are things that correlate to, or infer, another thing. So a dog's footprint in the snow indexes the presence of a dog. A limp could be an index of a wound. A frowning facial expression could be an index of displeasure. This is important for analysing action in photographs as we are not seeing actual events unfolding but are reading the indexes for what is taking place. For example, in a photograph we see a woman in a kitchen. On the table are two glasses of red wine and two empty plates. We do not see her sharing a meal and glass of wine, yet the objects index that she is doing so in the way that a footprint in the snow indexes the presence of the foot. Strictly speaking a photograph cannot code social action because there are no moving images, but it can index them. This is different from, for example, a film or commercial where actions unfold over time, which calls for a different and narrative approach, as we show in Chapter 7. In multimodal research relying on language theory, there has been a tendency to analyse actions in images as based on linguistic verb processes (e.g. Kress and van Leeuwen, 1996; Bauldry and Thibault, 2006; cf. the discussion in Forceville, 2007). In our approach, stressing semiotic materials and their affordances, we prefer to make an inventory of action processes in images departing from indexical links.

Emotional processes

This is when the pose and facial expression of a depicted person indexes an emotional state, as when a scowling facial expression indicates anger or concern. This is something natural and partly innate in both animals and humans. Charles Darwin (1872) himself took an interest in the evolution in common expressions of emotion in man and animals. Actually the invention of photography was crucial for this project, since such images could depict these expressions so that Darwin gave labels such as 'Angry Swan', 'Disappointed Chimpanzee', 'Disgusted Woman' and 'Horrified Man'. So the content of emotions are coded by bodily and facial expressions. If we compare the children in Figure 3.2 and 3.3 the contrast is obvious. The girl in the civil war takes a restricted pose and stands still with the hands on her back. Her eyes are open with a steady gaze and the mouth shut, with the lips slightly going down. This expression indexes, in our interpretation, that she is a bit melancholic. But her pose does not suggest fear or cowering. She stands like this, sort of at ease, even though the soldiers are there. In contrast to this complexity, there is no doubt the smiling children in the recycling image are happy. The pose of the man raising his arms and viewed from the back in Figure 3.4 indexes a feeling of freedom. This interpretation is supported by the rest of the image, since the man is looking out at a clean open space, a field of grass stretching to the horizon. A similar pose could also mean being tired when waking up and therefore stretching and taking a deep breath, but then the setting and composition of the image would be very different.

Mental processes

This is where we see a person who appears to be thinking and sensing, such as looking, listening and pondering. Once again this is indexed by poses and facial expressions. A typical example would be a lifestyle magazine where a woman is seen in close-up looking slightly upwards and off-frame. The text then supplies what she is thinking or worrying about: 'can you trust your boyfriend to be faithful', 'are you worrying about how to get that career boost'. We can compare that with Figure 3.1 where we are not encouraged to consider the mental processes of the soldiers. There is no sharp division between mental and emotional processes for the simple reason that thinking and feeling are not separated for humans. We can think of a man depicted sitting in a chair with his face placed in his hands. Knowing no more than this we can think of him mourning or deeply pondering a mathematical problem. The setting will often provide clues as to the more exact process. Perhaps he is wearing a typical funeral costume or we see a table with books and a computer screen with a complicated equation, which helps us to index the process as being more emotional in the former case and more mental in the latter case.

Verbal processes

This is where we see a person talking or shouting. The indexing will once again depend on the nature of facial expressions and poses. For example, a hospital website or document may show a doctor talking with a patient. In the present era of the priority of customer relations this may be important to connote 'taking an interest in' or 'giving time to' the customer. In the more recent IKEA catalogues, people who are depicted in kitchens are often shown to be talking (Figure 1.2). This relates to the way the kitchen is being marketed as a social space, whereas in earlier catalogues they were depicted as carrying or eating food.

Material processes

This is where a person indexes an action in the material world. For example, we see someone building a house, putting used food packaging in a recycling bin, a lecturer teaching students. The indexing here is about reading the photo as depicting something that unfolds over time. In Figure 3.2 the two NATO soldiers could be said to be protecting the civilians and consequently the girl. But here while the typical frame of childhood is used, the girl, as we said, gives a sense that life goes on. The girl holding the recycling bin in Figure 3.3 performs an action that helps to communicate an attitude to recycling, making it easy and fun and inviting the viewer to take part. A lack of material processes is also an important observation.

For example, in the university documents we never see lecturers actually teaching students. There are a few exceptions, such as a lecturer is seen with one student pointing at a computer screen. The actual material processes of what goes on in the institution are absent.

Positioning the viewer

If we look at the photographs in Figures 3.1 and 3.3 it is clear that how they communicate is not only related to how people, settings and objects are represented but also as regards how they position the viewer in relation to what is depicted. In Figure 3.1 we see the scene from behind one of the senior officers, almost taking their view of the row of soldiers awaiting orders. It all appears a bit removed. In contrast in Figure 3.3 everyone in the photograph is close to us and looks right at us. All of these create different meanings. In this section we break some of these down into an inventory that deals with different angles of interaction and with proximity to the scenes in the photographs.

Angles

Vertical angle   Vertical angles have long been associated in photography and film with experiences of superiority/inferiority or with strength/vulnerability. In Figure 3.2 we look down at the girl which helps to create a sense of her vulnerability. Often we find images of soldiers taken from below to emphasize their strength. A photograph used to advertise women's perfume which carries a semi-naked women may be taken from a very low point just below her navel to help communicate status. A photographer may even lay on the ground to make a person appear more powerful or intimidating. The photograph of the lecturer sitting on the staircase in Figure 3.5 could be seen as one part of showing academics not as elite and superior but as approachable. In the brochures we do not see women academics nor administrators sitting on the ground. Clearly here this points to other kinds of power relations related to gender and work roles. A male academic sitting on the ground appears approachable whereas a female academic appears vulnerable.

Vertical angles might also suggest a 'creative' way of looking. Here it may be used in extreme. For example, we may look up at some people from an odd viewing position. This has become more important in contemporary news to suggest 'engagement', 'opinion' and 'liveliness', moving away from former more static and formal images. The steep vertical angle in Figure 3.5 where the lecturer sits on the stairs is such an example.

Horizontal angle   This is to do with our viewing position around a horizontal axis and can relate to how involved or detached we are to the events we see. In Figure 3.3 we look on to the classroom scene from the front. To some extent this involves us more than if we saw the events from the side of the classroom, where we would have been more detached. On magazine covers we will normally see models from the front. If we saw them always from the side it would feel less engaged, like we were just onlookers rather than being addressed by the magazine.

In Figure 3.1 we see the scene looking on at the soldiers. But we have moved on the horizontal plane to take a position behind one of the senior officers. This can have the effect of allowing the viewer to take this person's perspective and can be a way to create a different kind of engagement with the scene, which in a sense is much more participatory. We might see a scene of a line of asylum seekers waiting at a checkpoint taken from behind the head of one of them. The impression is that we too wait in the line. In fact in Figure 3.1 our position from slightly back from the senior officer creates a sense of distance, a little like standing at the back in an audience for a talk.

Oblique angles   This is where the camera will be tilted in some way so that the vertical appears at an angle. These are usually used to bring a sense of playfulness, creativity or tension to a scene. It is now more common to find this used in all sorts of media images, combined with uses of horizontal and vertical angles to communicate 'new perspectives', 'dynamism' and informality. As theorists of photography note, such photographic resources, like slight blurring, or graininess, are ways that things such as 'informality' or 'spontaneous' can be represented where there is none (Barthes, 1977).

Proximity

Distance   In a photograph this is simply what we know as close shot, medium shot, long shot, and so on. And when we look at persons and even at scenes, how they work relates to the association of physical proximity. This works in much the same way as physical proximity in everyday social relations. Close-up we can have more intimacy with people. We have less intimacy with those we see across the street or in the far distance. So a close shot of a person represents them in greater intimacy than a long shot. Imagine if we looked on an Instagram or Facebook account of a person and all of their selfies were in long shot. There would be an impression of remoteness and isolation. When we see a close shot as in the left one in Figure 3.5 we feel more intimacy than if we saw these lecturers from the back of a lecture theatre. Intimacy could have been increased by seeing just an extreme close shot of the face of one of them. But this would have suggested more that we think about their own personal thoughts rather than simply seeing them as accessible and fun people. Close shots can also have a claustrophobic effect. A news photograph might show a crowd of asylum seekers at a border fence in close shot, suggesting threat and something unpleasant. The reaction may be to want to pull away from the scene.

Gaze   One other feature of photographs that can influence viewer engagement is whether or not the persons look at us or not. If they do look at us, as in Figure 3.3, there is a kind of symbolic contact between us and them. In Figure 3.2 in contrast, neither the girl nor the two soldiers look at us. It would be a very different image if they did. Kress and van Leeuwen (1996) suggest that it is useful to think about this difference in terms of 'offer' and 'demand' images (pp. 127–128). So, in Figure 3.5 the three lecturers acknowledge the viewer's presence and in a sense ask something of us as viewers. This is a 'demand' image. In everyday life we know that if someone smiles at us, or looks angry or sad, we might be obliged to respond in an appropriate way. Of course in the case of photographs we know there will now be the same consequences if we do not respond in the right way. But we have all felt the draw when we see a weak child looking out at us from a famine-struck village in a non-governmental organization call for charity. A politician must be seen to meet our gaze square on.

If the person in the photograph does not look at the viewer the effect is different since no contact, or demand, is made. In Figure 3.2 the soldiers do not look at us and consequently do not create a relationship with us. It would be a different photograph if they did. In this case we might assume that it was taken in the genre of a group regimental photograph, even if this would depend on what their facial expressions and postures indexed. In offer images we can also note where people are looking. Looking off-frame, even if the photograph has been cropped to remove what they were originally looking at, can give an impression of thoughtfulness. If they look upwards off-frame it can suggest more positive outward-going thoughts, such as ambition or 'looking to the future'. If they look downwards it can suggest more introspective thoughts. But these meanings will vary with other aspects of the image. An asylum seeker, seen alone in a squalid camp, shown looking sadly upwards off-frame, is clearly not thinking about promotional prospects for the coming year.

SUGGESTIONS FOR RESEARCH QUESTIONS

Throughout our account of applying this analytical tool kit we have been giving a sense of what kinds of issues these can be used to investigate. For a concrete research project we would need, however, a specific research question. This would guide us as regards which tools we may need to use. We do not need to carry out any kind of description or analysis that is not a part of answering our research question. Here are three hypothetical questions we might ask. These questions may be part of a project that also includes analysis of texts and other media, such as film clips and data presentation.

- Are there differences in the way that the politicians of different parties/gender/ ethnicities/countries are represented in photojournalism?

- How does a specific social media site represent environmental recycling?

- How do school text books visually represent poverty in Africa?

In each of these cases we may be interested in the kinds of people, places, objects and actions that we find and how we are positioned as regards these. Different politicians may be depicted in different settings and using different kinds of perspective. We may find that recycling is represented in ways that remove any actual concrete problems caused and those responsible. We may discover this also through looking at the persons, places, objects and actions represented.

One important part of the analysis would be to account for the kind of photographic use involved in our data, as we did in the first part of this chapter. In the news these are documentary type images. But on social media and in the school books these may be different, where we find more symbolic or artistic-type images. And here it is of vital importance that the research question in each case should be established through engaging with the existing research literature on each topic. So what is already known about these topics of visual communication in the domain in which the research questions sits: in political communication, in environmental communication/recycling and in the representation of other cultures? The analytical tools used should be suitable for revealing what kinds of discourses we find in the photographs, what kinds of scripts for carrying out social practices. Ultimately this will allow us to reveal the kinds of ideological interests that these discourses serve.

In each, the process of analysis could involve a larger-scale quantitative type study where we create a coding sheet for a larger sample. Or it could take place, as does must social semiotic work, by ways of collecting a large enough sample to allow us to understand what kinds of patterns are taking place, where we then carry out a detailed analysis of a number of selected typical cases.

4

DOCUMENT DESIGN

Introduction

In this chapter we are interested in how to analyse the design of documents. Documents, whether on paper or digital, are used to carry out established forms of communicative acts. They are experienced as wholes and are associated with different kinds of social practices. When we see a magazine on a table we know what that document aims to do, what it is for. The same is the case when we see a menu in a restaurant, or a utility bill. As with all the forms of visual communication we analyse in this book, document design must be seen as a fundamental part of social life, as part of specific social practices. As with photographs in the last chapter we take a critical stance on the design choices made, on the ideas, values and identities represented. In this case we are interested how such choices also involve other semiotic resources, such as typography, colour and borders. Of course documents themselves incorporate photographs, which we began to consider in the previous chapter. Here we are interested specifically in documents as structured wholes where the photographic forms of expression discussed in that chapter combine with other kinds of semiotic resources.

In contemporary visual communication, document design combines the functional with the affective. Since documents are intended to serve a specific task we can say that they must have functionality. They must be able to carry out their specific role. A menu must allow us to choose from available options. A tablet interface must allow us to navigate to different applications. A social media platform must allow us to easily and practically carry out a number of activities, such as editing and loading contents and posting messages that appear in some kind of order. But these designs also tend to communicate affective stances, for example what is lively or fun, or the romantic or fearful. It is this level of communication that we want to analyse in this chapter.

Document design in different social practices

To start with we look at three examples of document design that have evolved in different social contexts for different purposes, specifically movie posters, tablet screens and magazines. We use this section to show what we mean by approaching documents as forms of visual communication, beginning to point out what kinds of observations we may be able to make in order to ask concrete research questions about them and their role in visual communication. In the following section we present the tool kits we can use for this.

Movie posters

The movie poster is a very easy place to start in order to show how we approach document design in this chapter. Movie posters need to use a range of semiotic resources to communicate about the genre of the film, the kind of story we can expect, the kind of character and their relationships and also the mood of the film. All this has to be done very effectively on a single page. Over time, general multimodal patterns have evolved that are easily identifiable.

Figure 4.1 shows three different genres of film: sci-fi, children's animation and action. Even if we have never seen any of these films we could have a pretty good idea of what kind of viewing experiences each might provide. Of course the picture itself tells us a lot. In the *Cinderella* film we would not expect too much physical violence as compared with *The Expendables*, where there are weapons and muscular men aligned behind their super-macho leader. Nor in the *Alien* movie would we expect there to be too much cuteness or dancing. But we can look a little deeper into these posters. As we said *a propos* photographs in Chapter 3, we must not jump to quick interpretations, not just use superficial adjectives and say that the films are 'spooky', 'sweet' or 'macho'. These observations may not necessarily be wrong. But for the poster designer they need to be much more accurate. If we look, for example, at many movie posters that we might describe as 'macho' they are often slightly different even if they share many typical features. As analysts we need to be aware of both what these patterns are and also what the subtle differences may be. And in the following chapters in this book we show in regard to many other forms of visual analysis, of packaging, of films, of buildings, that we must begin from very careful acts of observation.

To begin with, across the three posters we can see that the typefaces used for each are very different. We would normally be familiar with using adjectives to describe such differences. So the *Cinderella* font is more 'feminine' whereas

Figure 4.1 Movie posters for *Alien, Cinderella* and *The Expendables*

The Expendables font is more 'macho'. But what we are interested in, in the first place here, is not so much *what* they communicate but *how* they communicate such things.

Here we can see that *Cinderella* uses slender and highly curved letters, all leaning slightly to the right. In contrast the typeface used for *The Expendables*, resembling a stamp on an ammunition, appears heavier and much more solid. It is also much more angular. What would happen if we changed some of these features around? Would it be a problem if we used some of the slenderness or curvature of the *Cinderella* font for *The Expendables* poster? In this case we can say that the semiotic associations of slimness, of curvature, of gently leaning are *how* the femininity of Cinderella is communicated. But really it is not just femininity that is communicated here. These font qualities communicate all sorts of ideas about the protagonist but also about what kind of film we can expect. Were *Cinderella* a film about a young woman who rejected the very idea of marriage finding it simply patriarchal, we may have needed a slightly different font.

On the *Alien* poster the font is different again. Here one key difference is the way that the letters are spread out from each other. We usually find the spacing of letters in this way used for things like the name of a modern art museum. The spacing seems to suggest something less easily defined, where there is room to think, or perhaps even something fragmented, or isolation. Again this would not work so well in a different context. If the letters in *Cinderella* were greatly spread out it would appear as if she was somehow less clearly defined, about ideas and creativity perhaps, a kind of philosophical or mystical Cinderella. Again what we see is *how* meanings about the Alien, about the film and the experience of being alone and isolated in space and under threat, are communicated.

On these posters we also find very different uses of colour. *Alien* and *The Expendables* are in some ways similar and both rely on a very limited use of colours. These are black, white and red with a little yellow and typical of what we often find in action movies. More monochrome colour schemes suggest more emotional containment. The red tends to be used as a representation of danger. The *Alien* poster is mostly black which brings a sense of darkness and concealment. But on *The Expendables* poster we also find a lot of very bright highlights. The actors are very well lit, unlike the egg object on the *Alien* poster. Extremes of light tend to be more associated with visibility, knowledge and truth. In the concealment created by the darkness we find something trustworthy perhaps? If we look carefully there are quite extreme levels of shadow and light. This seems to be less about concealment than a relationship between darker forces and the clear truth represented by the actors. And such highlighting of contours that this produces can be used to suggest grittiness and complexity.

In *Cinderella* we find a different colour scheme. There is dominance of the soft pale blue, but also a darker blue, reds of two shades, yellow and green. And we find a very pure white used on the clothing of the couple in the foreground. So we find a greater number of colours. Whereas limited colour ranges tend to be about more muted or constrained moods, so larger ranges tend to be more about fun, liveliness and energy. Again we can think about the effect should a much wider colour palette be used for *The Expendables* poster. In fact the impression would be that it was more of an action comedy film. The colours are also pure, like the white in Cinderella's clothing. We can see the difference in purity if we look at the red in the title of *The Expendables*, which carries some patches of black to suggest something worn, something more complex. Again we will be more likely to find pure colours on children's and family films and in comedies.

Our aim here is to show what kind of visual analysis we have in mind. It is about how meanings are communicated – through what semiotic materials. It is about paying attention to the details of visual communication. As we have already seen, this has allowed us to make more concrete and specific kinds of observations that would provide the basis for carrying out a more informed comparison between different visual designs. And fonts and colours are semiotic materials used across most documents, which we can analyse in this very fashion. Then of course we can look in more detail at the images. In part we deal with images in the previous chapter. And to a large extent we can draw on the same tools of analysis for film posters. We can ask what kinds of persons, objects and places we find. And we can ask what kind of actions and processes are suggested. In the case of the film poster we would ask how these work to communicate the same, or different, kinds of ideas, values and discourses as we find in colour and type. Sometimes, where a film is a parody for example, we may find that some elements suggest 'action' whereas others point to 'playfulness'.

Screen interfaces

In Figure 4.2 we see tablet interfaces of iPhone and Windows. Of course these may be often changing as regards content. But here we are interested in some basic features of the design. We look more at composition in terms of framing and in terms of what we call 'rhyming', which can involve borders, but also fonts and colour. This allows us to start to think more about composition and how different elements are placed on a page.

If we look at the design of *Dagens Nyheter* in Figure 3.1 in Chapter 3 we can see that certain elements are segregated from others by narrow lines. So one story is segregated from another. Such borders are a design feature long used by newspapers. It is a way of telling the reader that things in different frames are not related, or that things within the same frame are related. We can also see that some elements are separated from others by space. So a headline is separated from a block of text by space. Here the spacing indicates that the headline is different to the text, but related as it sits in the same frame. Looking at the different stories in the red tiles at the top, we can see that they are separated from each other a little by space. Yet they 'rhyme' in the sense that they are each placed in a frame of the same colour and shape. Therefore, in one sense they share certain qualities.

What is also notable about this particular newspaper design is that all the elements sit in space. Older newspaper designs tended to cram text into tight columns. If we look at the red tiles at the top, for example, we see that each photograph and text are given 'room to breathe' or 'the luxury of space'. The columns of texts are not pressed together economically using space but also have room to breathe. This in itself is part of a shift away from news as formal and authoritative to news which has to engage with readers, dress them as if they had opinions, and also where social media have changed reading habits. But as regards the design the space also creates rhyming across the page. And such designs must also be created with the need to be accessed and read across a range of platforms, for example on the web or on a mobile phone.

On the left in Figure 4.2 we have the design for the interface of iPhone. On the right we see the Windows interface introduced at that same time and combining applications with content. The two look different. We can use the ideas of framing and rhyming to think more concretely about these differences, to both describe

Figure 4.2   Screen interfaces of iPhone (left) and Windows (right)

them and also to point to the different ways that they communicate about what they do and the contents that they carry. This is important as both platforms must seek to communicate that they do a job well, or users may just cease to use them. As we discussed above, functionality in design now also works at the same time with affect. The meaning of the experience of using an interface becomes inseparable to how it functions.

If we look at the iPhone design in terms of framing and borders we can see that all the applications are represented by boxes of the same size and therefore comes out as being of the same order. We also see that they are separated by space, being placed at equal intervals. There is a sense of equality and regulation, even if four applications sit on a kind of shelf or work desk at the bottom. These are also regulated by size in the same way and by the same mutual distance. But the shelf position appears to give them more importance. These are those applications used most often. When this changes they can again take their place in the ordered system. There is permeability in this design. The boundaries are somehow open, porous or flexible. We can see that the icons themselves are slightly transparent as is the shelf at the bottom. This brings a sense of lightness and ease to the navigation. It also gives a sense that the apps are not so much boundaried from the system as a whole.

As regards rhyming we find that the applications are of the same size and same permeability. We find that all the applications have the same small white fonts. There is also rhyme and therefore connectivity created by the use of colour. There is a relatively large range of colours but a few dominate. Many applications carry mainly soft blue, suggesting science and technology. But we also find warmer yellows and oranges used to create links across the design and integrate the elements. Across all the colours we find bright white highlights which suggest truth and optimism. We also find the blue of the background which has the appearance of gentle ripples on a pond, serene and almost still. Water itself is often associated with life, with spirituality and purity.

If we now compare this with the Windows interface the significance of these observations becomes more apparent. We find that borders create three frame sizes. One in the bottom section contains more writing. Then the contents tiles above are found in two frame sizes. There are two larger squares and then smaller ones which are quarters of this. But the way they are positioned gives the impression of a much greater range of shapes and sizes, even of randomness. This creates a very different affect than the order of the iPhone interface. This creates a sense of dynamism and variety. Literally it looks like a range of many interlocking possibilities. It appears mobile and changing as opposed to the order, stasis and calmness of the iPhone design.

We see that each of the tiles is separated from its neighbours by a black border. This suggests clear segregation. Such borders can communicate degrees of segregation according to how thin or thick they are. So in one sense there is not the sense of permeability found in the iPhone design as each individual element is clearly segregated. But tiles of the same size clearly share some qualities as they are 'packaged' in the same way. In other words frame size and shape can create rhyming. They can be used to communicate similarities, differences and also hierarchies.

Frames can also create rhyme where they share the same colour. Across the tiles we find that there is the default background colour which is a warm orange. So the different applications such as the messenger and the email are clearly of the same order. We then, at least in the example we see here, find that the images carry neutral colours and rhyme with each other. The same thing happens with the blue and the white. And content providers simply must think ahead to how their material will appear not just on their home page, but as it will most usually be accessed embedded into such systems of tiles or in columns of 'trending' topics on social media feeds. In this case these colours create links across the document. In fact while it is much less obvious, the same links are present on the *Dagens Nyheter* design in Chapter 3. We can see in Figure 3.1 that red bullet points take the colour of the tiles at the top. A text box or border lower down may take a colour from elsewhere. But also the design uses three different kinds of modern types of font which are used to create more 'interesting' diagonal links across the page. On one level we may not see this so easily. But it is part of the way that documents communicate affect. Of course another news design may want to avoid such clean and subtle rhyming and use overlapping and different shapes and sizes of frames to suggest variety of content, fun and irreverence as do many tabloids. Overall the Windows design is about energy and dynamism. We find this in the tile sizes, in the different sizes of font uses, the way the tiles are arranged to give a sense of movement and lack of rigid order. Yet underneath this, or at least a different level, there is also order, just of a different nature than we found in the iPhone design.

So borders are created by lines and spacing and the resulting frame sizes can, as we have seen, create hierarchies, and also suggest rhyming, or shared qualities. Looking at a different news site, the BBC (shown in Figure 4.3), also designed for tablets, we can see again the use of space and 'room to breathe/think'. We also see the way that frame size gives salience to the new story on South Korea. In fact reading through the story it is not clear what is 'news' or hard information, and the page contains stories of different nature. The tennis report is an actual event. But the item on the London underground, 'The gruesome truth', contains very little other than some speculation about burial chambers. It is a story placed there for clickability, where the BBC can then show that it has high levels of traffic. The photograph is a stock image of a tube station. And it is often the

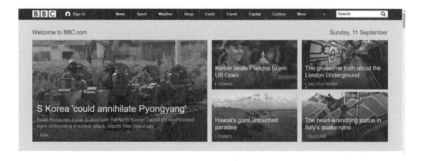

Figure 4.3   BBC web page

case on such tile displays that actual news photographs can be combined with stock images and also with highly symbolic photographs. While there have been changes to the more symbolic use of photographs in general, here it is design that in part allows these to sit together.

The menu bar on the top contains different content areas and have long been part of newspapers as a way of producing a sort of encyclopaedia of the world and making it accessible to readers, here by the categories 'News', 'Sport', 'Weather', 'Earth', 'Travel' and 'Culture'. This way of systematically accounting for the world dates back to the end of the twentieth century when newspapers, due to new printing technologies, could divide materiality, the pages, into sections and label them in recurring categories (Karlsson and Ledin, 2000). It affords the newspaper the ability to present the world as stable, even if the actual items in each section change. This gives the readers an important sense of recognition and ultimately a sort of security where the world always comes out as the same. So once again we see that semiotic materials evolve over time and are shaped by technology, where here the traditional and recurring headings on the top of pages have become a fixed menu on top of a digital web page, and are also present in apps. Of course these top headings/menus are ideological and naturalize a world view. In a traditional twentieth-century newspaper and before globalization the distinction of 'domestic' vs 'foreign' news would have been important, whereas nowadays, as the BBC web page shows, 'Shop' is a taken for granted category on par with 'News' and 'Culture', showing that consumerism has become a natural part of traditional news outlets supposed to be 'objective'.

Magazines

We use magazines to look at another important part of document design which is alignment. Lines of text, chunks of text, or even single words, as well as images and graphics must be aligned as regards space. This is also highly useful for communicating ideas and values and for giving meaning to different elements. In some of the documents we have analysed so far we can see some of these differences. On the *Dagens Nyheter* front page (Figure 3.1) the columns of text are level on both sides, which looks very tidy and slightly formal. The headlines are different. They are aligned with the left of each frame and are 'ragged' on the right. This looks slightly less formal. If we look at our two burger menus in the introduction (Figure 1.1) we see that mainly the text is aligned to the left. One difference can be seen where the text 'Gourmet Burger Kitchen: Gluten free menu' is placed in the centre. And the letters of the first three words have been designed to create straight edges. In the case of the use of single words on the Windows interface in Figure 4.2 we see that the word 'Adam' is left aligned, whereas the word 'Kindle' sits at the centre. This creates a very different effect in the two cases. This is all related to creating a sense of order, formality, lack of formality. It can also play an important role in creating what designers call different 'reading rhythms'. This can be seen clearly in the example of two sets of pages from the French magazine *Libération* in Figure 4.4, on the Italian Prime Minister Silvio Berlusconi being under pressure, and Figure 4.5, a feature about a gallery specializing in graphic art.

The designer of this magazine told one of the authors during an interview that one important aspect of the look is that it has two kinds of reading rhythms. These are 'condensed reading' and 'paused reading'. The difference can be seen in the two layouts in Figures 4.4 and 4.5 taken from the same edition. The first one clearly has a condensed section of text to be read and the other elements dispersed across the page. The second one has an integrated layout inviting the reader to choose which element to read. For designers such reading rhythms can be used to communicate the ideas and attitudes of the title

Libération was originally a radical left-wing newspaper launched in the early 1970s. While from the 1970s its contents ceased to be so radical, especially after financial difficulties in the 1990s, it is still very much associated with intellectualism and free thinking. But to a large extent it is down to the role of design to communicate such values rather than the content itself. This is accomplished by using typefaces and images but also, importantly, by framing and text alignment.

Figure 4.4 The French magazine *Libération* and the feature 'Berlusconi mis sous presse' inviting 'condensed reading'

In Figure 4.4 we can see there are no overlaps between elements. Segregation creates large areas of space around very condensed sections of text. Here we find both room to breathe and the luxury of space but also a sense of denser, more formal information or knowledge. As regards text alignment we find straight and even edges for the main body of text. This appears formal and regulated. But the headlines above where we see the words 'Berlusconi' and 'mis sous presse' are slightly uneven and staggered. Here we get a greater sense of creativity and informality. As regards the images we find contrast between frame sizes. But we find little segregation between the actual images creating a sense of intimacy between them.

In contrast, in Figure 4.5 we find integration and overlap, illustrating the graphic art of the gallery. The letter 'a' overlaps the fine borders and the photograph to the bottom left and the text follows the shape of the letter 'a'. This would not be suitable for a highly formal document. And above in the left and right corners we see that text for each image is ragged at the right margin. The magazine sometimes uses text that is ragged at the left margin to create an even greater sense of creativity and informality. Images too can be placed in relative ordered configurations, such as we see in Figure 4.4. Or these can be placed in a

Figure 4.5 The French magazine *Libération* and the feature 'comme anatome' inviting 'paused reading'

ragged column on the right side of the page where on the left is only space as in Figure 4.5. Again this can suggest something more creative, less formal. What we are seeing here is the visual communication of the ideas and attitudes of 'critical thinking', of 'creativity', of 'being intellectual', which in fact no longer actually lies so much in the text of the magazine.

We can draw out the meaning of text alignment even more by looking at the example in Figure 4.6 where we see a page from a web document where a university presents its 'Vision'. This is part of a set of pages that can be accessed by students who may be considering attending the university. Of course, it is by no means certain that any students actually read such a document. But presently such institutions are compelled to have them. Here a university uses text alignment to make fairly contradictory lists of things appear as somehow gravely important and momentous as part of the strategic plan that fulfils its vision (Ledin and Machin, 2016b).

We can see here that all of the text both at the top and in the four lower sections is centrally aligned. This has been done in a way that both ends of the text is 'ragged' rather than both being straight as we saw in the newspaper columns, or only the left side being ragged, such as in the headlines. This has

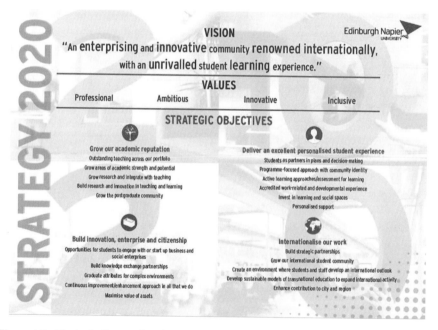

Figure 4.6 Strategic diagram from Edinburgh Napier University

more in common with the way 'Kindle' is positioned on the Windows interface. But rather than appearing as ragged it is here centrally justified. So we get columns of symmetrical chunks of text. If we look at the words 'vision' and the vision statement itself and the words 'values' and 'strategic objectives', these too are aligned in a symmetrical column. This kind of alignment is often found on memorials, on an invitation to a formal event, or perhaps on a certificate for a diploma. Leaving a notable gap between each line in the column can bring in a sense of separation, room to think. Simply, it becomes even more momentous and significant – more of a moment to stop and consider.

In fact the lists of items in the columns are little more than buzzwords. From the early 2000s it became increasingly common to see public institutions such as schools, hospitals, local councils, police forces and hospitals run along a management system used for private companies called 'balanced scorecard'. This is a system where all aspects of institutional processes, materials, persons, even things like 'organizational culture' and 'values' are treated like commodities. It is used in private companies to maximize productivity, improve competitiveness and ultimately to increase profits.

The problem of course for universities, as with other public institutions, is that they do not provide a product as such. Education is a complex thing. Why should education institutions or hospitals need to compete? But in the present political environment all public institutions such as universities are obliged to follow policy guidelines that governments feel will 'improve' outputs. Many of the semiotic choices on this document reveal strategies where the forced nature of this process has to be dealt with. It illustrates perfectly new writing, as discussed in Chapter 2 (p. 29). It relies on digital technology, fuses writing with other semiotic resources and is clearly symbolic. It decontextualizes actual work processes and commodifies what researchers, teachers and students do.

In the first place the use of extensive space helps to communicate the importance of the document. It is not a dense commentary as we find in Figure 4.5 from *Libération*. And sitting in space like this, with the different parts separated, there is a sense that these are the core elements, the components of the process of reaching a vision (comprising nonsense buzzwords). The use of text alignment suggests something momentous, significant, a time to pause and think. We also find the use of permeability where the strategies float over images of the university. They are therefore part of the university. And we find that each group of strategies is marked by an icon of the same size and style. Again we find clichés. A brick represents building, a tree growing. Internationalization is a globe. If we look at the contents of one of these lists it is certainly not clear how they will lead to the vision, not transparent how these could possibly work alongside the other strategies. Could there be contradictions, for example, between focusing on quality teaching and seeing students as partners? Close analysis of the document points to the use of buzzwords and themes that simply do not add up to anything systematic. But the document design, as in the case of *Libération*, is the level where the ideas of it being systematic and important are communicated.

Analysing document design

What we have done so far in this chapter is show how we can analyse documents as a form of visual communication. We pointed to the role specifically of fonts, colour, framing and alignment. All of these have affordances to communicate discourses. Fonts can tell us about the gentle fragility of Cinderella. Colour can tell us about the relationship between tiles on an interface. Framing and alignment can be used to tell us that a magazine is intellectually engaged. In this section we now go through these semiotic resources and provide tool kits.

Typography

Here we list features of letter forms that can be used as a way to describe how typefaces create meaning, drawing on Machin (2007: Chapter 5) and Lupton (2010). We have to remember, as with all the tools we present in this book, that the actual meaning is created through the 'whole', which will include combinations of different semiotic resources in the materialized design.

Weight

Typefaces can be of different weights. This can be used to create degrees of salience on a page where heavier fonts are used to signal headlines and titles. One level of weight may be used to signal that different titles or headings are of the same ranking. Weight in typeface can be used to communicate other ideas. Heavier fonts can mean 'solid', 'substantial', 'assertive' or 'daring'. We can see the case of the font used for *The Expendables* in Figure 4.1. In contrast lighter fonts can be used to mean 'delicate', 'insubstantial' and 'timid'. We can see this in the example of the font used for *Cinderella* in Figure 4.1. But these meanings can be reversed. A heavier typeface can suggest something 'clumsy', 'immobile', 'domineering' or 'overbearing' whereas a lighter font can mean something 'precise', 'mobile' or 'subtle'. We can see this on the Windows iPhone interface where lighter fonts are used to communicate the dynamic and mobile nature of the interaction with the flow of content.

Height and width

Typefaces can be tall and slim or wider and squat. The meaning here can relate to associations of tallness and upwards aspiration and sophistication, whereas squatter fonts can appear more grounded. But tall slim fonts can also appear pompous or less stable and squat fonts can appear immobile and heavy. The *Cinderella* font in Figure 4.1 relates to her aspirations. *The Expendables* font in contrast is much more grounded. A tall slim font would change the meaning here. Fonts that are very wide can be used in comedy to suggest clumsiness and inertia.

Expansion

Typefaces may be very narrow and condensed, or they can be expanded and wide. The meaning of this can relate to how we experience objects taking up space. Very narrow fonts can be seen as precise and economical. They can appear as if they are cramming a page with content, as if they are making the most of the space. Wider fonts can be seen as taking up space, using space up. These values can be reversed where narrow typefaces can appear as cramped or restrictive, and where wider typefaces can provide room to breathe, unrestrictive. On the *Dagens Nyheter* design (Figure 3.1) there has been a deliberate use of less narrow font along with increased spacing just for this reason. The word 'Kindle' on the Windows interface appears narrow and economical as it seeks to represent the space saving nature of the hardware (Figure 4.2). The word 'Expendables' uses a wider font to suggest the exuberance of the characters (Figure 4.1).

Curvature

A font can be angular or curved, or can combine both of these qualities. The meaning of these comes from the associations with angular or rounded objects. Angular fonts can mean 'harsh', 'technical', 'abrasive' whereas round fonts can mean 'comforting', 'soft', 'organic', 'feminine'. Depending on the context of use these can be valued both positively and negatively. In Figure 4.1 we see that *The Expendables* and *Alien* posters use angularity whereas *Cinderella* uses a curved font. The designer of *Dagens Nyheter* told one of the authors that more contemporary news outlets use more curved fonts as part of presenting news in a way that carries more emotions, that is softer, shifting away from an angular, authoritative look that is now alienating for readers.

Proximity

Letters can be pressed close together to each other or even connected, as in handwritten script. Or they can be quite separate, self-contained and considerably spaced from other letters. Where letters have closer proximity they can appear cramped. But this can also suggest 'integration', 'unity', 'coherence' and 'closed-up'. Where they are further apart there can be a sense of 'room to breathe', 'space to think' or 'easy going'. A modern art museum might use spacing between letters to suggest 'less closed-up' or 'room to think and experiment'. Contemporary newspapers use greater spacing between letters and words to suggest 'room to think' and 'room for your opinions' rather than 'this is authoritative information'. But spaced letters can also suggest 'fragmentation', 'lack of wholeness' or 'atomization'. If we look at the letters on the *Alien* poster in Figure 4.1 we see this sense of fragmentation creates a lack of certainty as to what the creature actually is. Such letter spacing would clearly be unsuitable for *Cinderella*.

Regularity

This can relate to how letters within a single word are the same and regular or to some extent different and irregular. This could be in terms of letter sizes where each is different. Words in a sentence may be of different sizes. Or different letters may have different features, for example where some letters have more roundness. Irregularity can relate to 'creativity', 'playfulness', 'liveliness' and 'irreverence'. The university vision document in Figure 4.6 uses irregularity in the size of fonts in its vision statement to communicate 'energy' and 'creativity'. We see the same on the page of the *Libération* magazine.

Slope

Sloping fonts can be associated with handwriting. In this sense they can suggest something less formal and more personal. An advertisement may use a sloping font to create such a meaning. We can see the use of this effect in the *Cinderella* poster in Figure 4.1. Such sloping fonts would be less suitable for more formal documents or where an advert may want to present technical information. We saw on the burger menu in Figure 1.1 that the words 'Gluten Free Menu' use slope and handwriting to suggest something more personal, handmade and organic. Slope can also carry the association of movement. This can be used to suggest something dynamic and energetic. A fashion magazine may use a sloping font for its title to suggest being up-to-date and as reporting on the 'latest thing'.

Flourishes

Fonts can carry a huge range of flourishes. These may be loops or elaborate circles for dots on the letter 'i'. These may bring extra curvature and emotional expression to a font. They may carry iconographic imagery such as a film website using a font comprising old film stock. Looking at Figure 4.4 we can see that the name 'Berlusconi' carries flourishes leading into letters and letters such as the 'c' carry a small node as if part of a swirl. This could be seen to be part of his self-styled extravagance.

Line spacing and alignment

While fonts can create a complex range of meanings through shape the way that they are arranged onto the page in terms of line spacing and alignment of text is also important, and below we describe these semiotic resources (cf. Machin and Polzer, 2015).

Spacing

Line spacing can carry similar meanings to letter spacing. Where words on a page or lines of text have small levels of spacing they can appear cramped and claustrophobic. But as with letter spacing this can also suggest 'integration', 'unity', 'coherence' and 'closed-up'. Where they are further apart there can be a sense of 'room to breathe', 'space to think' or 'easy-going'. A modern art museum might use spacing between letters to suggest 'less closed-up', 'room to think and experiment'. But spaced words and lines of text can also suggest 'fragmentation', 'lack of wholeness' or 'atomization', for example where on a page we see words and lines of texts scattered about. The *Dagens Nyheter* design in Figure 3.1 uses extensive spacing between lines of text precisely to give a sense of 'room to think', of 'openness'. This is a modern newspaper that engages with the view of its intelligent readers.

Alignment

Alignment of typeface relates to how the edges of the text are aligned with the edge of page or how each line relates to the others. Consider the following examples.

Even at both sides   Text can be even on both the left and right edges. Here the text appears bordered and controlled. This may be used to create a sense of efficiency, authority and formality. While the *Dagens Nyheter* page design uses many techniques to communicate openness we see that it uses straight edges for its main body of text (Figure 3.1). On *Libération* we see that one of the two pages (Figure 4.4) also uses such straight edges suggesting a more serious kind of content as compared with the other page (Figure 4.5).

Left edge is even, right is ragged   This creates a slightly less formal and more organic look to the text. The words are not controlled by the borders but take up the space they wish. It is therefore more relaxed. We can see this used on the BBC news website for the headlines on each image (Figure 4.3).

Left is ragged, right is even   Since in the West we begin reading from the left this kind of text is slightly more challenging to follow as each line takes up a different position. Such texts are highly informal and often found in advertising to suggest 'creativity'. We can see this in Figure 5.4 in Chapter 5 on the text on Ella's Kitchen baby products. There is a sense of fun and playfulness rather than formality. In the case of Ella's Kitchen this may also bring a sense of something more personal and natural, given that it also takes the form of handwriting. The effect of creativity here can be increased by the use of greater line spacing where groups of words can then appear like bursts of thought.

Both edges are ragged but the text is symmetrical   This kind of alignment is typical of invitations, commemorative plaques or greetings cards. Such alignments communicate history, formality and tradition. This effect can be made more pronounced by the use of line spacing. Here we get a greater sense of gravity and momentousness. We find this kind of alignment on the university vision document in Figure 4.6. Were these lists of strategies presented through a different kind of alignment it may become more immediately obvious that they comsist largely of an incoherent collection of buzzwords and even empty or weak notions.

Colour

As we have explained, colour has become a semiotic resource important for the design of all sorts of semiotic materials, and we refer to the tool kits in Chapter 3 (p. 49) and 5 (p. 102) for more observations on colour, where what we say about colour associations in Chapter 5 is applicable also to document design. The inventory of colour below makes a distinction between dimensions, such as brightness and saturation, and the role of colour in composition.

Dimensions

As for dimensions, colours have qualities that can be placed on scales, such as light and dark, saturated and dilute. These combine both cultural and experiential associations.

Brightness Colours can be on a scale from brightness to darkness. This has to do with what is light and dark, which obviously is a rich source of meaning-making, including associations with clarity and obscurity, from brighter more optimistic moods to those that are solemn or reserved. In Figure 4.1 we can see that the *Cinderella* movie poster uses brightness to point to clarity and optimism. In contrast the *Alien* poster uses darkness for obscurity and darker moods.

Saturation Colours can be rich and saturated or more dilute and muted. Saturated colours can be associated with higher emotional temperatures whereas more diluted colours evoke more muted and reserved moods. The reds on the *Alien* poster in Figure 4.1 point to the intensity of the emotions in the film. On the Windows interface in Figure 4.2 we find much more muted blues. Here truth and purity appear at a more gentle and soothing level.

Purity Colours can be pure or they can be blended or contain shades, or elements of other colours. Historically, pure colours have been associated with truth, order and simplicity. Impure colours are associated with complexity and ambiguity. On a movie poster for a children's film such as *Cinderella* we might find more pure colours. On an adult drama film poster, less pure colours might be used to suggest ambiguity and complexity.

Modulation Colours can be flat and featureless or they can carry grades of colour saturation. Or they can have different degrees of graininess, where they carry lighter versions of the same colour or another colour. The meaning of this can also relate to simplicity. A flat unmodulated colour can appear idealized, simple. On the *Cinderella* poster in Figure 4.1 we can see that many of the colours are flat and featureless such as the trousers worn by the prince and the uniforms of the soldiers. In contrast there appears to be an exaggeration of contrasts between light and dark on *The Expendables* poster suggesting complexity or grittiness.

Colour range This is to do with how many colours we find on a design. A higher number of colours will tend to be used to communicate fun, liveliness, playfulness. A smaller number of colours reducing to monochrome will communicate something more reserved and contained. A high number of colours can also look crude and garish whereas a limited number can appear dull and lifeless. It is of interest that in Figure 4.5 we see that the *Libération* page is for the most part quite muted as regards the colour palette but on the upper part of the design a wide range is used. As we have seen already on this skilfully produced design, it seeks to communicate both 'ideas' and 'seriousness' but also 'energy' and 'lively creativity'.

Composition

When analysing and documenting design or form of visual communication such as product packaging we must also be attentive to the way that colour is used in the composition. Colour can be used to create links between elements or to distinguish them from others. On the *Dagens Nyheter* page design the three items at the top are coded as being of the same order through frame shape, but also through colour (Figure 3.1). On the Windows interface in Figure 4.2 we see that colour is used to code the tiles as being both the same and different categories. Often on a document border colour, font colours and key colours in images will be used to create coherence and links across a design. Again this can suggest that they are fundamentally connected or belong together.

Borders

Borders point to the way that elements are shaped and related to each other. A border might be a line dividing a space and delimiting it from other spaces, and also space itself, together with alignment, makes differences between elements. In a document design this is a way of telling the reader that things in different frames are not related, or that things within the same frame are related, or that an element separated from others by space has a certain function in the layout (cf. van Leeuwen, 2005: Chapter 1, whose analysis of 'framing' is close to our analysis of 'borders'). The meanings of borders draw on associations with thickness, with the strength or relative permeability of boundaries and with distance created by space.

Segregation

This is where elements are separated from each other by a border. They therefore occupy different domains. The meaning here is that they are of a different order. Examples of this can be seen on the university vision document in Figure 4.6 where the vision itself, the 'values' and the 'strategic objectives' are separated from each other by borders. In these cases the thickness of the frame can indicate the strength of the boundary. In this example the boundary is narrow. Boundaries can be much thicker or can be permeable which suggests possibilities for movement and integration of meanings.

Separation

This is where elements are separated but by empty space. Here the elements may be part of the same domain but have some similarity since they are separated by space. In Figure 4.6 we can see that the different strategic objectives are separated to a considerable degree. Yet they are classified as being in the same domain. Such a design feature can have the effect of communicating that things are of the same order which in fact have very little in common or are highly contradictory.

Integration

This is where elements occupy the same space. For example, in the *Dagens Nyheter* layout we can see that in the tiles at the top of the page images and text sit in the same frames (Figure 3.1). This communicates they are of the same order. A photograph of a person can be related to a story purely though integration. On an advert or brochure a smiling person becomes integrated into the meaning of the product or the service. To some extent they operate as one element. On the university vision document the text sits over the images of the university therefore communicating as one element (Figure 4.6).

Overlap

This is where an element partly crosses over a boundary or space. We see this in the *Libération* design in Figure 4.5 where the letter 'a' spreads out making other elements adapt to its form. In this case this helps to communicate 'crossing of boundaries' and 'creativity'. This can happen to different degrees. On the *Dagens Nyheter* page in Figure 3.1 we can see that a cut-out of a person may subtly bleed out of the frame. On a cover of a children's magazine this may be more dramatic to suggest fun, irreverence and lack of boundaries.

Rhyme and contrast

Different elements can be linked where the frames have some kind of common quality. This can be that the frames are the same shape, colour or size, for example. We see this on the BBC news site where very diverse content is presented as the same by the use of frame size and shape and by the ordered way they are presented. In the same way elements may be presented as different through things like shape, colour or size. We see this on the Windows interface where we are given a sense of variety through frame size (Figure 4.2). The BBC news site creates ranking of importance through different sizes of the same frame (Figure 4.3).

SUGGESTIONS FOR RESEARCH QUESTIONS

Throughout this chapter we have given a sense of how this form of analysis can be used to analyse documents as part of a research project. For example, we have carried out comparisons of movie posters for different film audiences, of different kinds of mobile interfaces and magazine page layouts. In each case we showed how such analysis allows us to reveal the kinds of discourses that these carry. Concrete research questions for such a project could be:

- How do different sports web pages communicate to their specific audiences?

- Is there a difference in visual design between medical social media sites targeted at men and women?

- How have the visual designs of school history textbooks changed between 1975 and 2015?

In each case we would have to make clear what specific examples and cases we were using in order to carry out the analysis. For example, we would not want to look at all history textbooks, but focus on the representation of the Middle Ages or the Second World War. As regards the medical social media site we may specify a particular kind of site, say for example for cosmetic surgery, or for dealing with depression.

In each of these cases we may combine the tools presented in this chapter with those in the chapters on photographs and data analysis, since, for example, school books may carry photographs and present data in different ways. Tools will be chosen to allow us to reveal the differences in each case. Taking the example of school textbooks representing war, how do document design, photography and data communicate different discourses about that event? Do they use colour, layout and photographs differently?

Again, as we emphasized in the previous chapter, the basis of the questions that we ask should be informed by engaging with the existing research literature on each topic. So what is already known about these topics about visual communication in the domain in which the research questions sits: about film genres, about gender in health communication, or about the representation of war in the media?

In each, the process of analysis could involve a larger-scale quantitative-type study where we create a coding sheet for a larger sample. Or it could take place, as does most social semiotic work, by way of collecting a large enough sample to allow us to understand what kinds of patterns are taking place, where we then carry out a detailed analysis of a number of selected typical cases.

5

PACKAGING

Introduction

In this chapter we turn our attention to packaging. Here we are interested in the kinds of boxes and bags used to carry and present our breakfast cereal, the variety of bottles and containers used for shampoo and deodorants, or any kind of packaging used to help sell products. Such packaging brings new kinds of challenges as regards analysis compared with photographs (Chapter 3) and document design (Chapter 4) which are only two-dimensional. Packaging is three-dimensional, having not only height and width but also depth. It comprises objects that we can pick up and feel, which we carry away from a shop and place in different rooms and storage spaces, such as the larder or fridge in the kitchen or a bathroom cabinet where we may interact with them as we use them. This calls, we show, for other types of tool kits than in the previous chapters.

Packaging draws on and communicates wider discourses about things like health, safety, gender, nature, learning and pleasure (Wagner, 2015). A shampoo can indicate a gendered use; a yoghurt can signal vitality; or a biscuit can tell us that it is something traditional. These are complex ideas, values and issues that, of course, are re-contextualized for the purposes of selling products (Ventura, 2015). For example, product packaging and branding invites us to participate in being responsible for the environment through a collection of minor consumer acts. We can buy coffee from a local Latin American producer who uses sustainable farming, a fruit drink where the container is made from recycled material, an organically fed chicken in a textured package with a card surround carrying images of an idyllic farm and portraits of the farmers. Yet what is not communicated here is that more environmental cost is accumulated in the production of a product, in its transportation, storage, in the creation of the complex packaging, the design of the brand, the promotional work, than can ever be recouped in its recycling. One might not unreasonably suggest that the environment might be best served by banning such packaging in the first place, or by wholesale government policies. But recycling and saving the planet are sold to us as a kind of personal moral and even aesthetic choice. As regards things like the environment, gender or health, we might argue that it is through consumer products and their associated discourses that we most engage with them.

Discourses of packaging

Packaging communicates by combining many different semiotic resources into a coherent whole, using the material package and its shape, be it small or large, angular or circular (Klimchuk and Krasovec, 2006). The material could be paper, plastic or aluminium, all of which have different textures and connotations. The packaging may carry a typeface that is ornamented and old-fashioned or modern and regular. Writing on packaging has many functions, such as carrying a slogan like 'Have a Coke and a smile' or formally stating the ingredients of the product. Colour too is important in communicating values and ideals, for example luxury, where often black and gold are used, or child-friendly by means of a bright colour palette. All these resources are combined into a whole to communicate to specific consumer groups or to communicate specific discourses about products. We begin by looking at three examples of how packaging draws on different discourses to addresses consumers and communicate values, specifically 'gender', 'innocence' and 'value for money'. We then present the tool kits for analysing packaging.

Grooming products: communicating gender

In Figure 5.1 we see two grooming products that are very obviously gendered: a shampoo from Garnier Fructis and a shower gel from Axe. Without knowing anything about the contents of these packages, or having tested, smelled or touched the products that they contain, nor experienced the cleaning results they offer, we immediately, due to the packaging, sense that Garnier Fructis targets a younger female consumer, whereas Axe is directed to male consumers. Already the brand names suggest this. Even if, in principle, nothing hinders a woman from using an axe, we normally do not associate it with female beauty products. Also, the Garnier Fructis product name 'Strength and Shine', with for example 'Triple Nutrition' and 'Body Boost' also being part of the range, is to be compared with the product name 'Apollo', pointing to explorations of space and with 'Jet' and 'Anarchy' as other products of the Axe range. Both brands encompass a broad range of female and male grooming products with a recurring design and visual identity.

Figure 5.1 A shampoo from Garnier Fructis and a shower gel from Axe (Photographs by author)

The communication of gender, however, goes beyond the names of the products and is found fundamentally in the shape of the containers. And these examples are a very good place to start with this kind of analysis, since, in a sense, they are so obvious. But we are less familiar with asking more systematic questions about three-dimensional shapes.

These two plastic containers contain the same amount of liquid, 250ml, but we see that the Garnier Fructis container is tall and slender in comparison with the shorter and thicker Axe container. Such a design choice is precisely the kind of deployment of semiotic resources that interests us in this chapter. Consequently, the Garnier Fructis bottle needs a bit more protection or handling in the sense that it might fall, whereas Axe stands steady. Even if the actual product weight is the same, Axe appears heavier and more robust due to the packaging. But the difference is also about the way that the height and slimness gives a look more of elegance and aspiration in contrast to the more grounded and substantial look of the Axe container.

As well as height and width we find that the two containers deploy curvature and angularity differently. The Fructis container curves gently outwards from the base and then inwards towards the top. Roundness is clearly an important design principle for Garnier Fructis. Axe, in contrast, uses inward curvature, to create a 'grip' look, including angular cuts going upwards. The container is therefore textured to the touch and feels tougher and more substantial. The grip, found on tools, machinery and motorbikes, helps to point to toughness and robustness. The lid too is thick and angular, alluding to the rocket theme, but also resembling broad shoulders. The angularity suggests something more aggressive than the gentle curves of Fructis.

Since packaging is three-dimensional it can communicate what is front, back or on the sides, or not do so. Garnier Fructis has a clear distinction between front and back with no sides foregrounded. The Axe container also communicates a clear back and front, also using the sides to create the grip look, integrating the two. As we will see in this chapter, these dimensions can be used in different ways. For example, we may find a design used to create a clear front, or an illustration, such as on a milk carton, can wrap around several different sides and so contain the whole product. What we find on the Fructis container is that the sides are reduced and not used to carry text in order to help communicate slimness. In the case of Axe the sides are used as part of the design of the grip.

Colour is also an important difference between the two containers. Garnier Fructis has a bright and shiny, lime-like, almost neon-green colour. This has a highly glossy quality that communicates qualities of the results of the product. The Axe container has a sober black nuance and cold colours, grey and aqua blue, in the angular graphic symbol, with possible associations with power and calculation.

The typeface of the Fructis brand name has curvature and letters with a low weight and thin strokes, including a dot over the upper case 'I', giving extra ornamentation, with possible associations with elegance and emotions. Another ornamentation is the characteristic knob on the lid in darker green. In the latter and male case we find large and broad letters in the brand name, where the length of the horizontal strokes gives a distinct graphical identity to the brand and makes it stretch out in space, following an overall Axe design principle that has been called the 'square round edge' and devised to give a sense of sophistication, no doubt with sexual undertones, to their male grooming products.

On the two containers we also find iconography. On the Fructis container we find a round icon that has the appearance of a cutaway of fruit labelled as 'Grapefruit Extract'. We also find this round icon repeated at the top of the container. Here the emphasis is on roundness and the natural, but the cutaway suggests something more connected to processing and science, rather than an organic kind of natural. On the Axe container, we find a symbol resembling lightning is used, alluding to energy and movement. This symbol has angularity, which relates to the angularity in the shape of the container. We could ask how the women's product would communicate differently were it in a smaller, fatter, squat container, or if the men's product was taller, slimmer and more elegant, with gentle curves.

Honest branding: communicating innocence

Since the 2000s 'honest' branding has become widespread, which in the case of packaging means that the 'natural' and 'organic' are visually communicated in new ways. This can be seen as a response to the increasing awareness of environmental threats and healthy eating and also to low consumer trust, where scandals such as horse DNA traces found in beef burgers in British supermarkets or minced meat being re-packed in Swedish grocery stores and given new best-before dates. It is also related to a rise in interest in ethical and healthy diets. Scholars have suggested that these more natural kinds of food are interrelated with a middle-class notion of taste, status and power (Shugart, 2014).

The organic must suggest slowness, the personal, the opposite of processing and impersonal manufacturing process. The idea of 'local' can also be important, which can be accomplished by a range of semiotic means and may be broadly thought of in terms of a less mediated form of product that goes directly from the farm to the table (Shugart, 2014). Such ideas are infused with romantic ideas about purity and innocence of nature and simpler ways of life (Hansen, 2002). The idea of honest branding therefore is to communicate messages such as 'nothing but nature', 'unadulterated food', 'clear conscience' (Burrows, 2013). As with the case of gender, packaging here is an important part of communicating this honesty.

In Figure 5.2 we see juice bottles from the UK brand Innocent, sold in many countries around the world. Important three-dimensional qualities here lie in the bottle being designed as a carafe with a neck and thick lid, evoking something home-made and also robust and authentic, as if we were being served a good wine in a rural area. Here too the stockiness of the bottle appears less elegant and more grounded. The transparent plastic material is also an important choice here, which, unlike the washing products above, unmasks the content, allowing it to speak for itself. As we know, an honest person has nothing to hide, and this trustworthiness is part of the brand message.

The plastic itself is thin. On the one hand the manufacturer promotes their aim to use less plastic in packaging and that it should all be from food-grade recycled materials. So on one sense this in itself brings more 'naturalness' and 'uncorrupted' association to the package. But on the other hand this also creates a different feel to the more robust thicker plastic of the Axe gel above. In the Innocent case the thinness of the plastic relates to the unmediated, 'just product' idea. It also in itself,

Figure 5.2   Juices from the brand Innocent: a promotional photo to the left and drinks on the shelf to the right (Photographs by author)

once empty, appears insubstantial and a modest item to recycle. Again to draw out these meanings we can think of the effect were a male washing gel packaged in this transparent type of thin plastic container.

Given that Innocent exists in an already crowded market of juices the logo of the brand and package imagery are important. And given these juices are sold often at three times the price of other products some work must be done to show why. The logo here, shown in Figure 5.3, combines something almost childish to represent simplicity and innocence, with something more modern and measured. We see a face with a halo, where the uneven strokes seem drawn by a child, or at least someone not taking too much care to make it perfect, and the use of the halo of course suggests something guilt-free, pure of thought and intention.

The fonts used, in contrast, are even, regular and modern. Letters are rounded and gentle and are slightly spaced out, giving a sense of 'air' and 'room to breathe' as designers say. Such products communicate lack of artifice, serene moods and slower paces. It is also important that the font is rendered in black bringing more sober associations. This contributes to an overall limited colour palette which makes it clear that colours here are not combined to signal what is fun, but measure and restraint.

Figure 5.3   The logo of Innocent

The label on the Innocent packaging divides the bottle into a clear front and two different sides. While one side contains the mandatory copy on contents, the other side is used for what is commonly called CSR or corporate social responsibility. On the front panel of the bottle we see a call-out with a hat and the text 'the big knit', with an arrow connecting image and text, a feature quite common in honest branding (Burrows, 2013). In this case the headline reads 'Small hats, warm hearts' and is about knitting a hat which you can then send to Innocent who may then put a photograph of it on the bottles. For each sold bottle wearing a hat Innocent donates 25p to Age UK. The light-green arrow connecting the image and the text is curved, connoting simplicity and informality, saying 'see for yourself!' and inviting consumers to take part.

In Figure 5.4 we see another example of honest branding that codes 'innocence' with a very different kind of package. Here we find two products by Ella's Kitchen which is UK's biggest baby-food brand and established in many European markets. In this case the aim is to promote baby food that communicates cleanness, being simple and unadulterated food. For their smoothies we see 'the red one' has a simplified strawberry symbol and 'the yellow one' has a stylized banana.

We find pure saturated primary colours which on the shelf create a lively colour palette. Here we see even the product names 'the red one' and 'the yellow one' avoid 'strawberry' or 'banana' as product names, which means that language is used for labelling in a way akin to a picture book, where a simplified illustration of a bright yellow or red car can co-exist with the word 'car'. The product descriptor 'ecological smoothie' is written in a small font below the logo. The typeface is also childish, with uneven strokes, appearing hand-drawn.

Figure 5.4 Ella's Kitchen and the smoothies 'the red one' and 'the yellow one' (Photographs by author)

Specific to this product is the use of a thin plastic packaging which is accommodating. We can compare this to the majority of baby food which is packaged in see-through glass containers which are hard and unyielding and not for children to touch. Here the child can hold and feel the package. And the package, with its rough and unregulated contours, also comes out as less regulated. It adjusts to the touch of the hand, rather than being a food stuff that we take out of the pot with a spoon. This physical closeness in itself can communicate a kind of intimacy as opposed to the remoteness of artificial processes. We also find a stark contrast between the thin and square body of the package and the big, round and solid lid or head, which once again evokes a sense of the playful, of the package being almost a toy. It is also interesting that the colour nuances slightly change and underpin this contrast. The lids are bright red and yellow, of the kind we also meet in children's toys, but the body has more muted nuances. The yellow is darker, almost mustard-like, and comes out as more 'adult' or measured, as directed to parents.

What we begin to see here is the way that colours, fonts and iconography can communicate ideas and values, but so too can materials, sizes and textures. Of course, we experience these as a single material object. But we start to see the value in looking more closely at these semiotic choices.

Discount brands: communicating value for money

Figure 5.5 shows a form of packaging used to communicate 'value for money'. We see the red and white packaging of the Swedish brand ICA Basic, part of a Dutch-based European food retailer which runs a set of products called Euro Shopper. This is the local ICA version.

What is immediately striking is that the products are given a coordinated colour and design scheme to be easily identifiable on the shelves. But when we

Figure 5.5   The Swedish discount brand ICA Basic

look closer we also find something very specific as regards the shape and textures of the packages that unite them. And all of these semiotic materials are deployed to communicate 'basic', 'no fuss' and 'value', without suggesting that quality is lower. Of course, what stands out from other packaging is the use of two colours only which together create a quite stark effect and suggests simplicity, something direct, ungarnished. The UK food retailer Sainsbury has a similar design of their basic line where orange and white are used. It is no surprise that ICA's logo is red and Sainsbury's orange, fusing the products with the brand. Also important is that neither of the colours has contours. They are flat, unmodulated, regular, without relief. Such flat colours tend to be used to communicate constancy and truth. There are no subtle shades or nuances here.

The red and white are used to create rhyming across the designs. The red 'speech bubble' stating the nature of the product, rhymes with the 'table' surface upon which the products sits. The font colour rhymes with the white. The surface too communicates something basic, uncomplicated and functional. The choice of the glossy is slightly garish. Upmarket versions of frozen vegetables, for example, will contain more iconography of serving equipment and the textures of the plastic packaging may be slightly rough. Such textures feel like they invite touch more than the glossy. We can see in Figure 5.5 that the glossy plastic appears to catch the light in a way that is less flattering. Again this can help give a sense of lack of artifice.

If we look at the baby-food packaging in Figure 5.4 we also find a glossy surface. But here the effect changes with the soft textures created by the colour effect, the typeface and the stylized drawings. And in the case of the whole it is a playful design compared with the starkness and emptiness of the basics design, where also traditional photographs are used to display the product on the front of the package. ICA uses a modern typeface with curvature and a horizontal orientation. It is un-aspirational yet modern and suggests softness and nurturing. A more angular or traditional font would have been too harsh and logical for the rest of the composition. In sum we see that while packaging may to some extent be required to protect, store or transport a product it can also be used to carry very specific discourses and ideas to sell the product.

Analysing packaging

In this section we begin with materials, and then look at the shape and form of the packaging. We then turn to colour, typeface and writing, and finally iconography. We refer back to some of the examples above and also introduce some new ones, especially those that allow us to carry out the kinds of comparison that tends to be useful for drawing out affordances.

Materials

Packages are manufactured from physical materials, and we will here make comments on some affordances of such materials. In an actual package such materials will of course be manufactured and shaped into a whole. Furthermore, after the packaging and product have been used, materials become part of processes of not only recycling but also 'upcycling' (Björkvall and Archer, 2017). So discarded materials are reused and their semiotic values and affordances are transformed. A metal food container can be made into a lamp, a torn ladder into a bookshelf, a PET bottle into a broom.

There are clearly a number of key materials used in packaging: paper, card, plastic, glass, metals and wood, as well as a new range of bio-materials made from plants. And these materials can, as we have seen above, communicate ideas and values. A plastic bag can be thin and mainly transparent to hold budget apples. It can be glossy and white for a basics line, or it can be given a texture and pastel colour scheme to hold a product like an organic chicken. Below we present an inventory of some basic affordances of typical packaging materials (cf. Klimchuk and Krasovec, 2006: Chapter 8).

Wood

We begin with a much less used material, which is useful for drawing out the affordances of other materials. We only tend to find wood used for packaging of products such as cigars or a bottle of expensive whisky. Clearly there is a sense of something special here, that such products are associated with craft, with being handmade, with something artisan. The artisanal connotations suggest slower, careful processes, which translate onto a product that must be appreciated and savoured at the same slow pace. Increasingly we can find things like cosmetics packaged in ways to connote naturalness. Although in such cases we do not find the rougher wood-casing look of the whisky, but wood that is more fashioned and shaped; for example a blusher is placed in a round wooden pot where the grain of the wood can be seen through a metallic coloured finish.

Glass

This is a more traditional form of pre-plastic and pre-mass production packaging and much of its meaning can relate to these associations. Glass can suggest something older or traditional. It gives a sense of something created to endure longer and can communicate substantiality through weight. Beers sold in bottles feel different than those sold in cans which appear more practical, and attempts to use plastic bottles have not been successful (Wagner, 2015). Shops now stock ranges of newer specialist beers where much thought has gone into the design of the glass, as regards form and colour, often to bring connotations of tradition in brewing. The weight of the bottle here can be important to carry associations of provenance and substantiality and again of artisan honesty. It feels more ceremonious if you eat in your local Indian restaurant and two specialist beer bottles are placed on the table rather than two cans of beer. And of course glass can be used to allow us to see the contents, which can be another way to communicate honesty. We often find cosmetics in coated glass can suggest quality and expense.

Carton

Boxes can give an extra layer of protection. But they can also suggest higher quality. Some deep-freeze foods, such as pizzas, come in clear plastic sealed covers, whereas others are also placed within a box. A basics range breakfast cereal will tend to come in a plastic packet whereas a branded cereal will be in a box, although of course boxes can then carry colour and compositions that tell us that it is nevertheless a more economy brand. Cartons can also have different thicknesses, which can also signal quality through weight, durability and solidity. A box of special occasion biscuits, made for taking to an event, will likely use thicker card than cheaper biscuits or say for a pizza packaging. Cartons can also be used to communicate 'no frills' in a specific way when they are used in a form that looks bare, as is the case of the brown, rough, packaging in IKEA stores (cf. Ventura, 2015).

Paper

Paper gives an impression of more fragility and tends to be associated with something more handmade or traditional, where formerly goods were hand-wrapped in paper. So we may find bread in paper and find it more traditional than the loaves packaged entirely in a plastic bag. A bar of soap in an organic shop may be wrapped in a stiffer form of paper. When we buy fresh fish at a counter some supermarkets may use a plastic bag, or seal the fish into a polystyrene tray. But others may wrap the fish in paper which is sealed on one side, which appears more hand-served. We may also find an addition paper layer of wrapping inside a tin of biscuits.

Plastics

Here we find a wide variety of forms and their meaning will depend upon textures and shapes as we saw above as regards the washing products and the baby food.

Plastic can communicate modernity and processing, in the way that a manufacturer may feel the need to add elements of card, texture or colour to help add a sense of quality or honesty. For example, an organic, free-range chicken may be sealed in a plastic bag, but if there is a thin card band fastened around it and if the plastic is textured this will give it a different meaning than the glossy polished plastic of the basics range. A bottle of face cream may have a basic plastic container but has a fused outer card surface, again for texture. But even very cheap clear plastic can be used to communicate expense and quality. For example, you buy some Apple hardware, such as an iPhone. Each individual item, the cable, a connector, the device, its container, are all wrapped in their own tiny plastic bag or sleeve. And this early interaction with the product can be part of the message about it being an event.

Metal

Metal, like plastic, can be used to make lightweight and thin yet highly resistant containers. For preserved food they have the disadvantage or advantage of concealing the product. In this case a picture can be used, either printed onto the can or by using paper. The look of the contents is then not that important as the cultural meanings which the packaging can load upon it. But metal can also bring a sense of quality, given it is durable. A metal lid on a bottle appears more high status than a plastic one. And the metal can be covered with lacquers or paint. Some coffees such as Lavazza produce options in metal cans with a re-sealable lid. We also find this with some branded cooking ingredients such as gravy powders. Often food for Christmas such as biscuits or chocolates come in tins bringing a sense of tradition and luxury. Here, neither wood nor plastic would do the same job.

Textures

It is clear from the above account of materials that the kinds of textures that they are capable of, or which can be designed onto them, is important as regards how packaging communicates. Like materials themselves textures are infused with social meanings and values and are experienced in all human activities. Here we look at textures using several categories of analysis, drawing on Abousnnouga and Machin (2013), van Leeuwen (2016) and Ledin and Machin (2017b). As with materials, the meaning of these will depend upon how they are used in other design combinations. But here there is value in exploring these in this atomized manner. In practical analysis we would tend to use them together with the other tool kits to look at a single package.

Rigidity

Surfaces may be resistant or they can give more or less to the touch. A resistant surface is a hard surface, and as surfaces get softer their resistance to pressure decreases. The floor of an entrance hall may be a marble floor which is unyielding to the touch. Another may have a cork or rubber floor which gives very slightly. In theory we could make a highly resistant sponge floor that had the texture of a mattress. This may be okay for a children's play centre but not for a corporate building. If we look at the two washing products at the start of the chapter we find that the Axe container is more rigid to the touch than the Fructis shampoo in Figure 5.1. Simply the surface is stronger and less yielding. The whole package feels more stable. We can say that this works alongside the angularity and colours as part of communicating toughness. The more giving container of Fructis, in contrast, could suggest something more accommodating, or comfortable. The baby food in Figure 5.4 suggests softness, yielding to the touch, which contrasts with the more usual use of transparent glass jars. The Innocent bottle in Figure 5.2 is made of very thin plastic that yields slightly. In both cases this yielding could be better than glass for communicating accommodating to the environment. In the case of the baby food the softness can also go along with nurturing.

Relief

Parts of surfaces can extend below or above a horizontal plane. This can suggest the difference between something that is natural and uneven, with imperfections, or something that is artificially flat. Relief can signal 'authenticity', 'simplicity', something worn, used over time, a lived surface. Relief can also hinder movement and touch, as the bumps on a road. The flat and smooth surface might, on the one hand, be considered un-authentic, dull and pre-fabricated, but could, on the other hand, come out as pure, practical, efficient and easy to use. We can see in the two washing containers in Figure 5.1 that Fructis has a flat unhindered surface. Here we might say there is a sense of something pure and efficient. In contrast the Axe container uses relief on the sides with the grip look and for the lid with the angular shapes. Here there is a sense of something more authentic, less easy. The Innocent bottle in Figure 5.2 is very flat. The smaller version of the bottle has no relief at all, emphasizing simplicity and ease. The larger version has a very gentle ridge which sits around the label area. But for the most part we still find lack of relief. We can contrast this with contemporary traditional ale bottles which often have ridges, lettering which is raised, other emblems and icons which raise the relief of the bottle. And other products, like chocolates or perfumes, may have raised letters and designs on boxes. Here too there is a sense of a personal touch, of something hand-embossed.

Regularity

Regular textures are predictable and can mean homogeneous, lack of surprise and consistency. Or they can be irregular and mean different, playful, creative, or inconsistent. Irregularity can also suggest something handmade as opposed to being manufactured and standardized. The Ella's Kitchen baby food in Figure 5.4 uses irregularity, also to point away from the idea of processing and regularity. We can see how this rhymes with the irregular appearance of the fonts and colour scheme. And many organic products might seek to use less regular surfaces, such as through paper or card packaging which is slightly uneven. Other products that may use irregular packaging are breads. We could imagine buying a bread in a sharp-edged regular surfaced box. This would not tend to work as breads should bring some sense of being handmade, or as having provenance or a link with nature, as we see in the commercials that market them. Where we would be less likely to find irregularity would be on medical products where regular surfaces communicate predictability, standardization and science.

Naturalness

Textures can also communicate naturalness or artificiality. This is partly because materials may have their origin in nature or be manufactured and artificial. Natural materials include wood, bark from trees. But naturalness partly involves cultural experiences and knowledge in determining the origins of different materials. So a rough paper might appear more natural than a shiny plastic. A glass bottle, such as used for a traditional ale, might appear more natural, due to the association with traditional and natural methods of production. This is one reason a beer bottle appears less intrusive than a can of beer when placed on a table in a restaurant. Naturalness can be associated with what is authentic and organic. Textures that are less naturalistic can suggest technological progress, high competence, the predictable, and also the impersonal and artificial. In the case of the ICA Basic, we find mainly plastics with glossy surfaces, which points to the predictable and the impersonal. The packaging communicates little of personal touch as regards texture. On beauty products we may find wood used for make-up containers or plastics that are moulded in the form of wood grain, bark or leaves. Other products might use tin to deliberately communicate older industrial processes.

Viscosity

Viscosity is about how sticky different surfaces are. Of course, this can have positive and negative meanings, depending on context. Sticky can mean dirty and unwashed, which is not very useful for food packaging. But more sticky can also be achieved through rubber-like or foam textures, which can add comfort and grip. More often in packaging this is accomplished by shape, which we deal with in the next section. But, nevertheless, viscosity may be used on lids to help them be gripped and unscrewed. Men's washing products may use viscosity as part of a handle-type grip design. A type of canned energy drink may use viscosity, in the form of a polystyrene layer, to communicate its practical use during fitness. A branded detergent may have a small viscous section to help grip, or a trigger section where spray action is involved. Such additions may be practical, but they also help to communicate functionality as a kind of affect as would a male deodorant that was slightly viscous. For a branded product such extras can be important as part of communicating its robustness in doing its job.

Liquidity

Surfaces may be more or less wet or dry, which can relate to life and vitality or to rot and decay. Liquid is a prerequisite for humans and living organisms. Surfaces that are wet can mean vitality and purity. This is one reason a corporate entrance hall may install a wall fountain. Sexuality is tied to what is humid, which often makes a 'wet look' stand out as sexy and also young. Dryness consequently can connote ageing, a lack of vitality. But dryness can also signal comfort, cleanliness and order, as when we do the laundry or wash the car and then dry it to get a smooth and perfect surface. We may find a wet look surface less often in food packaging, although this may be of value in drinks and ice cream sold in summer. But dryness seems of high importance. Dryness can be used as part of communicating oldness and tradition as in the dry and crispy-type paper found to wrap some brands of crackers. While the inside of a cheese packaging may be glossy and liquid to suggest moisture, the outside may be dry and slightly lacking in vitality to suggest aging. The dryness of breakfast cereal packaging can also be important to communicate crispness and freshness. The packaging for washing products such as Garnier Fructis may have a surface that appears to have liquidity connecting it to the shampoo within.

Shape

Since packages are three-dimensional manufacturers naturally take a lot of interest in shape. Again, to some extent, there are practicalities as regards storage and transportation. But important too is how the product looks on the shelves, the physical appearance and feel when we pick it up and its possibilities for use in domestic space. In the inventory below we list three-dimensional features of packaging.

Front and back

Important for packaging is that there is a front and a back. Packaging designers call the front the 'primary display panel', or PDP, and here colour, symbols and typography come together, not least to emphasize the brand name, as we see in the examples above (Klimchuk and Krasovec, 2006: Chapter 4). There is a clear parallel with humans. We also have a clear front and back and interact with others this way. The front is our face, our eyes and sensory organs, and displays who we are, and we look into the eyes of friends to see how they are or feel. This is an important explanation as to why packages are designed as they are and as to why the communication comes out as direct.

Vertical and horizontal

This is simply whether a package is tall and more vertically oriented or squat and more horizontally oriented. Here taller slimmer packages can appear more elegant, aspirational or even delicate. A shorter fatter package can be more stable, durable or practical. Also the reverse meanings can be realized, where taller can appear pompous, insubstantial, fragile or delicate and where shorter packages can appear clumsy and immobile. We see this difference in the two washing products in Figure 5.1 where Fructis uses a more vertical orientation to suggest something more elegant and perhaps delicate, as compared to the squatter, more stable-looking Axe. So a bottle for a white wine may be tall and thin, to suggest elegance while such a form would not be so appropriate for a beer, a whisky or even for a fruit juice.

Curvature and angularity

Angular packaging can suggest something practical, technical, harsh, efficient, even masculine. In contrast curved packaging can suggest emotions, the organic, expression, luxury and feminine. We see curvature in the shape of both the washing products in Figure 5.1. Of course in the case of Garnier Fructis we find a gentle curvature of the container combined with vertical orientation and slimness. In the case of the Axe container we also find curvature. But this is used to create the shape of the grip handle. And we also have other aspects of angularity in the surface relief. And we have much less horizontal orientation. We can see that the orange-juice package in the ICA Basic range in Figure 5.5 is a square box in contrast with the curves of the Innocent bottle in Figure 5.2. In the case of the basics range the use of the box can communicate practicality and efficiency, whereas the curves of Innocent can here, combined with other aspects of the packaging design, communicate something more natural and organic. A perfume bottle may use curvature in more complex ways to communicate emotional expression and femininity. In the case of Ella's Kitchen in Figure 5.4 we find the use of roundness as part of communicating something natural and emotional. The oversized lid is highly rounded. The 'shoulders' of the packet have been rounded and the base given a rounded form.

Opacity

Packaging can be opaque, as in the case of the Axe container, or transparent, as with the Innocent container. Other products might have a small plastic window so that the product can be glimpsed. Where we can see inside there is a sense of revealing the inner workings, or a sense of lack of concealment, of openness. In many contemporary public and corporate buildings glass walls can be used to suggest such transparency, communication and open interaction. A jar of asparagus where the product can be seen may suggest something more honest, a more open and simple relationship between production and consumption than a can of asparagus that carries a photograph with a serving suggestion. In the ICA Basic range there is no transparency or intimacy, but a consequent use of photographs that appear bright and optimistic. We can also get degrees of transparency and opaqueness created by coloured glass. The greens and browns used in traditional ale bottles, as well as signifying older, artisanal types of glass, help to bring a more rustic hue to the beer.

Size

Size is of course related to practicality, to how large a package must be to contain the product, but we can think about size where it has been used deliberately to communicate something about the product. Larger size can then be used to communicate value. The package may still contain a lot of air, as we find in breakfast cereals or potato crisps, but this may still be a good way to communicate 'more'. When we buy electronic products, for example a new electric toothbrush, we might find padding used in a larger-than-necessary box. This may be moulded plastic or polystyrene. Here the size of the packaging and the sublayers of wrapping help to give value to the product. Other packages may seek to be smaller and discreet, as opposed to taking up space. A luxury product or particularly something wholefood may work better in a smaller container. This may be related to preciousness, about quality versus quantity and also about communicating less packaging and environmental friendliness, even if this product's processing and the creation of the packaging in fact was highly costly to the environment.

Colour

In this section we make an inventory of colour as used for packaging (Klimchuk and Krasovec, 2006: Chapter 6). We also deal with colour in Chapter 3 (p. 49), and in Chapter 4 (p. 80) we look specifically at colour in composition. Here we start with experiential metaphors involving colour.

A colour has a range of associations that arise from experiential metaphors, our experiences of life and culture (Gage, 1994). We know, for example, that the sky is blue, as is the sea when the sun shines. And blue has come to be used to communicate reflection, science and objectivity. This may be related to the way that the blue sky is not confined and allows us to see and think clearly. Blue has also come to be used to communicate purity since water is viewed as soft, pure and cleansing. A toothpaste might use such associations to create a 'burst of freshness' type design, which we see in Figure 5.6.

When a person becomes tired or exerted the face can become reddened as the heart speeds up. When we are wounded, of course, we bleed. Thus, red is a common signifier for energy, for being active and on the move. A red price tag on a package means a special offer, something immediate and on the move. Red can also communicate fire, heat and therefore, passion or aggression. Red can be used on the label of a beer bottle to suggest warmth. Orange can, like red, be associated with warmth, and be the colour of sun. Orange is a popular colour for skin-care products, or, if we associate it with flavours, it can signify fruitiness, as from peach or tangerine. We often find red and orange are colours used by discount brands to suggest simple optimism. Yellow is associated with the brightness of sunshine whereas colours like green and brown are related to the earth and to nature.

Black and white are associated with seeing a vision. Black can mean darker moods, seriousness, secrets, concealment, and it is a typical colour of up-market products, for example champagne. White is associated with purity and with softness. It is also common that the colour of the package simply depicts the product, so that tomato ketchup comes in a red bottle. Lemon juice might be packed in a yellow plastic container with relief having the exact shape of a lemon. Due to the fact that blooming nature is green, there can be a 'green product line', signifying that the products are ecological. When carrying out analysis we must be mindful that colours carry many different meanings and therefore these kind of associations are wide-ranging and ambiguous out of context.

Dimensions

As for dimensions, colours have qualities that can be placed on scales, such as light and dark, saturated and dilute. They combine cultural and experiential associations.

Brightness   Colours can be on a scale from brightness to darkness. This has to do with what is light and dark, which obviously is a rich source of meaning-making, including associations with clarity and obscurity, from brighter more optimistic moods to those that are solemn or reserved. In the process of analysis here we can look at the relative levels of brightness found on different packages. For example, in the case of the two washing containers in Figure 5.1, we find that Fructis uses a brighter colour for the plastic material and also brighter colours for some of the design. It is simply more optimistic. In contrast Axe uses a black material, suggesting something more reserved. The fonts use a brighter white and also aqua blue and a neutral grey. This helps to bring some brightness to the overall design. If we look at the ICA Basics design we find a bolder red, but these packages are dominated by white and by brightness. While the white and the form of the composition communicate simplicity and emptiness, they are also therefore optimistic. Such a design would not have worked with an overall darker colour scheme.

Saturation   Colours can be rich and saturated or more dilute and muted. Saturated colours can be associated with higher emotional temperatures whereas more diluted colours with more muted and reserved moods. We see saturated colours on the packaging of ICA Basic in Figure 5.5. The red here shouts out. As regards the Aquafresh toothpaste in Figure 5.6 we find rich emotional reds and bright whites but also a more muted sea blue-green, suggesting something more soothing.

Purity   Colours can be pure or they can be blended or contain shades, or elements of other colours. Historically pure colours have been associated with truth, order and simplicity. Impure colours are associated with complexity, ambiguity. Children's toys and products, of course, tend to use pure and highly pure, saturated colours. A toothpaste may use pure blues and whites to communicate simple direct cleaning actions as we see in Figure 5.6. ICA Basic will use pure colours to communicate simplicity and the truth if basic products. But we may find that natural products will tend to use less pure-looking natural types of colours, such as browns with blues in. Combined with a rougher textured card these can suggest something less purified, and therefore natural.

Modulation   Colours can be flat and featureless or they can carry grades of colour saturation. Or they can have different degrees of graininess, where they carry lighter versions of the same colour or another colour. The meaning of this can also relate to simplicity. A flat unmodulated colour can appear idealized, simple. The ICA Basic range uses such flat colours in the red. Even where we see the surface areas where the dishes stand, we see only minimal evidence of shadow.

Colour range   This is to do with how many colours we find on a package. A higher number of colours will tend to be used to communicate fun, liveliness and playfulness. A smaller number of colours, reducing to monochrome, will communicate something more reserved and contained. A high number of colours can also look crude and garish whereas a limited number can appear dull and lifeless. Typically, packaging for children's products will carry a wide colour palette of brighter colours. In Figure 5.6 we see that the Aquafresh toothpaste uses dark blue, blue-green, white and red. This is a relatively small colour range. Here the 'energy' is supplied by the pure, saturated, white explosion.

Writing and typography

Typography is a crucial part of packaging and we have made many typographical observations of packages in this chapter; for example a bold font with weight giving emphasis, as in the ICA Basic design in Figure 5.5, or a curved font suggesting something gentle and feminine, as was the case for the Garnier Fructis shampoo in Figure 5.1. As for analysing typography, the tool kit presented in Chapter 4 (p. 78), based on dimensions such as 'weight' and 'slope', works also for packaging so we refer to this tool kit.

Here we will concentrate on writing, which clearly is part of the design of packaging and also subject to regulations of law, which Figure 5.6 illustrates. This toothpaste carton comes from the US National Library of Medicine, which points to the regulations for packaging (and in this case medicine). As for the different types of writing we draw on Klimchuk and Krasovec (2006: Chapter 5). It is worth noticing that packaging designers make a general difference according to the three-dimensional shape of packaging and talk about the 'primary display panel', or PDP, as we discussed above, and 'secondary panels'. Here the primary front panel always contains the brand and product name and often call-outs, whereas the mandatory information to a large extent is given in the secondary panels. Below we account for our inventory of different types of writing.

Brand and product name

This is placed on the PDP and in this case reads 'Aquafresh' and with smaller upper-case letters 'fluoride toothpaste' and 'triple protection' placed above and

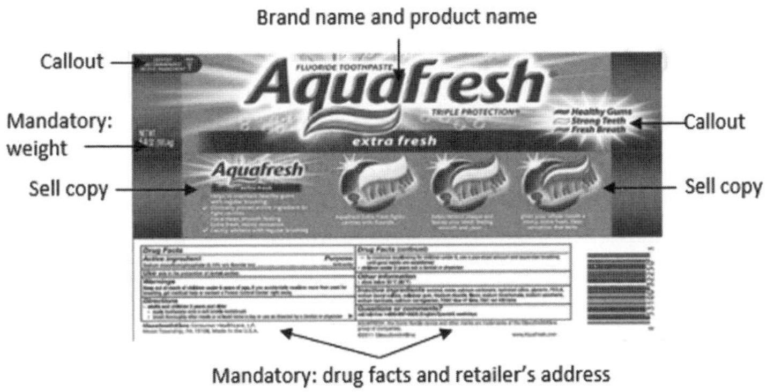

Figure 5.6 The carton package of Aquafresh as stored in and approved by the US National Library of Medicine and with categories of writing added by us

below the logo. In lower-case but larger letters in a dark-blue ribbon we see the text 'extra fresh'. So the product is, unsurprisingly, given positive qualities in order to sell.

Callout

A callout is writing inserted in graphics, in an icon or box of some kind. It is printed on the PDP. The Aquafresh carton has two graphically separated callouts with icons, to the upper left about being recommended by dentists, and to the right about improving gums, teeth and breath. As we saw in Figure 5.2, Innocent used the callout 'Small hats, warm hearts' to involve customers.

Sell copy

This is often placed on a secondary panel, in the case of Aquafresh on the side of the carton. To the left we meet bullet points saying, among other things, that it 'Helps to maintain healthy gums with regular brushing' and that it has a 'Clinically proven active ingredient to fight cavities'. The rest of the panel has another lay-out and displays toothbrush heads but with similar and overlapping messages: 'Aquafresh Extra Fresh fights cavities with fluoride …'. Similarly Innocent in Figure 5.2 uses sell copy on the 'sides' of the bottle to explain their knitting campaign where money is donated to the elderly.

Mandatory copy

This is copy enforced by the law, which explains why the net weight must be given on the PDP. Otherwise we find the mandatory copy in small fonts (but it must be legible according to law) on the back of the carton, on the side opposite the PDP. Here we find ingredients and the obligatory address of the retailer. In practical analysis different categories of mandatory copy can be separated according to their contents and legal constraints.

Overall, the writing of packages is very functional and connected to shape and three-dimensionality. We find strictly informational text but the promotional text is also striking, where graphics and writing come together in selling and branding the product.

Iconography

Packaging tends to carry a range of drawings, more abstract designs such as wavy lines as well as photographs and icons (Klimchuk and Krasovec, 2006: Chapter 7). Here we look at how we can guide the way we can make observations about these and draw on Barthes (1977) and Panofsky (1970). Both of them were interested in the way that elements in visual representations could be used to communicate wider associations. Panofsky's interest lay in art while Barthes had a wider interest in popular culture. Often such elements become invisible as they become part of more established discourses. The job of the analyst for these writers was to denaturalize them. Drawing on the work of both we have constructed the tool kit below.

Objects

Here we can ask what kind of objects we find on a design. This can be a kind of animal. Such an animal may be a bird to suggest lightness, or a monkey to suggest fun and playfulness. We may find an item of machinery involved in production. We may, for example, find a farm tractor, or simply icons for technology and power such as a battery or cogs. We may also find a leaf, or an item of fruit. The Fructis shampoo in Figure 5.1 has several scientific diagrams. Here too we find a cutaway of fruit, but here rendered as if seen through a microscope or in a petri dish. Of course, the meaning here is a mixture of natural refreshing cleaning ingredients from fruit along with science. Of interest was that men's cosmetics tended not to carry such scientific diagrams but rather icons representing machines or energy.

Settings

We can ask what kind of settings are represented. We might find nature (Hansen, 2002). This could be a farm, one that is idealized with a winding brook and happy animals, or a wild meadow. Or it could be a mountain, where nature becomes a natural wilderness, or ocean. Nature may be in the form of a deliberately exotic setting for coffee or global foods. Or we might find scenes such as an old-fashioned factory, a distillery. In, for example, the Innocent juice in Figure 5.2 the fruit appears to sit in an empty white space infused with brightness. Some fruit juices choose to show fruit placed in fresh growing grass. But here the light infused space seems to suggest a step further into purity and innocence.

Persons

We can ask what kind of people we find on packaging. We might find a farmer, often used to represent honest work, even where the producer is a huge corporation. Such pictures can be used on meat and dairy products to point to traditional production processes, free from worry of the use of toxic feeds, and so on. We might find an attractive yet unstriking woman used on a hair-colouring product. We might find a child on the side of a carton of organic milk, to help communicate health benefits. We might find generic ethnic people for coffee from Latin America, or Chinese people for a brand of soy sauce.

Emblems

Products carry all kinds of emblems, brand marks and crests. Here we can look at things like experiential associations such as angularity and curvature (for the meaning of such associations see sections on borders in Chapter 4), colours and the kinds of objects they carry. The Axe container in Figure 5.1 carries an emblem that resembles a kind of burst of electricity, yet in Aqua blue and grey. The Aquafresh toothpaste carries three circles that are glinting with light. Out of each comes a toothbrush that carries one of the three colours contained in the toothpaste used to visualize the sell copy.

Stylization

Barthes (1977) called this 'photogenia'. By this he meant the kind of style that is used. For example, do we see a 'real', more naturalistic scene, such as a farmer in front of a farmhouse. Or does it appear more in the form of a children's drawing, as on the Ella's Kitchen packaging in Figure 5.4, or a scientific diagram as on the Fructis package in Figure 5.1. Does it suggest a particular style of art? We might find a kind of impressionist art used, for example, on an organic range to connote high culture, yet at the same time something gentle. All such associations will depend on cultural experiences.

SUGGESTIONS FOR RESEARCH QUESTIONS

Throughout this chapter, through showing how packages communicate, making comparisons within product types and showing what kinds of discourses they communicate, we have given a clear sense of what kinds of research questions can be answered using these tools and how the analysis would take place. But here we can think about some specific research questions and how we might answer them:

- How are ecological/organic toothpastes packaged compared to 'regular' products?

- How are children's versions of dairy products packaged in three different countries?

- What is specific about the packaging of healthy products?

All of these questions imply some kind of comparison. In the first case we would need to collect a range of different toothpastes that were branded as organic and not branded as organic. We could then compare things like shape, materials, iconography, colour, texture, and so on. We would most likely establish that there are a number of basic rules for 'organic-ness' which we find to greater or lesser degrees. There is an organic shop near to where the authors live that sells very small and very expensive tubes of organic toothpaste. At this level great care must be taken to signal the correct meanings to justify the price. As part of this research project we would need to carry out a literature review on media representations of nature and the environment, some of which we referred to early in this chapter.

In the second case we would need to collect children's dairy products from different countries. This would then allow us to compare the uses of materials, colours, iconography, and so on. This may give us insights into the different ideas of things like childhood and health in different countries. Of course, many products may have many similarities across countries where there is only translation of language. In such a case this may indicate a global homogenization of children's foods. But we may find many differences too. Such a project would engage with literature on the representation of childhood in society and in the media.

In the third case we may need to narrow the question down to one specific kind of product. 'Healthy' is a broad and vague notion as regards food products. It can be associated with added ingredients and supplements, or with the 'natural' which is often again very vaguely defined, or with 'wholegrain', with 'goodness', with weight management. In this case a research project may be better aimed to investigate 'healthy products' as regards one type of food stuff, such as drinks, or breakfast cereal with an aim of looking at the different discourses that are communicated and at *how* these are communicated at a semiotic level.

6

SPACE DESIGN

Introduction

In academic work it has long been thought that space, how we design spaces, like urban parks, school rooms, town-centres, shops, and so on, tells us something about our ideas, values and priorities. This work crosses many academic fields, such as anthropology, cultural studies and critical theory. In social semiotics, space design is mentioned in the classical work of Hodge and Kress (1988), Kress and van Leeuwen (1996) and van Leeuwen (2005). In recent years it has attracted more and more interest, as we see in studies of elite tourism (Thurlow and Jaworski, 2012), the design of cafés (Aieillo and Dickinson, 2014), offices (Roderick, 2016) and IKEA kitchens (Ledin and Machin, 2017c), and the use of space in fitness regimes (Kerry, 2017; Ledin and Machin, 2017b). Importantly, space is three-dimensional, which shapes how we orient ourselves in relation to others. This means that space regulates how we can position our bodies and sets up possibilities for interaction. Teachers and management consultants, for example, are very aware of this and arrange spaces and furnishings to scaffold ways of behaving and interacting.

We present a set of tools that allow us to describe and analyse designed space, which includes both the interiors and exteriors of buildings. As in previous chapters the purpose is to allow us to draw out the kinds of ideas, values or discourses communicated by these forms of visual communication. We show that spaces are infused with the discourses that tend to dominate a society at any point in time and that these discourses are realized through the kinds of materials, colours and textures that are used, and through the formation of boundaries and front-and-back and sides. Specifically we show how we can study how space is shaped by its three-dimensional design. Such a design will have what we call 'interactional affordances' (cf. Goffman, 1993, on 'interaction order'). It will shape movement and interaction and consequently facilitate or restrain how we can engage with others.

How space shapes behaviour

There are a number of types of spaces that are obviously designed to channel our behaviour, to foster particular kinds of experience. The designs of airports, for example, are carefully devised to encourage people to act in certain kinds of ways, to foster a sense of ease, to channel movement. Supermarkets too are thought through as regards how they encourage us to spend more money. But we are less familiar with considering how other kinds of space shape interactions and identities. We will look at three examples – classrooms, restaurants and offices – in order to point to what kinds of tools would be needed to carry out an analysis.

Classrooms

The design of schools and classrooms has been a major project in Western societies and related to the forming of the national state and the disciplining of the population. From the beginning of the nineteenth century, primary schools (a notion coming from the French *école primaire* first used in 1802) were constructed with the idea that everyone must master the basic skills of reading, writing and numeracy, plus the proud history of the nation. Core principles of education at this time were that it brings both discipline and prosperity.

That schooling is historically connected to discipline is suggested by the US architect's drawing in Figure 6.1. It dates to 1838 and was at its time connected to a vision of both democracy and order (Weisser, 2006). Hitherto, American schoolhouses had mostly been wood-frame buildings located on a spare plot of land. They were often dark and cold, with small and irregular windows and all sorts of chairs, benches and pupils gathered around a wood-burning stove needed to keep warm in wintertime. What Figure 6.1 shows is an attempt to strengthen public education, to make it efficient and accessible for everyone, by modernizing the school building.

As we see, the building's capacity for reform relies on the teacher as the undisputable authority. The teacher's desk (A) is located on a raised platform and is the focal point, where the height in itself signals power and of course facilitates surveillance of the class. The area of the teacher is separated from the rest of the room with all pupils turned against her. It is a layout that relies on symmetrical framings, where the rows of desk create partitions. The 56 desks are neatly ordered and channel behaviour – anyone entering this room would know where to go and how to behave. The architecture is devised to bring order where chaos had reigned and to implement a large-scale pedagogical programme based on free schools paid by local taxes. We clearly see how space shapes and here restrains bodies and movement. It is laden with 'interactional affordances', meaning what kinds of social interactions and movements are built into the design. In this classroom no one but the teacher speaks unless told to, and social and also visual interaction between pupils is constrained due to the layout with fixed desks many rows deep.

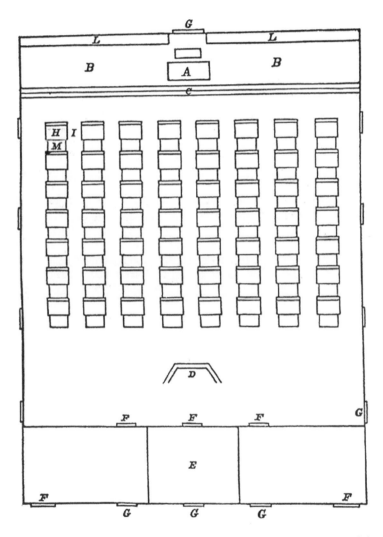

Figure 6.1 Drawing of an American schoolhouse from 1838 (from Henry Bernard, School Architecture, 1848, also published in Weisser, 2006)

The growth of the educational system made architects construct huge school buildings with multiple identical classrooms. In the UK this took the form of Victorian buildings, and one of the authors attended such a school in the 1980s which was later demolished. It was a place where the dark tiles on the walls and floors made it feel inhospitable. No talking was allowed. Windows were positioned high so that children could not look out, isolating them from the outside world. There was still corporate punishment in the form of caning. Learning subservience and obedience was as much a part of the purpose of these rooms as was learning about ideas. Externally these buildings tended to appear as any other state building, such as council offices, libraries, hospitals or court-rooms. Scholars have written on the way that these schools were in a sense primarily about creating a more submissive working class ready for labour in factories (Willis, 1977).

In Figure 6.2 we see a classroom that resembles the one where one of the authors started primary school in Sweden in the late 1960s, soon to be replaced with more open-plan layouts connected to the progressive pedagogy of the 1970s. The photo dates to 1956 and is typical of many Northern European classrooms that were constructed after the Second World War, during the post-war boom, when compulsory education was prolonged and the idea of the welfare state gained ground (cf. Depaepe, 2000). Now the more severe and classical building

Figure 6.2 Northern European classroom from 1956 (Getty Images)

styles were abandoned and one-storey, flat-roofed structures with standardized concrete wall systems became common – simply more schools had to be built quickly and affordably.

As we see in Figure 6.2 discipline is still important as the row-and-column lay-out suggests. So pupils are separated, each one having her own fixed space with books and school work on her bench, and the objects have permanence. Even if it is not impossible, which it would have been in the layout of Figure 6.1, it would take some effort to rearrange the benches and, for example, connect them in hori-zontal rows to afford interaction and group work between pupils. The room has, as before, a focal point connected to the teacher and blackboard, as evident from the boy who stands up. He meets the face of the teacher, whereas the children behind him just see his back.

That this is a standardized space connected both to mass production and to mass education is also suggested by the textures. Wood is the major material for the desks and shelves, and it is manufactured and varnished to be durable and resistant to the impact of the never-ending arrival of new pupils. There is rigidity and regularity, pointing to what is homogeneous and consistent, to the lack of surprise, and overall these manufactured surfaces suggest institutional control. Yet in this case we can sense some individuality where we see that clothing is varied and personal, and the pupils have different postures towards the boy. In the UK Victorian-style school clothing and postures were also regulated. The huge amount of different teaching materials and artefacts in the shelves also brings a sense of some dynamism: there are maps, books, a globe, different posters, and so on. Within the bonds of the overall order and discipline, different activities and lessons are to be carried out, so that every child eventually can contribute to the prosperity of the nation.

In Figure 6.3 we find a modern and corporate-style classroom from Canada. It is filled with light. Windows are used to allow the outside world in and do not hold the gaze of the children within the room. Furniture does not encourage children to sit individually in regimented rows. Colours communicate fun and energy, and textures are designed to create softness. This affords movement and interaction, learning together. This room clearly carries very different ideas and values as regards the purpose of education, the nature of learning and also of the identities and behaviour that are to take place there.

What is striking is the emphasis of the dynamic and flexible. The classroom layout in Figure 6.1 was designed for 56 pupils with fixed places supposed to sit still and quiet. Here we see a 'team', a teacher with five children, all unique indi-viduals and populating a multipurpose space where you can interact and adapt to new demands and challenges. There are no clear partitions. Space opens up and

Figure 6.3   Contemporary, corporate-style classroom (Getty Images)

has no clear limit, just as learning and outcomes have no limit but can improve continuously. The textures are accommodating and give to the touch, unlike the mass-produced wooden benches in Figure 6.2. We also see organic textures in the background where green plants are allowed to grow wild, making possible a parallel to how the children are rooted and will grow. The soft pastel colours are both controlled and optimistic. In this particular image promoting this kind of classroom we also see that the grey of the teacher's cardigan matches the ceiling. The pink of the trousers of the girl by the whiteboard rhymes with the pink seating behind her. At a different level, clearly, some kind of order and regulation is highly important.

Of course you can ask how comfortable it is for a child to have a seat with no back if the point is to listen to presentations. We can also consider the pros and cons of the separated benches in Figure 6.2, where each children had a personal space designed for concentration on school work. The one resemblance to the earlier classrooms is that we still have a sense of a focal point, which, and very typical for schools, is the place where the whiteboard, the former blackboard, is placed. And in social semiotics the very existence and placement of such objects has been shown to have huge ideological importance and play a big role in shaping teaching and learning activities (Jewitt, 2013; Jewitt and Jones, 2005).

From this brief account of classrooms we begin to see that there are a number of key changes as regards things like layout, how the space is segregated or integrated to regulate movement and interaction. We see changes in materials and in textures. And fundamentally we see changes in interactional affordances. What we begin to get a sense of, therefore, are the tools we will need to carry out more systematic analysis and ask specific research questions. In this case we may want to ask how space in these classrooms carries discourses about learning and education.

Restaurants

Restaurants and cafés are places we might associate much less with the shaping of identities and interactional affordances. Although we may have some sense of the way that they now tend to certainly have specific designs to code what is 'exclusive', 'homely', 'ecological', 'romantic', or for socializing and fun. In Figure 6.4 we see the interior of the café Supreme Burger in Stockholm, a brand launched with the slogan 'welcome to your second home'. It is located in a gentrified district populated by the wealthy middle class.

Of note in the design of the café is the large communal table dominating the room, designed for social interaction and chatting, even if in reality pairs tend to sit and talk separately. In the image to the right we also see that chairs are placed by the window bench, where visual interaction with the outer world, or people passing by on the street, is afforded. In many traditional restaurants (see Figure 6.5 below), tables would be arranged to create a personal space, where friends, couples or families can sit by themselves. The kitchen itself here is open-plan and can be seen from within the eating area over the low counter. So overall there is no clear focal point, but focus can shift depending on the circumstances and the people that might come to the place. Flexible and dynamic use of space for groupings is important here.

What we see is an open-plan layout in which texture is important, as it has become in trendy urban cafés around the world. At the level of texture the

Figure 6.4 An urban hamburger café (Photographs by author)

'authentic' is communicated. The naturalness of the wood of the table in the left image is evident since it has irregular planks that differ from each other slightly. And while the tables are varnished for durability the surfaces remain uneven and slightly unfinished. Such textures would not, for example, tend to be found in a fast-food restaurant.

In the image to the right we see that the walls are hung with old newspapers, where the paper is worn and torn by time. Like the uneven wooden plank tables, this contributes to the sense of a space having historical roots in the twentieth-century low-tech culture. The menu is written on a torn and previously folded paper which has a rough texture. The font is Courier, once again imitating twentieth-century print culture, where typewriters were used, and it contrasts with the digital tablets or elegant menus of other up-market places (compare Figure 1.1). The rough textures of the napkins on the table are also important – certainly soft linen napkins are ruled out – and in the ceiling the ventilation pipes are bare. All this contributes to the communication of a kind of authenticity and simplicity, and lack of processing, and is devised to evoke the idea of a local community.

These design ideas have spread throughout the world. In the redesign of Starbucks in the beginning of the 2010s, first introduced in Seattle in the US, similar textures were used to evoke a new and much more local sense of 'authenticity' (Aeillo and Dickinson, 2014). Different materials were deployed in the redesigned stores to signal provenance, and consumer-citizens were construed as part of a local community, for example through large communal tables made of old and irregularly shaped wood planks from a nearby area, a design strategy that made each store stand out as seemingly unique. We see the same in the Stockholm burger café. Here, 'uniqueness' and 'locality' are communicated through a limited repertoire of symbols that can be bolted into an overall global template and aesthetics. As Figure 6.4 shows, this also comes with careful coordination of colour. This is as regards the use of browns and colours which suggest nature and the organic. We find this in the table, floor, walls, the colours used on the menu. The chairs are sleeker metal, suggesting something more industrial and modern, yet rhyme in colour and have a slightly rough texture, just like the table, menu and counter.

In Figure 6.5 we see a traditional Swedish pub in a rural area. The contrast with the hamburger café is striking. Here tables are separated from each other in order to give every group and visitor the opportunity to sit in a space that is at least to some extent disconnected from other guests. There is flexibility so that the square tables can be rearranged to form a suitable space appropriate for the size of each group. This means that interaction is afforded at each table but, contrary to the burger café, restricted as to other guests, who usually would not, at least not without politely asking for permission, sit down at your table. There are two general focal points in this space, which are the TV, allowing single guests to sit alone and watch sports, and the bar with the waitress, ready to take orders. In such a pub it is common to see family groups eating together and also people alone sitting with a beer, watching football.

There is a lot of brown and wood, but these are of different shades and textures and not carefully coordinated as in the Stockholm café. The bar area carries a more textured wood, whereas the tables are very glossy to be functional and quickly cleaned. The wall panel with its decorations is of yet another shade of wood. The grey seating, striped floor and the metal counter used for salad to the right are in no way used to create effect or coordination. Even if the brick chimney and the bar as a whole give a sense of something rustic, there is no rhyming between materials and textures. This rural pub feels rather like eating in a café from the 1970s before affect became so important, before space was coded so carefully.

Figure 6.5   A traditional and rural Swedish pub (Photograph by Johanna Björck)

What we see in these two restaurants is that materials, textures and layout can be designed for different kinds of interactional affordances. And such affordances are infused with discourses that carry ideas about history, authenticity, identities and the meanings of interactions. Whereas the rural pub is in some ways more functional, eating in the Stockholm café is much more clearly loaded with affect, with meanings of urban chic through decontextualized symbols of history and authenticity. There is a sense of integration with the wider urban setting, whereas the rural pub is a more self-contained place.

Offices

Office designs have changed in the last decades. There has been a shift away from more fixed spaces with individual work desks designed to carry out individual work tasks to flexible, open-plan solutions created for adaptability and social interaction. Below we see the offices of two different universities. These are from where we work in Sweden, but the two types can be found in public institutions around the world. One is an older-style office from Stockholm University in Figure 6.6 and the other a new-style office from Malmö University in Figure 6.7.

The buildings of Stockholm University were inaugurated in 1971 as part of a new campus. The architecture is modernistic and based on square and regular modules. If we look at the corridor in the middle image in Figure 6.6 it is narrow and straight with solid doors, all of them closed, so that each individual and member of staff is allowed a private space. Inside each individual office we find a personal type of space. Here, as we see in the right image, the office

Figure 6.6 The traditional office design of Södra husen ('south buildings') at Stockholm University (Indoor photographs by author)

118

can be slightly messy with piles of book and papers spread out on the desk. Such office spaces are segregated from the rest of the working environment and from the individual work of colleagues. The only permeability in these offices is given by the window through which you can get a glimpse of people working in the opposite building. Such a space is good for work which requires longer-term periods of concentration, quiet focus and having personal resources at hand, such as books and files. Such a space is also good for having private conversations such as meetings with students about progress. And these can take place in a more personalized environment – staff may have posters on the wall, plants or rugs on the floor.

In 2015 Malmö University built a new campus area in the now gentrified harbour area. Here the decision was that it should have an open-plan style. Many newer university buildings around the world have this kind of design. Externally we see that the building, called Niagara, has a rounded and slightly irregular shape where the two connected buildings also have a different height. This can be compared to the regularity of the Stockholm University buildings. Such designs communicate 'creativity' and 'interest', and appear more dynamic than the older square functional looking designs. The newer buildings also favour larger glass sections and larger atrium style entrance and 'social' areas.

If we look inside at the design of the offices we find an open-plan layout. There are no walls between work spaces. There is some separation created by low-level storage units, but even here, as seen in the middle image, there is use of glass, which also creates permeability. There is no allocated personal space nor storage and staff are to bring their laptops and sit at any free space in a system of 'hot-desking'. We also find screens separating spaces but anyone walking through the office will be able to observe or hear any kind of work or interactions taking place. This means that there can be no private work, nor can there be

Figure 6.7 The open-plan office of the building Niagara at Malmö University, built in 2015. Indoor photographs by Patrik Hall

any longer-term, focused work that requires concentration – which characterizes much of academic work such as research, writing, marking, administration. And the furniture that we do find is designed to be moved, to be flexible, so that the open space can be easily and quickly reconfigured.

In such an environment it is simply hard to get things done. As a result staff work from home, which is ironic since the idea of this space is to afford dynamic interaction. If students meet staff in such an environment they are aware that their comments are all public. They do not address the staff member as an individual but as part of a group. This is interesting as in Chapter 3 on analysing photographs we looked at the way that universities market themselves by presenting a highly personal and informal relationship between academic staff and students (Figure 3.5).

In his work on office design Roderick (2016) has argued that these changes relate to wider shifts in social organization and in the nature of the workforce. Since the 1990s society has changed with the rise of what is called 'neoliberalism'. This is a shift from a society with a strong central state, which in part maintains society by ensuring that everyone has work, which stimulates the economy. Here the state has responsibility for welfare of the citizens. It is a shift to a society where government declines, where full employment is no longer a priority. Here labour is temporary and impermanent, and the works must adapt and be flexible. There is an emphasis on 'innovation' and 'creativity' where competition is supposed to ensure a good economy. And individuals now have responsibility for themselves. We can see this realized in the shift from the older offices where the individual has a static private space to the newer office where the individual passes through. Here, only very immediate types of activities can be carried out and the emphasis is on social interaction, which also was the case in the corporate-style classroom in Figure 6.3. The individual ceases to be part of the institution in the way that they were formally when they had an office with their name on the door. And in universities, indeed staff, as students, become simply one other set of assets, or components in the company.

Analysing space design

Through the examples of the classrooms, the cafés and the offices, we see patterns as to what is required for a tool kit suitable for analysing space. In this section we begin with meaning potentials which allow space to become structured, for example as regards the way the school rooms or offices were more or less segregated or open-plan. We look at how we can approach the way that space can become loaded with interactional affordances. We then move into texture and materials and finally colours. In developing these tools we have been inspired by the approaches of 'semiotic landscapes' (Jaworski and Thurlow, 2010) and 'geo-semiotics' (Scollon and Wong Scollon, 2003), which both stress that discourses and semiotic interpretations are place based. We show how the tools can be used to make more detailed observations of the examples given above as well as others. At the end we reflect on how these can be used in a research project.

Partitions

Any designed space forms an overall shape. And it will comprise interrelated elements. For example, in a café you may have a counter, a food preparation area (which may be closed off or open for view), a serving counter, an arrangement of tables, an entrance space, a games machine area, a TV, a border created by a row of plants to create a sense of privacy. How these are arranged gives meaning to the space, to how people can behave in that space. We show here that if we look more carefully at such forms of arrangements we can reveal something of the ideas that lie behind them. The analysis of partitions clarifies how elements can form frames or be framed in terms of degrees of connectedness and disconnectedness. It is akin to what van Leeuwen (2005: Chapter 1) calls 'framing', a notion applied to both two- and three-dimensional space. In this book, and due to our emphasis on semiotic materials, we prefer to analyse framings occurring in two-dimensional space as 'borders' (see Chapter 4 on document design, p. 82), and when they, as here, are part of three-dimensional space as 'partitions'.

Separation

This is how 'open' or 'closed-off' different spaces are – by walls, curtains, or being distant in space from each other. We have seen that this can be to different degrees. In the open-plan office in Figure 6.7 storage units frame working and meeting areas from the main area but do not close them off. We also see separation in Figure 6.4 where the food preparation area in the restaurant is placed next to the eating area. The closed-off-ness could have been strengthened by using high storage units or simply walls with doors.

Where spaces run into each other we can talk about 'integration'. This is when, for example, a kitchen opens up into a living room. In the new classroom design, as seen in Figure 6.3, the learning spaces of the students become integrated into other spaces. And teachers would often police these boundaries should they see a student crossing them. Where spaces are closed off from each other we can talk about 'segregation'. In the case of the older-style university offices, as in Figure 6.6, lecturers work in spaces which are segregated by walls and doors. In the integrated designs such segregation is reduced as working spaces become more integrated, as Figure 6.7 shows. The twentieth-century classroom in Figure 6.2 is certainly a segregated space where bodies are meant to be contained in one room and where the school bell will ring and announce the end of the lesson. Segregation and integration will be seen in terms of the boundaries that your neighbours erect around their property. If the neighbour on one side has built a 4m high brick wall there is clearly a sense of segregation. If the neighbour on the other side has created a boundary with small and pretty flowers, we might expect, perhaps, that they wish to remain more integrated into the immediate community.

Permeability

This is the degree to which partition elements afford interaction be it visual, auditory, or both. Buildings and rooms have openings – doors, windows, curtains, or perhaps a book shelf with gaps that can divide a work area from a relaxation area with a sofa, a lounge from a kitchen. Such elements allow the possibility to hear sounds from, and partly see into, the other area. So in the older-style university offices there was little permeability between individual offices and between the offices and the corridor, as we see in Figure 6.6. With the door closed you can certainly not see anyone else, and you may be able to hear muffled conversations. There is of course some permeability with the world outside afforded by the window.

In the new office in Figure 6.7 each workspace has high permeability with other workspaces and with the corridor. There is some segregation through the storage units and through the use of space. But there is always a high degree of permeability as regards both what can be seen and heard. Other more newly built university office spaces we have seen may have complete glass walls separating workspace. Here there may be less permeability as regards sound, but complete permeability as regards seeing. Our own offices have doors that contain windows, so the staff do not have visual privacy. This has provoked some people to put more or less permeable curtains over the windows, since they feel uneasy with the visual interaction always being possible and have a sense of being watched.

We can see increasing permeability if we return to the development of the IKEA catalogue kitchens since the 1970s shown in Figure 1.2. In the 1970s the kitchen forms a closed-off discrete space, since we see no view into other rooms, with the curtains closed, nor indications of an open-plan design. Today's kitchen are suffused with light and often opens to both a balcony, or garden, and other rooms. This permeability is akin to use of an open space in the contemporary corporate style classroom seen in Figure 6.3.

Permanence

This is the degree to which framing is dynamic. Curtains, doors, and so on can be opened, locked or unlocked, furniture can be designed to be easily moved or changed according to the task to be carried out. In a modern classroom a teacher may tell the students to move the arrangement of tables for a particular activity. In the old-style classroom there would be no change of furniture position regardless of the subject being taught.

We can see a contrast as regards permanence in the case of the changed designs in IKEA kitchens in Figure 1.2. In earlier designs objects in the kitchen appear to provide fixed functional purposes. The kitchen is a place where you cook and eat, as the family sitting at the dinner table illustrates. The kitchen of today is by contrast marked by impermanence; we find an emphasis on moveable objects such as open storage in a kitchen island, where boxes can be taken out and rearranged, the movable stool on which the child stands and the set tray that indicates that dad and son are either going to sit down in some other place soon or that they together have brought the tray back to the kitchen. Broadly speaking, the kitchen from the 1970s is part of the functionalism of the twentieth century, where parts serve fixed purposes, while the contemporary kitchen codes a 'liquid modernity' (Bauman, 2000), where parts and persons are flexible and dynamic, and where the kitchen brings solutions to different life challenges, here to have quality time with your child.

One striking feature of contemporary office designs according to Roderick (2016) is that furniture is designed to be easily movable, so that it can be quickly reconfigured to adapt for the immediate needs. Looking at the open-plan office in Malmö University in Figure 6.7 we can see that all of the furniture is of this nature. In a short time the whole setting could be reorganized to create new configurations of team work, subject-groupings or accommodate more members of staff. The storage units that carry glass panels can be quickly repositioned to create new forms of permeable segregation or integration.

Interactional affordances

As we have noted, spaces shape movement and interaction (Goffman, 1993; McMurtrie, 2016). Where we put walls, staircases, serving counters, tables and chairs may be driven by practical matters. But these are never independent from what is felt as the priorities for that kind of space and inevitably bring about inter-actional affordances. Those of us who have visited IKEA will be familiar with the way the stores are designed such that we are forced to zig-zag on a path that takes us through the entire store. There are a few short-cuts, but they are generally well hidden. We are encouraged to see as many products as possible. If we do not buy this time, next time we may do so. Here the layout clearly channels behaviour, and the different areas of the store will be carefully devised. Except the zig-zag trail between departments there will be a restaurant and also a supervised children's play area, all this affording different types of positioning of bodies, of movement and interaction. The analysis of partitions in the previous section partly points to interactional affor-dances, but in this section we will be more precise as to how such affordances arise.

Areas

A space layout will comprise different areas that are more or less segregated depending on the partitions. An obvious example is the classroom design in Figure 6.1. Here the elevated teacher area is clearly separated from the children's area with 56 benches, coded both by the small staircase and the separation in space, where the benches are close to each other and distant from the teacher's desk, signifying power and control. In the case of the traditional pub in Figure 6.5 areas are more dynamic. The bar and the counter is obviously a separate space where the guests can order drinks or in this case also catch the attention of the waitress and be served. The area of the guests comes out as one functional space but is, due to the placing of tables and chairs, divided into sub-areas, where every table affords interaction between the guests there but not necessarily with other tables. In the case of the open classroom in Figure 6.3 the flexible furniture will be arranged to foster different interactions in pairs and groups or adjusted to listening to a presenter.

Focal points

Spaces and areas are designed to create focal points, to have different centres of attention, which frame interaction. Simply speaking, a focal point will be some-thing that we experience to have a front. As humans we have a front, which is our face and our sensory organs, and we approach others in communication with our fronts. Similarly we can have a sense of a room having a front, which certainly is the case for classrooms, where the blackboard or whiteboard is the artefact to receive attention, the focal point that provides 'the law', where the writing is to be learnt and obeyed. Bodies are positioned in relation to the whiteboard, so that typ-ically the teacher is the one writing on it and the children or students are placed so that they can look at it. It is telling that the blackboard/whiteboard is in the centre of attention in all our school examples (Figures 6.1, 6.2, 6.3), despite the fact that they date from the nineteenth to the twenty-first centuries.

In restaurants and cafés (Figures 6.4 and 6.5), an obvious focal point is the waitress, who has her usual position in the kitchen or bar area behind a counter. Her job is to be a 'front', to look at us and communicate. If there is a TV, as in Figure 6.5, that is another focal point that we take to have a front and affords communication as long as we position ourselves in relation to it. Obviously not everyone goes out to watch TV, and different pubs will have different policies, for example whether the sound should be on or not, depending on culture.

Channels

That space channels behaviour is clear already from the obvious examples of supermarkets and IKEA stores that we have mentioned. This is done through degrees of segregation and integration which prevent or allow us to move in different ways through the product displays. Since space is tied to behaviour and movement there will, as long as there are humans, be certain paths or passages used, what we call channels. Already in nature people will, even if no one has planned it specifically, create and follow trails and thus show regularity in movement when going from one place to another. In space designs, channels are of course carefully devised by architects and then by people responsible for a certain space, for example a tenant or a house or shop owner.

If we look at the traditional office in Figure 6.6 movement between areas is channelled in a clear way. The corridor is the passage that gives access to different spaces. You go to the offices and choose, as part of the staff or as a student or visitor, which one to enter, after having knocked on the door. There is in fact an electric display beside each office, where red could be lit to signify 'occupied', even if nowadays it is seldom used by the staff. The corridor also links to a few meeting rooms, the kitchen and the lunch room for the staff, all of them places that invite groups of people, in contrast to the segregated offices. Thus, the architecture is devised to give choices of space depending on work needs and tasks, and therefore channels behaviour to make the spaces involved available.

In today's prestige architecture, new ways of channelling behaviour and affording interaction have been developed. In Figure 6.8 we see the Oslo Opera House. It appears as technical and geometric. But it also gives a sense of the organic as it is integrated with the surroundings and the sea. The roof angles to the ground level become not only functional parts of the building but form part of a plaza and invite pedestrians to walk up and enjoy the panoramic view and sit down at a café. The large windows with minimal framing invite interaction between inside and outside. The white stone materials are constructed to fade away on a sunny day, in the sense that the reflections of light make the corners and sharp edges hard to discern, and the thin angled columns of the roof are designed for maximal openness, not to interfere with views and sights.

In one sense here we could argue that traditional, modernist distinctions between inside and outside, the manufactured and the organic, culture and nature, reason and emotion, and so on are consequently blurred. In short, the building invites 'readings', its qualities are in the eye of the beholder and always contingent. The visitor is programmatically part of some kind of interaction. The same kind of postmodernist architecture is seen around the world as a means of branding cities and to indicate 'success on the global market'. Obvious parallels are the opera houses in Sydney also located by the sea, blurring inside and outside and evoking ideas of both the highly technical and the authentic and affective.

Materials and texture

The materials and textures we use in spaces, or the textures that they acquire through use, have meanings for us. They can, for example, give us a sense of a locality being warm and welcoming, cold and hostile, formal or informal, or more or less secure. Obvious examples are in the case of the classroom above. We find different materials and textures in the older and newer rooms in Figure 6.2

Figure 6.8 Oslo Opera House (Getty Images)

and 6.3. The old room had mass-produced materials, with benches and chairs of wood that was manufactured to be hard and resist impact. There was an emphasis on regularity, where bodies were divided from each other in rows and fulfilling a function for the sake of the progress of the nation. In Figure 6.3 we see glass and light and seating without backs made of linen in saturated colours with less rigidity but flexible and adaptable to different needs. The furnishing is used for group or team work, and clearly different ideas and values about learning and being in a school are communicated.

We have elaborated on materials and texture in the case of packaging in Chapter 5 and we refer to these sections (p. 96) for an extensive account. Here we will make brief observations to point to the use of materials and texture in space design.

Rigidity

A resistant surface is a hard surface, and as surfaces get softer their resistance to pressure decreases. The degree of rigidity carries many and often metaphorical meanings. What is hard and rigid can be seen as strong, powerful, stable or harsh and unfair. Softness can mean, or be interpreted as, weakness in certain contexts, but in others it may be accommodating or forgiving. In the example of the class-room above, the old design in Figure 6.2 certainly communicates resistance and hardness rather than giving and yielding which we find to greater degrees in the newer design in Figure 6.3.

Relief

Parts of surfaces can extend below or above a horizontal plane, which can point to what is natural and manufactured. For example, a surface such as a shiny and polished kitchen surface or a perfectly shaven face can bring a sense of perfection, suggesting control, but also give the feeling of the artificial or non-interactive. The surface of the floor in the traditional university in Figure 6.6 is flat, smooth and polished. It suggests not a lived surface, but is manufactured to be pure, clean and efficient. Were the surface uneven as in older wood or uneven tiles it would suggest more an organic type of variation. Many schools in the UK, as part of a process of privatization, build new entrance halls often using patterns of glass and polished steel – compare the exterior of the new university building in Figure 6.7. Here we find a kind of relief created through surfaces meeting and interacting at different angles, as we also see in the Olso Opera House in Figure 6.8, where also the expensive marble has been manufactured to enhance relief. This can be seen as part of a modern, systematically controlled and managed kind of 'innovation'.

Regularity

Regular textures are predictable and can signify the homogeneous, lack of surprise and consistency. Irregularity can signify less predictable, the whimsical, the heterogeneous or the natural. The building of Stockholm University in Figure 6.6 is about regularity, and its façade has a systematic pattern based on angular shapes. Squares are evenly distributed all over the building, and this points to a vision of society where individuality is erased, to the homogeneous, where each part has the same role in the working of the overall system. Similar meanings are evoked by the regularity of the classroom layouts in Figures 6.1 and 6.2. The Oslo Opera House in Figure 6.8 has regularity in the sense that the overall whiteness, and the stone materials, unite the parts. But within these bonds the construction is about irregularity, where walls are sized unevenly and the roof angles in different ways to the ground. It is an architecture that has a programmatic interactivity and is designed to invite people to explore the building, to walk around it both horizontally and vertically. This irregularity thus codes playfulness and activeness.

Naturalness

Materials may have their origin in nature or be manufactured and artificial. Manufactured materials include steel and plastic. Meanings can involve technological progress, high competence, the predictable, and also the impersonal and artificial. Of note is that natural materials are also submitted to industrial process or advanced handicraft. The stone and granite in Oslo Opera House are natural materials, shaped by craftsmen (of course using highly technological tools) and evoke the authentic, a building – and metonymically also people and a nation – related to nature and origins. Its tower is made of aluminium, which seems to counter this interpretation. But in order to make the visual design and the social values coded it is white as the rest of the materials, reflecting the sun, and with weaving patterns inscribed, adhering to the idea of nature and history. In the burger café in Figure 6.3 we also find the use of old wooden tables, which bring a sense of provenance and authenticity. We would be less likely to find such surfaces in a traditional fast-food burger restaurant such as McDonald's.

Liquidity

Surfaces may be more or less wet or dry, which can relate to life and vitality or to rot and decay. Or dryness can relate to comfort. Monuments can be designed to incorporate wet surfaces and water. In the case of commemorative monuments this can communicate purity. But corporate-style monuments or art placed inside atrium spaces can use walls of water in order to communicate life, vitality and also bring serenity into the otherwise manufactured and controlled space of the spacious flat polished surfaces. In this way we find affect included into the design but also a kind of spirituality or morality.

Viscosity

Viscosity is about how sticky different surfaces are. Here both positive and negative meanings arise, depending on context. On the one hand, what is dirty and unclean is a bit sticky. On the other hand, sticky can mean support and safety. In traditional gyms surfaces can be a bit sticky, such as practical rubber-foam grips on treadmills. We could imagine that we may find sticky strips on stairs in a public library or a hospital. But it may be odd to find sticky surfaces on the floor in an entrance to a typical atrium building where it is important to communicate through smoothness and regularity. In our country where there are long winters, there is a very practical problem of wet floors and slipping. In the new atrium building at the university of one of the authors, the solution has been to use a large section of matting placed over a sort of concealed grille. The matting itself has very low relief and high regularity. The avoidance of slipping can be accomplished without compromising smoothness and flatness. The ideas of managed creativity are not compromised by textures that might communicate support and safety.

Colour

We do not say too much about colour in this chapter since we address this in detail in Chapters 3 (p. 49), 4 (p. 80) and especially 5 (p. 102), and the categories provided there can be applied to colour as found in space and materials. But here we say a few things about colour that may be specific to space.

Colour hues

Here we can have more natural hues such as found in the burger café in Figure 6.4 which are dominated by earth tones and muted nuances – brown, grey, off-white – giving a sense of a place in contact with nature, with an origin. In the case of the modern classroom in Figure 6.3 we find warmer colours like pink and light blue, evoking, together with the light, a bright optimism.

Colour palette

Larger colour palettes are associated with fun, liveliness or garishness and restricted colour palettes with more measured moods, or dullness. In both the burger café and the traditional pub in Figures 6.4 and 6.5 we find a quite limited colour palette, which is associated with more muted or reserved moods.

The contemporary classroom in Figure 6.3 has a wider colour palette where grey provides a background for brighter colours. This palette is associated with fun, liveliness or with garishness. Of course we might find such a wider colour palette in the furnishings in a fast-food burger restaurant.

Colour saturation

Saturated colours are associated with emotions and warmth. More diluted colours are associated with more muted emotions and distance. In a contemporary kitchen design we may find a predominance of more muted neutral colours such as lighter yellow-browns in natural wood surfaces, along with more saturated whites which suggest cleanliness and purity (Figure 1.2). We may be encouraged to use one exciting saturated colour such as blue or red in the design which can be coordinated in different places, such as a red kettle and red coffee machine.

Colour purity

Pure colours can be used to communicate simplicity and truth whereas impure and hybrid colours are associated with complexity and difference. The contemporary classroom in Figure 6.3 uses muted pastel colours, and these tend to be more hybrid. This hybridity is also seen in the materials where we have steel combined with organic plants. Such uses of colour can suggest complexity of ideas, ambiguities, challenges, although these are combined with the smooth, polished, controlled and managed surfaces. In the fast-food burger restaurant we will be more likely to find pure colours to suggest simplicity and practical food.

SUGGESTIONS FOR RESEARCH QUESTIONS

Throughout this chapter we have given a sense of the kinds of research questions that these tools can be used to answer. For example, we can look at the way that spaces of teaching and learning have changed, or how domestic spaces have changed. In such cases the tools for analysis can allow us to draw out the ideas and values about things like learning, children and the family, and the kinds of priorities that are valued in society at any time. We could also then relate these to wider ideological interests, where learning becomes a little more like a corporate activity, where domestic life becomes more of a self-management project in a world

(Continued)

that requires solutions and flexibility. But we can also here consider some concrete research questions. Here are two examples:

- What are the differences in the design of space between 5 star and 2 star hotels?

- How is space used on management training courses?

In the first place we would need to choose a number of hotels and visit them, make short films and take photographs. We would then need to compare things like entrance halls, breakfast spaces and guest rooms. What kinds of partitions do we find, what kinds of interactional affordances are set up, what are the focal points and how is movement channelled? Are these different in each case? We can also look at textures, colours and rhyming. Of course here the aim is to establish what kinds of patterns seem to be associated with luxury. What are the discourses of luxury and how are they communicated?

In the second case we would need to be able to take photographs, and make short films to allow us to map out how people move and interact in different kinds of training courses of management events. In such cases the discourses may be communicated in the first place as regards how interactions are channelled. For example, one of the authors recently went to a research 'ideas sharing' day where the point was to find ways to foster interdisciplinary projects. Over 100 staff sat around in a huge circle. Here there is a sense of equality, of being in a group, rather than if we had all faced the front in rows. A consultant facilitator walked around in the circle. The focal point for activities here was the centre of the circle. We were called to go to the centre of the circle and use a microphone that was placed there on the floor to say who we were and what our research idea was. We then had to describe it in a few words on a small piece of paper (writing on the floor) which we were to stick to a board where later people from across all university disciplines would 'buzz' around, ask questions and 'think creatively together'. Since people were 'buzzing' around there was little chance to really explain a research project and presenters found themselves repeating the same answer many times as people came and went. But the space communicated 'equal footing', 'movement' and 'no boundaries'.

7

FILM CLIPS

Introduction

In this chapter we focus on video adverts and promotional film clips. This is a form of visual communication that developed in the form of TV commercials, but which with cheap digital technology has become hugely commonplace. Every business and organization has a YouTube channel, or have short films on their website. When we open our social media home pages, or visit a sports site, we will usually come across some kind of embedded commercial. When we apply for jobs through an online system we may be directed via a number of pages that carry films about the 'mission' of the company, or that give 'success stories' of notable employees as a way of both personalizing the organization and as a measure of its culture and ambition.

A film clip comprises moving images and evokes time. It invites the reader to meet characters in a story. Compared with the semiotic materials that we have targeted in the previous chapters this calls for new tool kits. In this chapter we show that the best way to understand these short films is in regard to the kind of story or narrative that they tell along with the way that they represent characters and settings. These narratives are communicated in many ways, by different uses of language, by kinds of generic and individual characters, by the way that scenes are composed and by the nature of settings. All these play clear and identifiable roles in telling the viewer the point of the narrative and communicate the discourses that are required for the purposes of marketing and branding. In other words they code ideologies and tell us, for example, what it is to be a true friend, a sexy woman or man, a good parent, or how we should fight for social justice and a sustainable environment. And in each case the type of narrative structure allows this to be done in different ways.

Types of film-clip narratives

In the first section of the chapter we make a broad distinction between three types or genres of promotional film. In the tool-kit section that follows we then show how these genres have a very specific structure or formula. It is useful to know this for several reasons. First, it allows us to break down the clips into their basic building blocks. Second, it allows us to quickly get a sense of how events are being shaped for us, or what the film is trying to do. Each of these three types tends to be associated with a general communicative purpose. Here we want to simply point to the differences between these films and gather a sense of what other kinds of analytical tools are needed in order to carry out an analysis.

The entertaining narrative: the case of banking

These kinds of short film clips have their history in TV commercials, and they often deploy qualities from the TV medium, not least from TV series of the sitcom type, for example *How I Met Your Mother* in the US or *Two Pints of Lager and a Packet of Crisps* in the UK. These kinds of entertaining narratives, unfolding in chronological time, rely on a recurring set of contrasting characters that we get to know and identify with, and the setting usually comes from everyday life or work. In marketing campaigns such an outline can be useful. It builds on the idea that the recurring characters should become sort of mascots for the company, building trust in the brand, and ideally the audience looks forward to new episodes or video adverts, so that the series takes on a life of its own.

We begin by looking at a film from a campaign by the Bank of Ireland which introduced a young nerdy couple, Steve and Rachel, which ran between 2014 and 2016. These commercials should be understood against the background of the banking collapse in 2008 leading to years of austerity budgets and a situation where banks reached record levels of mistrust, meaning that a brand such as the Bank of Ireland had overwhelmingly negative associations. The campaign was directed at gaining market shares in residential mortgages, one of the most profitable businesses for a bank. The commercials came with the promise that the bank would pay part of the stamp duty.

In the film clip 'Stamp Duty' the setting is a house-share scenario, specifically the living room, where Steve lives with two flatmates. Immediately this kind of everyday setting, restricted in time and space, where a funny dialogue between characters with some special and annoying qualities unfolds, signals the similarities with a sitcom. In order to evoke humour there must be a narrative with a tweak, or some kind of problem to be resolved, and also the bank must be introduced. Here we look at the 30-second commercial, presenting the basic stages (Iedema, 2001) the story takes in this genre, which are orientation, complication, resolution and coda.

0.00–0.05: The stage of orientation: the setting and characters are introduced.

Steve and Rachel, shown in Figure 7.1, enter the living room where Steve's two housemates sit in the sofa playing a video game.

Steve: 'alright lads'

Housemate: 'Steve'

Rachel (engaged): 'how you guys'

Housemate (reserved, concentrating on the video game): 'hi Rachel'

Steve: 'who's winning? it doesn't matter'

Figure 7.1 Steve and Rachel enter the living room

0.06–0.18: The stage of complication: a problem occurs.

Steve and Rachel announce that they are moving together; in fact Rachel is moving in to the house. The camera moves between the happy Steve and Rachel and the two shocked housemates.

Steve: 'anyway, Rachel and I have decided to take the next step'

Housemate: 'moving out, Steve?'

Steve: 'it's even better than that, Rachel's moving in with us'

Rachel makes a jump and shouts

Steve: 'isn't that great'

The two housemates stare at each other

Rachel: 'listen, we're gonna have charades and secrets and dares, gonna be awesome'

Housemate (shocked): 'deadly'

Voice-over: 'need to move?'

Figure 7.2 The housemates are not happy with Rachel moving in

0.19–0.25: The stage of resolution: a solution appears (Bank of Ireland helps you).

To escape Rachel's moving in, the housemates consult the Bank of Ireland mortgages on a tablet as seen in Figure 7.3.

Housemate takes up his tablet with the Bank of Ireland website and a page about mortgage

Voice-over: 'if you need to move, talk to the only bank that helps to pay your stamp duty'

Rachel giggles, says 'hooo' and puts her finger on Steve's nose

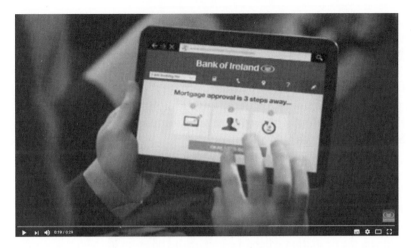

Figure 7.3 One of the housemates looks up Bank of Ireland's webpage on mortgages

0.26–0.30: The stage of coda: the final point is stated

A slogan from the Bank of Ireland ends the video. The living room fades out to show that this is the general point and Bank of Ireland's logo is displayed on the screen.

Voice-over: 'Bank of Ireland, whatever your next step, big or small, we're there for life'

So this is an entertaining and funny narrative, relying on the contrasting characters and their lines and with a voice-over explaining the point. We can see that it is made up of a number of stages, related to scenes and shots. A scene is what occurs in one time and space, and, as we said, in this sitcom-like video the idea is to use a limited amount of scenes. In this case it is the living room in the house shared, where the lines of the characters push the narrative forward. The scene comprises different shots, where camera movement is uncut. Here the camera action, as shown in Figure 7.1 and 7.2, is mostly about moving between Steve and Rachel and the housemates, depending on who is talking, but in the resolution the shot of the tablet with the homepage is important, as we see in Figure 7.3.

The shots foreground the characters and their lines, and these unfold in a narrative with stages based on chronological time. In the first stage, the orientation, Steve and Rachel exchange greetings with the housemates in the living room. Here the greetings themselves convey the antagonism between the characters. The housemates utter a very reserved 'hi Rachel' in response to her enthusiastic 'how you guys'. The complication starts after the greetings when Steve says 'anyway', which is a discourse marker that signals a new topic. Here we get to know that Rachel is moving in. The shocked housemates stare at each other making it clear that this is a huge problem (Figure 7.2). It is such problems that drive the genre of the entertaining narrative. The characters must start to search for a solution, and this allows the introduction of the Bank of Ireland where the two housemates check mortgages online. This is the stage of the resolution. At the end there is a coda, also typical of this kind of promotional film. We cease to see the living room and find a black screen where the Bank of Ireland takes over and makes it clear they come to the rescue in these situations.

Unlike TV sitcoms this kind of film advert has a voice-over, belonging to the narrator, which represents the Bank of Ireland's perspective directing attention to their products. This voice sets up the resolution with the line 'need to move?' and triggers the resolution where the housemate takes up his tablet. The offer and resolution put forward is that the Bank of Ireland helps with the stamp duty. So while the characters in the film talk in the orientation and complication, only the narrator's voice provides the solution.

The ideological effects are clear. The Bank of Ireland is represented as fun and trustworthy, as a friend that helps you in life, not as a company making most of their profits in the cynical, yet profitable, product of residential mortgages. In this instance building up a portfolio of mortgage debt is placed in a narrative of mild comedy, with everyday characters, the video-gaming flatmates, just back from work, and the clash with the geeky couple.

Projecting possible worlds: the case of universities

We now move to a different type of film narrative that is not built on chronological time, but that sketches a future or fantasy in rapidly changing scenes. Car adverts are often of this kind and use the setting of natural landscapes which suggest exploration and adventure. In the example we have chosen here we find a university communicating the future as a space of openness and potentiality. Anything is possible in this bright future, if you go to the actual university. This space has agency in relation to the viewer and the basic message is 'this could be my future life'. There is not, as in the previous example, an overall chronology of events, nor is there a complication that is to be solved. We call this narrative genre a 'projection' (cf. Hogan, 2016, on narrative simulations that sketch possible worlds).

We look at a 1.18-minute-long promotional film clip for the University of Michigan: 'Come to Michigan'. Below we show the outline of the narrative in the form of a table so that we can compare what is seen and what is said. In such films there are usually interesting patterns of relationships in this regard. In the first column we note the time, in the second column we note and number the stages and scenes, and in the third column we transcribe the voice-over in italics. We have inserted stills to give an idea of how the scenes look, and marked the overall structure. In the previous example, of the Bank of Ireland, we found the stages orientation, complication, resolution and a coda. In this case most of the film comprises the stage of 'simulation' which is framed by an orientation and a re-orientation.

Time	Stages and scenes	Voice-over
	Orientation	
0.00–0.05	Logo	

Time	Stages and scenes	Voice-over
0.05–0.07	Fade out, black screen	
	Simulation	
0.08–0.10	(1) Young man and woman running over a green field in what could be the campus area	*come*

Time	Stages and scenes	Voice-over
0.11–0.12	(2) A group dancing in a room where a computer screen with a graph is zoomed in	*come create and calculate*
0.13–0.14	(3) The Michigan stadium, a group of young students carrying a hovercraft	*shatter both records and stereotypes*

(Continued)

Time	Stages and scenes	Voice-over
0.15–0.20	(4) A close-up of the face of a young woman/student sitting in the driver seat of the hovercraft	*build improbable machines and impossible medicines*

Time	Stages and scenes	Voice-over
	(5) A robot running around in a circle in some kind of laboratory	
	(6) A dark woman in veil looking into a microscope	
0.21–0.24	(7) A man walking in a huge and elegant entrance hall	*unleash masterpieces and birth theories*
	(8) A laboratory with equally shaped water tanks on shelves, a man and a woman in work coats	
0.25–0.30	(9) Three young men holding up an object which we then see flying, camera shifts to a man with a remote control	*come because there is so much to be done out there, and to be undone*
	(10) On the country side in a foreign country, dark people walk on a path	
	(11) A white woman tapping water from a barrel	

Time	Stages and scenes	Voice-over
0.31–00.34	(12) The upper body but not the face of a man holding a white object in paper shaped as a fan	*come find out everything of which you are capable*
	(13) Camera zooms out, we see him in a room lifting up a long wreath	

Time	Stages and scenes	Voice-over
0.35–0.37	(14) An outdoor evening scene with men standing at telescopes on a hill	*come believe in something greater than yourself*
0.38–0.41	(15) A woman with 3D glasses against a digital wall, moving and playing some game	*an experience unlike any other awaits up here*

Time	Stages and scenes	Voice-over
0.42–0.44	(16) A memorial plate on the ground, 'Class of 1953' (17) The back of a male student raising his arms, wearing a hat with the university logo	*here dreams are in need of your voice*
0.45–0.47	(18) Female students of different ethnicity sitting in a classroom with sculptured technical objects	*fragile ideas await your strength*
0.48–0.50	(19) Students sitting outside in a ring in a garden	*come answer the call*
0.51–0.53	(20) An engaged teacher (male and white) lecturing	*join this assembling of minds*
0.54–0.56	(21) A woman playing cello in a narrow room with technical machines of some kind	*put your grand imagination to work*
0.57–1.02	(22) The female soccer team playing in rain, one player makes a header (23) An ancient medieval-looking tower on a hill shot from below in the sun (24) Student/man rolling a big cube in a park	*come let your visions rattle these walls, and help move the world forward*
1.03–1.04	(25) A man running on the pitch of the stadium with a Michigan flag	*come join the leaders and best*
1.05–1.07	(26) A gymnast making a vault in an old and solemn locality	*the victors valiant*
	Re-orientation	
1.08–1.10	(27) White students come out from a building into the sun, a dark female student sits on the stairs, the logo appears in the middle of the screen	*come to Michigan*

(Continued)

141

Time	Stages and scenes	Voice-over

| 1.11–1.13 | Fade out, black screen | |

| 1.14–1.18 | Logo | |

The simulation is framed by an orientation and a re-orientation where the logo and a black screen reappear in a circle composition. These stages anchor the middle stage, the simulation of the future in the university. It is not random potentialities we are invited to witness, but futures dependent on University of Michigan. Also a darkness is shown – the black screen lasts between 2 and 3 seconds, the same length as each of the scenes in the simulation. This can be given a metaphorical interpretation. Before life there is darkness, when born we are thrown out to a bright world with endless possibilities, and eventually we all die and re-enter darkness. This is a narrative about how to live your life.

It is the speaker's voice that creates the coherence to the simulation. Sometimes the voice-over points to one scene, sometimes it unites several scenes, which helps to make the future projection dynamic and flowing. The language is clearly poetic and used for triggering imagination, as a means for inviting the viewer to decide on her future, to shape and tell her story. This poetical use of language is evident in lines like 'come create and calculate' (scene 2) and 'come let your visions rattle these walls' (scene 22). There is lots of rhyming and repetition of the same phrases, words and sounds. In scene (4) the structures of the grammatical units used echo each other – the phrases 'improbable machines' and 'impossible medicines'. All such uses of language help to create a sense of wonder and fantasy (cf. Jakobson, 1960, on poetic language and Cook, 1994: Chapter 4, on the uses of it in advertising).

We also find that imperatives are used throughout. These are verb forms that issue commands and sound forceful, confident and energetic. This is typical of advertising where we are told 'drive a Ford today', rather than 'why not drive a Ford today'. We find this in the way the speaker codes future action, with 'come' as the main verb, used in 9 of the 18 utterances. We also find the viewer addressed directly through second-person pronouns 'you' and 'your', as in scene (18), 'fragile ideas await your strength', where 'fragile' and 'strength' are rhetorically contrasted. This form of personal address is important and also a typical feature of advertising language.

Each scene is in itself chronological where we see a character involved in a short series of events. But there is no chronology between the scenes, which is the point of this genre, to sketch potentialities, and here the huge amount of scenes that stands out. In the 1-minute simulation we see 27 scenes, which means that each scene only lasts for about 2 seconds. This can be contrasted with the Bank of Ireland video, based on just one scene. The core message is that it is up to you to form your future life and the possibilities are endless.

The scenes function differently. Some mostly project the simulation and others work more to ground it, making the link to Michigan explicit. Examples of typical projecting scenes are (4) with the young woman in the hovercraft or (11) and (12) where we see a white and more elderly woman pouring water from a barrel and then darker skinned people in the countryside in a foreign country. These seem to evoke a sense of advocating for social justice, a message clearly part of the video. Of note is that technology appears to be a saviour of mankind, with all sorts of inventions from engineering and science deployed throughout the fast-moving scenes. Of course there are debates on technology in many social contexts, also on its dangers, but here, as is typical in advertising discourses, it simply makes everything better.

An important difference from the Bank of Ireland film clip is the way that people are represented. In the Bank of Ireland advert characters were individualized, in the form of the annoying couple Steve and Rachel. As for the University of Michigan, there are no individuals, only glimpses of persons. What we meet is a collective. Different persons with different backgrounds, genders, ethnicities and nationalities appear, and we are invited to become part of this dynamic collective, of a multi-faced, positive world.

Recounting events: the case of the credit card

The next example is another very typical case, here of the genre 'recount'. The structure or set of events involve a simple sequence of events being told. These films can be used to show how a product is used to make things better, or simply to align a product with qualities of a sequence of events. These often feature celebrities who recount their use of the product. The example we look at here is for a credit card, MasterCard Black Card, and it comprises the three stages orientation, series of events and coda, which we show in the table below with stills inserted. There is very little language in this film but music has an important role.

Time	Stages and scenes	Sound
00.00–00.06	*Orientation*	
	 We see a businessman who gets a pleasant phonecall.	Music begins. Tentative building to have rhythm.
00.07–00.18	*Series of events*	
	 We see an episode where he puts on his biker gear, walks to his motobike, drives through the city, and arrives at the restaurant to meet friends and a partner.	Music picks up rhythm, becomes flamboyant and show-tune like. Instrumental 'stabs'.

144

Time	Stages and scenes	Sound
00.19–00.21	 In the resturant he greets a partner (he kisses her) and other people and has conversation	
00.22–00.27	 We see a hand (of what we take to be the man) place a credit card on a surface	Sound of slim metallic object falling on surface. Voice-over: 'To apply for your Mastercard Black Card visit Luxury Card or call 844 Luxcard'.
00.27–00.29	*Coda*  We return to a more distant shot of the man.	Scene shown over final horn section stab with the caption 'Life Without Limits'.

In the orientation we find a generic attractive businessman in a rather extravagant, highly designed office. He is working late, since it is dark and lights are on. He receives a phone call that makes him smile and he walks around the office. The phone call triggers the next stage, the series of events, which is the part where he goes out in the world, or city, to fulfil a project, which is also coded by the music picking up rhythm. He gets on his motorbike and rides to a restaurant where he unites with a partner, whom he kisses, and a group of friends. There is then an extreme close-up scene where we see the credit card placed on a well-lit table. We hear the voice-over telling us how to obtain the card. There is then the final shot and the coda when the series of events is evaluated by the caption and slogan 'Life Without Limits'.

The structure is different from the two previous examples. There is no complication, no urgent problem, and therefore no need for a resolution. This is simply a sequence of events that are recounted chronologically in order – and not, as in the university advert, a simulation where a huge amount of scenes are projected without chronology. The point is that the credit card gives you freedom and frees you from everyday obstacles and strains. Thanks to MasterCard you can go to an expensive restaurant whenever you like.

The scenes and shots work differently to the other two films. We see some broader shot scenes that identify settings, such as the office and the city. These are important to point to the stylized lifestyle and idea of success. But much of this comprises intimate close-up shots. For example we see a shot of the man on his bike pulling onto the street. Then we see his face in close shot as he is riding. We also see close-ups of objects such as clothing and shoes and of actions where he picks up the jacket. We do not, therefore feel that this man, or his way of life, is remote and distant. We meet a main character whose life can be our life, provided we get a MasterCard. The card is part of this level of blissful success where you can work late, look great and maintain good relationships.

Evaluations in this film are partly created by the music that resembles a show tune played by a big band, but with a fusion beat and addition of synths. It is slightly showy and flamboyant. But as often in commercials, language is employed to make the point of the story explicit towards the end. A voice-over tells us to apply for the card that gives you 'life without limits'.

Analysing film clips

In this first section we show how to go through the stages, scenes, settings and characters of film-clip genres in order to pin down their meanings and take a critical stance on the ideologies at work. We also point to the way music can give films a rhythm. Finally we look at language and evaluations.

Narrative genres and stages

We have pointed to narrative genres in film clips. Film genres, as Keith (2007) explains, have typical characters and settings – think of a western or sci-fi. They also, as Iedema (2001) explains, have an overall structure made up of stages and related to the communicative purpose, which is the case for genres in general (van Leeuwen, 2005: Chapter 6).

The genres entertaining narrative and recount are in fact both used spontaneously in everyday life. The entertaining narrative as an oral genre is extensively described by Labov and Waletzky (1967) as a way of conveying personal experience on how to cope with life. The recount is a genre that occurs in speech when you ask your child 'what did you do in school today?' and get told what happened. Both these genres, because of their everyday nature, are part of the writing curriculum in primary school, with their stages as a point of departure for instruction (e.g. Martin and Rose, 2008; cf. Berge and Ledin, 2001, on genre conceptions in linguistics and rhetoric, and Barthes and Duisit, 1975, on narratives where 'nuclei' is the term roughly equivalent to stages). Then they are written in the first person, with an 'I', whereas in film clips they are in the third person and invite viewers to relate to the characters and their life. In film clips these genres are useful for visually communicating how to live our lives, conveying the basic message that buying the product makes everything better. In short they naturalize a consumerist ideology. The genre of projection is more filmic and elaborate in the sense that it relies on evoking fantasies and futures without chronological connections between scenes.

We will go through these genres and their stages in turn and start with the entertaining narrative. The stages we can use to understand an entertaining narrative, such as in the case of the Bank of Ireland, are shown below (cf. Labov and Waletzky, 1967).

Narrative stages	Applied to the Bank of Ireland film clip
Orientation: the setting and the initial situation	Steve, Rachel and the two housemates exchange greetings in the living room. We understand that the housemates think Rachel is embarrassing
Complication: something disrupts order and triggers a chain of events	Steve's use of the discourse marker 'anyway' signals a new topic, which, to the shock of the housemates, is that Rachel is moving in
Resolution: a new order is achieved	The housemates look up mortgages on the homepage of Bank of Ireland on their tablet
Coda: the final point of the story	We see Bank of Ireland's logo and hear the voice-over say 'we're there for life'

This narrative structure makes it possible for the company, here Bank of Ireland, to take part in everyday life and come to the rescue, to solve a problem, here about moving. An analysis of this genre is found in Ledin and Machin (2017a) and targets how the IKEA kitchen solves everyday problems in commercials. In one advert we meet a man deeply engaged in cooking creative food, which is the orientation. The complication is signalled by a caption saying that parents want to spend more time with their children, followed by no less than six children entering the kitchen and creating chaos, which is the complication. As we are familiar with this genre, we know that order must be restored, that the stage of resolution will follow. This happens when we see the facial expression of the man change from a sulky frown to a warm smile. He and the children unite as a team and happily cook together. In the coda, making the final point, the man and the children sit in the dining room. He uses the remote control to dim the light over the dirty dishes and the IKEA logo appears.

The basic ideological message is that you should spend 'quality time' with your children and that IKEA brings the solution to this problem. In this sense life becomes a series of challenges, and the IKEA adverts also draw on other ideas prevalent in society at the time, which can be successfully managed through the right consumer behaviour. Domestic life must be improved, so that we can be more creative, more social and deal with the fast pace of life. An ideological reading of the Bank of Ireland film would be about the cynical nature of enticing people into debt as a way to expand a bank's portfolio by placing this issue in the realm of mild domestic comedy.

The different stages are normally easy to point out. That we have a complication is evident when we see the shocked housemates in the Bank of Ireland film and the children creating chaos in the IKEA film. It is also coded by language and the shots, where the camera focuses on these characters. The resolution is also evident, where the housemates use their tablet to consult the Bank of Ireland and the man and children unite as a happy team in the IKEA kitchen. The coda is, in both cases, coded by a change of settings, where the living room and kitchen fade out and the logos appear, also with slogans.

Moving onto the projection genre and the case of the University of Michigan we have a very different structure and series of stages, where a simulation is framed by an orientation and a re-orientation. Here we have three stages. To help illustrate this we introduce another narrative projection, a car advert for the Renault Kadjar, from which stills are shown in Figure 7.4. This allows us to show how the same structures can be used for different kinds of content.

Narrative stages	The case of University of Michigan	The case of Renault Kadjar
Orientation: introducing the product	The logo of the university followed by a black screen	A car with three men driving in a barren terrain
Simulation: a variety of scenes without chronological links	Rapidly changing scenes sketch possibilities. Characters and settings are continuously changing. An emotional voice-over ties the scenes together.	Rapidly changing scenes. Some include the car, others show the care occupants doing extreme sporting activities. Romantic music gives the scenes coherence.
Re-orientation: returning to the starting point	The logo of the university followed by a black screen.	The car is back in the original barren terrain. We see the logo and the slogan 'Renault Passion For Life'.

The projection narrative uses the stage of simulation to construe a general structure of potentialities, a possibility that we (as customers) are supposed to take a stance on. In the case of the university it is to imagine our own future, or, if a parent is involved, the possibilities available for your child. In the Renault case it is to imagine a life where the car is part of fun, friendship and adventure – of 'passion', we are told. In this structure the simulation is part of a circle composition where the initial orientation comes back as a re-orientation at the end. Furthermore, a poetic language (University of Michigan) or romantic music (Renault Kadjar) runs through the changing scenes, as a way both to create coherence and to infuse the product with emotions. Again this is ideological. Education is not about ideas, about different ways of thinking, about hard studies – but a euphoric journey that has tangible and honourable outcomes. Cars, easily associated with congestion and environmental problems, become loaded with emotional discourses of adventure, empty nature and friendship.

Moving onto the recount film structure, using the example of the MasterCard advert, we find the stages of orientation, series of events and coda.

Narrative stages	Applied to the MasterCard film clip
Orientation: the setting and the initial situation	We see a businessman in an office who gets a phone call
Series of events: events and scenes follow chronologically	He puts on biker clothes and walks out to the motorbike, rides through the streets and arrives at the restaurant where he greets people and sits down
Coda: the final point	A close-up of the credit card is followed by the slogan 'Life without limits' as we return to the restaurant

This is like the entertaining narrative since it is chronological and has a main character. Also the initial situation, the orientation, starts the narrative – here we are given the sense that the phone call is the reason the man leaves the office on his motorbike. But there is no real suspense. There is no complication or explicit problem and therefore no clear resolution. The ideological effect presupposes that we look up to the main character and envy his popularity and easy life. The genre of report allows us to follow a day or evening in his extraordinary life. Here using a credit card becomes related to success, style, flexibility. And debt becomes naturalized and interwoven with a desirable lifestyle which itself is based on consumerism.

It is common that celebrities are used in advertising, not least in US credit card commercials, for example Gwen Stefani endorsing MasterCard and Samuel L. Jackson Credit One. The product is then communicated as contributing to superstar status and the advert is devised for evoking desire. The genre of report can be efficient in such cases, because it allows us to see 'everyday life' of a celebrity. The rationale is of course that we should purchase and use the product in question if we also want to be successful.

Scenes

In this section we look at scenes and relate them to settings. Film narrative is basically visual. Its structure comes from combining narrative stages with scenes and shots, which we define below following Iedema (2001). We then apply these to the example of the Renault car advert.

Stage Stages unfold over the film and mark beginnings, middles and ends. Different film-clip genres have different stages, as we have seen above. This may be several scenes that are linked in the same or different setting and indicate chronological time or a mixture of scenes in a simulation.

Scene In a scene the camera is located in a time and a space, where it moves in different ways to combine shots. Sometimes scenes unfold in sequences, as when we follow the man on the motorbike in the MasterCard advert.

Shot It is useful to distinguish between shots when accounting for scenes. A shot is when the camera is unedited. If we have a scene with people talking, the camera will often move and have shots of the speaker through a close-up of their face. Importantly, shots can have different types of camera movement to create effects, such as zooming or panning.

To show how this can be useful analytically we look here at the use of scenes in a Renault Kadjar narrative projection. This commercial is 1.03 minutes long. During the film we see scenes where the car moves in different types of landscapes. Other scenes show spectacular sports such as parachute gliding. The film uses what we have already called 'grounding' and 'projecting' scenes. The grounding scenes focus on the car by shooting it on the road. The projecting scenes show adventures, as we see in Figure 7.4.

The film starts with the car moving in a sort of barren terrain, in a semi-desert region with scrub vegetation, sharp cliffs and a sandy road. In another shot these three men are walking in the barren terrain where they wear hats and quilted jackets. A bridging scene that we see in the upper-left image follows, where the camera zooms out and we see the car from above on an asphalt-covered road on a bridge with water squirting above the river, and then we suddenly meet the car in a winter mountain landscape. Once again the men walk in nature and then two of them, as we see in the upper-right image, jump out from a mountain with paraglider wings, conquering nature and climbing towards the sky. Another spectacular scene shows high-wire walking in a city, seen in the lower-right image.

Figure 7.4 Shots from different scenes in the US commercial for Renault Kadjar

These scenes naturally evoke time as the car is moving. But it is not about characters changing over time, and it is impossible to discern an overall chronology. What we meet is a simulation where mastery over wild or 'raw' nature is a key message and projected in different ways in a variety of scenes. We once again meet a general structure of potentialities. Very few people would actually drive around in a deserted barren terrain or land on the roof of a car paragliding, as in the lower-left image, so this structure is about fantasy and creating emotional bonds to the car.

So a mixture of different scenes is used for 'excitement' and 'imagination' in such film clips, not least for cars and universities. In the entertaining narratives there are fewer scenes since we follow how actual characters develop over time, and it is through relating to their experiences that we are supposed to identify with the brand values. In the recount example we also see fewer scenes: office, city, interior of restaurant.

Settings

Scenes have settings, which is the place where action unfolds. Certainly settings are important both for communicating the idea of the narrative and the values of the brand. Typical qualities of settings in film adverts have to do with communicating aspirational ideals connected to, for example, beauty, prestige, health, recreation and honesty, and might also, and at the same time, include different problems of everyday life that the product in question solves. In analysing settings we first point to the kind of space that is used and second the qualities of this space. As for the space we can make a simplified distinction between nature and culture and the actual qualities of these.

The qualities of natural settings

Nature is a setting used in all sorts of advertising, including, as Hansen (2002) shows, film clips. In this case, for example, food and body products, as well as many drinks, evoke nature as something good in itself. This can be nature as something 'genuine' and 'authentic' so that nature here suggests that products are somehow 'healthy' or 'fresh'. This can apply to things like bread or frozen foods. But it can also apply to washing products, alluding to the restorative powers of nature. In our discussion of packaging in Chapter 5, we saw that the shampoo Garnier Fructis was branded in this way and that the Innocent fruit juices evoked nature as something unadulterated and pure in their 'honest branding' (Figures 5.1 and 5.2).

What is not common in commercials, or advertising in general, is to portray nature as a threat or endangered, and consequently in need of protection.

In the Michigan video there was a quick scene from an underdeveloped or poor country where a white woman tapped water from a barrel. So here the university hints at its powers to help produce solutions to environmental problems. In this sense nature is used to point to social responsibility. It becomes one part of the many 'solutions' and other examples of 'progress' we see in the other stills. In the fifth still we see a woman experimenting with virtual reality seen in a dynamic 'explorative' pose suggesting physical engagement and immersion in the research journey. In the third still the young woman sitting in a hovercraft also points to the wonders of high-tech science. Here we see her utterly absorbed in the research project, inviting applicants to imagine how they themselves may be completely immersed in this future projection. In neither of these scenes are any actual solutions specified. Nor do they raise things like contradictions between the development of science and caring for nature. Yet the scenes of nature coupled with those where we see hovercraft development and innovations in virtual reality help to signify a set of activities that are part of producing some greater value. The expression of the woman in the hovercraft leaves no doubt that this collection of students are absolutely committed to this cause. The physical engagement of the woman wearing the headset points to a kind of study experience which is about go-getting, about making the future.

In the Michigan video nature also appears in a different form where we see a couple running energetically across a green field in the beginning of the simulation. On one level this works in the manner of signifying 'open spaces' and freedom. Life at Michigan is certainly not about being stuck alone in stuffy 'private study' booths. But here the patterned undulating form of the field also suggests something 'intriguing', something 'unique'.

In car commercials, as the Renault film makes clear, nature often appears as something to master, as a wilderness, untouched by humans, seen in two of the stills in Figure 7.4, at the bottom left and the top right, but possible to conquer with the car in question. To the top right the two friends glide over a snow-covered mountain top and then over a high ravine. This points to nature as raw and a place of excitement and bonding. In the bottom left still, in what seems to be an entirely different landscape, although still open and rugged, we are able to more literally link these meanings of adventure with the presence of the car itself.

It is also common to find the idea of 'nature as distance', as a space to be traversed. As in the Renault film, this is made clear by showing the advertised car as the only vehicle on the roads displayed, as we see in the still to the top left. And this can also be shown by men alone in nature when hiking, paragliding and canoeing, as seen in the top right still in Figure 7.4. Such open spaces can suggest metaphorically 'freedom from worry'. Of course what is of interest is that things like 'freedom', and to have agency, become associated not with freedom of thought, nor things like social agency to make the world different as regards social justice, but one that is about freedom to have fun.

So this part of the analysis is about specifying the qualities attached to different types of nature. Recurring qualities in film clips include 'nature as healthy and fresh', 'power over nature', 'nature as a nice place to visit', 'recreational qualities of nature' and 'nature as distance or obstacle' (Hansen, 2002: 508).

The qualities of cultural settings

We have dealt with the meanings of settings in Chapter 3 on photographs (p. 51). Film clips tend to deploy kinds of natural environments to communicate adventure, something romantically pastoral, or as a place of escape. But we also find sports arenas used to communicate strength and victories or scenes where we see highly sanitized technical or scientific spaces as in a toothpaste advertisement. We may find different kinds of generic domestic settings, as in the case of IKEA and the Bank of Ireland. In each case, as we showed in Chapter 6 on space, we can think about meanings of how that space is organized, what objects and forms we find in that space. In each case we can think about the way that these settings help to create problems, or form part of the solution, or simply give us status and success. We can look for the way that these spaces are carefully designed, for example to communicate levels of naturalism that give meanings to a product or service.

In the second still of the MasterCard film we also see a setting typical of advertising which is the cityscape at night. In this still we do not find a busy city centre with traffic and congestion but a still evening with empty streets. The scene in this image connotes a more romantic view of the city, not as a place to work, not as a place of stress or pollution, but for excitement and for romance, perhaps, allowing the man to signify an easy, independent lifestyle, as he drives freely and uninterrupted by other traffic from his office to meet his friends. And of course in this scene the motorcycle itself suggests 'disposable income' and 'independence'.

We also find the city used in the bottom right still of the Renault film. Here we see a man tight-rope walking, alone, between two buildings. Here the city, where we see no other people, and indicators of mundane everyday activities, such as shopping, parking cars, and so on becomes itself able to signify freedom and individualism. It allows us to remain with the idea of adventure and freedom, rather than the detailed nature of each activity (which notably would have taken extensive planning, cost and technical support, which is re-contextualized to a few smiling friends in a car).

When analysing settings we can also consider the extent to which settings are clearly articulated. For example, if we look at Figure 7.3 we see presumably one of the flatmates using a tablet to access the Bank of Ireland website. The setting is out of focus. In contrast the office setting in the first still for the MasterCard film is shot in high detail. In fact in the whole of the Bank of Ireland film, as seen in the stills, the flat is slightly out of focus. This has the effect of making the characters more salient. We are not encouraged to spend time studying the flat itself. In contrast the office in MasterCard, shown in longer shot and in sharp focus, is part of the important information provided about the man's enviable lifestyle. In the still where we see him in the restaurant, however, we do find a less clearly articulated setting. Here what is important is not the setting per se but the idea of friendship and intimacy. When we finally see the Black Card in the final still, a plain white, well-lit surface is chosen rather than a more realistic restaurant table top, to give the card salience. The film can then cut back to a restaurant scene where the friends chat warmly after paying – the energy and pleasure in company to stay into late hours. As a viewer our awareness is not drawn to these out-of-film moments represented by the white surface.

We can also look at the way that cultural settings have been 'managed' in order to help produce different meanings. In the University of Michigan film, for example, we find the yellow colour of the logo coded into the scenes digitally. This is important as it provides a link to the yellow touches that appear in many of the scenes throughout, helping to provide a sense of coherence and cohesion. For example, in the scene where we see the girl in the hovercraft, the roof section of the hovercraft is coded in the same saturated yellow colour. In one scene a peasant pushes a basic, yet innovative, farming device which has a yellow highlight. In this sense the settings are also coded into the overall meaning of the projection. In the final scene where we see the student relaxing, as if somehow the journey is achieved, or where it is to be contemplated sat next to classical architecture, the yellow logo returns completing the cycle. And of course this coding through yellow is found in the opening still where we see the logo against a black background and then at the end where we see it now superimposed over a relaxed, perhaps contemplative student, sitting against a piece of classical architecture. And here it is notable that while the projections in the film point to a future through science and technology, to rapid movement and change, it is at the end that the film uses the sense of the 'eternal' and a more classical notion of knowledge as higher-level thinking as a coda.

Characters

Characters too are very important as regards the way that we understand narratives. Toolan (1988: 98) gives an example of the reader meeting a 'beggar' in a narrative about Victorian Britain. He suggests that the reader may immediately expect therefore a narrative where the person represents some kind of social injustice. Barthes and Duisit (1975) discuss how the character of James Bond gives rise to different narrative expectations. We use the same set of tools as in Chapter 3 on photographs (p. 54), but adapt them to characters in film clips.

Individualization

In film clips unfolding over chronological time, there is often a main character, or characters, who, according to narrative theory, is called the protagonist. This points to the individual who is foregrounded and who we as viewers are supposed to relate to, and often also to identify with. In some commercials this may be some kind of celebrity. We might feel that the Bank of Ireland's couple Steve and Rachel are embarrassing, or that the IKEA man, with six children, is ridiculous, but the success of such commercials comes to a large extent from our interest in how such characters will cope with the problems they face, how they are forced to make difficult choices. Looking at Figure 7.1, Steve and Rachel are given quirky, nerdy type of traits, with slightly unfashionable hairstyles and clothing and exaggerated poses and gestures which indicate gawkiness. These help to create highly memorable characters.

In such film clips there can be someone functioning as an antagonist who opposes and tests the strengths and weaknesses of the protagonist. In the Bank of Ireland advert the housemates have this function and are in conflict with Rachel. In the IKEA video the children take on this function in the complication, disturbing the man's artistry.

Specific and generic

Individualization is also related to uniqueness, to what extent characters come out as unique individuals, if they are specific or generic. As we know, an individual has a name that singles him out and is the basis for his identity. So by their sheer names, Steve and Rachel are made unique and specific, which of course is crucial when making a sitcom type of commercial. By contrast, the housemates are not given names, which underlines that they are not the ones we should identify with or follow. They are individualized to some degree as seen in Figure 7.2 where we see their reactions in close-up. Yet on another level they are signalled as 'regular guys', through clothing and actions.

The men in the Renault advert in contrast are generic. They are attractive, adventurous and appear as very similar to each other. We are not encouraged to see them specifically as individuals but as types who inhabit the simulation. When we see them in close-up laughing and enjoying the adventure and each other's company there is nothing really to distinguish them. Clothing, hair-style, postures and reactions are highly similar across the group. In Figure 7.2 we learn little about the two flatmates as individuals but smaller details, like the suit, the casual, clothing and the beard, signal specific individuals.

In the MasterCard film we find classic generic characters in the final scenes, as we see in the last still. We recognize the protagonist, who, helpfully, wears a white shirt to stand out from his friends who wear darker colours. At no point does the camera encourage us to connect to any of these friends. Yet from the glimpses we get, they are attractive, at ease, warm – in fact the generic types of friends that populate such films, as found in the Renault film, for example.

Collectivization

People in films can appear as part of collectives. This can be where we see people are part of a group, where they are shown in a way that makes them appear as sharing qualities with a group. In an advert it may be useful to show a particular collective of people in order to emphasize the individual nature of the protagonist who makes the good consumer choice. To an extent the children in the IKEA commercial are collectivized. We do see them briefly in close-up but they wear the same kind of clothes and behave in the same way. Nothing in the sequence asks us to engage with them as individuals. The same goes for the different people in the University of Michigan film clip. If we look at the people we see in the stills from the film it is clear it is not in the first place about them as individuals. We do not expect them to return later in the film. And in three of the scenes (4, 8, 15) we see that the young women bare very similar facial expressions of focus and absorption. The student body is collectivized as part of this journey to the future, absorbed deeply in its moral worthiness.

Categorization

We can ask to what extent characters have some kind of biological or cultural categorization. This can be both positively and negatively evaluated. In the Michigan film we clearly find an emphasis on ethnic heterogeneity. Many universities use such representations, both to attract international students, to suggest openness, liveliness and being 'international' which is an important marketing idea. In some universities, in our experience, this certainly does not represent the reality of the proportions of different ethnic groups studying at an institution. In the IKEA film the children appear to be culturally categorized. They all wear clothing that points to natural fabrics, handmade, which coordinate with the natural materials in the kitchen.

Rhythm and sound in scenes

One important part of the way that these film clips communicate relates to rhythm. Music plays a big part here. The IKEA commercial deploys changes of music to communicate the narrative stages, and Renault Kadjar uses a romantic folk song to infuse the car with emotions. A rhythm in a film clip may suggest something easy and smooth, or something more stuttering and difficult, or even have variation to communicate lack of conformity or creativity. Films may be edited to the rhythm created by the music, or ride over this.

Here we draw on Cooke's (1959) inventory of rhythm, used by Machin (2010) to look at popular music (cf. van Leeuwen, 1999). This is useful for thinking about film clips since it draws attention to the way that music implies different kinds of movement. This can be used to activate a set of associations. Sound qualities can therefore evaluate what takes place and evoke associations of 'speed', 'weight', 'evenness', 'intensity' and 'intimacy'. These are associations that can be useful for marketing and branding and that may be harder to communicate through other semiotic materials. Below we point out some important features of rhythm and sound.

Even and uneven

Rhythms can be even (as in much pop music) or uneven (as may be the case in jazz). Uneven rhythms can communicate a sense of difficulty, or if the unevenness is repeated a sense of being prevented from moving forwards or remaining in one particular place. Unevenness can also suggest creativity as movement changes, reacting and refusing to conform. In our IKEA commercial above we find that the music of the complication, a funky piece, is highly uneven as if stuttering. Once the resolution starts the rhythm evens out. In the Michigan film we find evenness throughout. The future offered by the university is part of a smooth and regular journey.

Fast and slow

Rhythms can suggest energy or relaxation or sluggishness; hurry versus leisurely; rush versus patience. In the IKEA commercial we find the slow relaxation and pondering in the orientation, also coded by a piano that tinkles and suggests thoughtfulness, and the increase in speed when the complication starts. The Michigan film moves along quickly throughout.

Lightness and heaviness

Rhythm, due to instrumentation, for example if it is dominated by a deep, loud, bass drum, or in contrast by a flute, can suggest heaviness versus lightness, clumsiness or mobility, strength or weakness, important or unimportant. The Michigan film while fast and even also begins lightly and delicately. There is a sense of lightness and of mobility. As the film moves along it becomes heavier and more substantial as the emotion builds. This gives a sense of building which is part of the 'building of possibility' communicated by the film. The music acts as a kind of conjunction binding the short scenes together.

Stasis and motion
Through constant beat tones (such as a single bass drum pulse or repeated strike on a piano keyboard) rhythms can suggest stasis, waiting, hesitation or restriction. There are many ways in music that motion can be communicated, but here we need to think about what kinds of motion we are dealing with. Forwards motion can be suggested by the alternating tones of a snare and bass drum, the meaning of which will depend on things like lightness or speed. Also some music suggests a side-to-side or rocking movement rather than a forwards motion, which is often used to suggest emotional dwelling. The rhythm in the Michigan film suggests a combination of swaying and light steps forwards. While at the start this sounds thoughtful and cautious, as the heaviness increases with volume it becomes more confident. In the still where we see the couple running across the field there is a sense, therefore, of something gently moving. By the time we see the still where the woman wears the 3D glasses, more pace and significance is taking place.

Metronomic and non-metronomic time
Lack of rhythm can be used to suggest timelessness, sacredness or spirituality (Tagg, 1984). And we may find bank or life insurance commercials which use such meanings to suggest 'freedom from worry' and 'simplicity'. In the Bank of Ireland commercial, relying on speech, we find no musical rhythm until the announcement is made that Rachel is moving in. Here the bank information appears on the tablet and an easy, light and airy piece of music with some warm xylophone type sounds. There is little motion in the rhythm and even a sense of unevenness which appears rather to indicate 'thoughtfulness' and 'reacting'. Before we hear the music, there is more of a sense of film realism or drama.

Language and evaluations
A story must have a point, otherwise it would not be worth telling (Labov, 1997). The many semiotic resources used in film clips make it possible to use different types of evaluations, but language tends to be a major resource here. Below we account for different uses of language in evaluations.

Types of language

Our examples clearly point to different types of language used for evaluations. These are of three types. First we have lines delivered by characters, as in the Bank of Ireland film. So here, through their utterances, we get to know the main characters and can follow how they react. Second we have voice-over. This voice is obviously not belonging to the characters but to a narrator that guides us though the narrative and tells us what is noteworthy. Both the Bank of Ireland and University of Michigan rely on voice-over. In one sense the song lyrics to a piece of music work in the same way here, offering more abstract ideas about 'searching' or 'travelling', for example. Third we have captions, which is what IKEA uses. Of note is the difference between using spoken (lines, voice-over) and written (captions) language. Using written language, as IKEA do, the evaluations come out as more factual compared with the spoken lines of, for example, Rachel, which we take as belonging to her. And in the analysis of film clips it is important to think about which level evaluations take place.

Character and narrator evaluations

The three types of language must be related to the characters and the narrator, because here we meet different evaluations (Young, 1982). We meet clear character evaluations in the case of Steve and Rachel. Here the lines make clear the clash between Rachel and the housemates, as when her enthusiastic evaluation 'gonna be awesome' is met with 'deadly'. In the University of Michigan commercial the voice-over is, as we explained, highly poetic. The many characters have no lines and our emotional attachment to them must come through the voice-over, as we are invited to be like them. The folk song in the Renault advert works similarly, using a romantic and poetic address to evoke emotions. Also in the IKEA film the characters do not speak. But we can get a sense of their evaluations through their posture and facial expressions (cf. the analysis of such indexing of emotions in Chapter 3 (p. 56)). For example, everyone looks happy once they start to work together as a team. But the main evaluation comes from the narrator and the written captions stating the point of the story, that parents need to find time to be with their children.

Evaluations and narrative stages

As we have seen, evaluations can be made in different parts of the narrative and also in different ways. In the Bank of Ireland film, we meet the lines of the characters in the orientation and complication, and then the narrator takes over in the resolution and coda. In the IKEA advert the captions are distributed in the narrative stages as follows.

Narrative stage	Evaluations in captions in the IKEA kitchen advert
Orientation	'7 of 10 children want more time with their parents', 'Why not give them more space'
Complication	no captions
Resolution	no captions
Coda	'Together everything is possible' followed by IKEA's logo with the message 'Shop whenever you want at IKEA.se'

So the narrator sets up the complication as being the point of parents wanting and having to spend 'quality time' with their children. Then we meet the chaos in the complication. From the point of the narrative it is of course important with this disorder that it can be brought to a new balance and harmonious teamwork in the resolution – all this, as we explained above, also coded by changing music. In film clips, a coda is important, because the narrator must be explicitly linked to the company and the brand. Here it becomes clear that IKEA brings solutions to life problems, which is also what Bank of Ireland's coda accounts for. And the university and car commercials that we have discussed obviously end with a coda to show that the exciting futures and fantasies shown are dependent on the company.

SUGGESTIONS FOR RESEARCH QUESTIONS

As we have applied our analytical tools in this chapter we have begun to show how they could be used in a research project. We have shown how they could be used to look at the way that educational institutions sell themselves, how banks use them to sell debt and how cars are marketed. But we can think about this as regards what the specific research questions might look like. Here we give two examples. These use quite general examples, but could use much more specific ones related to smaller-scale organizations.

- How have banking commercials changed over the past 30 years?

- Compare the videos of three different political parties leading up to an election

In the first research question we might collect films from a number of banks over 30 years. These can often easily be found on social media. We could then begin to look at the kinds of narrative structures that are used; what kinds of people, place

(Continued)

and settings do we find? How are evaluations carried out? We may indeed find that some core ideas and values about banking have changed over this period. Has music and rhythm shifted to suggest more drama, or lightness and carefree for example?

The second example is more of a title than a research question. But this could be followed up by specifying that the aim was to compare the ways that three or more parties provide different narratives about themselves and society, about issues that need to be addressed. Here we can look at the kind of persons and ideas that dominate the films and how and where the evaluations are provided. Of course, the ultimate aim is to draw out the discourses used by each.

8

DATA PRESENTATION

Introduction

In this chapter we are interested in the way that data and information are presented. In contemporary media we tend to find more and more numbers, statistics, graphics and classifications of things. This, of course, is now very easy to do with software for analysis and data and information presentation. But we can also relate this increase to wider cultural and political changes that we discussed in Chapter 2. There has been an increasing 'technologization' of semiotic resources (Fairclough, 1992) which accelerated sometime in the mid- to late 2000s. Language and other semiotic resources become more codified in order to have greater control over communication. This has been harnessed by certain threads of political thinking where all parts of life must be managed to improve outputs, such as in hospitals and schools. Such outputs are to be measured and presented as statistics presented in league tables. But this also leads to a culture which begins to prioritize the value of classification and quantification for its own sake. All sorts of things become subject to such codification, even where, from one point of view, this would seem entirely inappropriate, such as the way the emotional and attitudinal development of a pre-school child must be subject to classifications and worked upon.

In fact classification is a part of everyday life. We classify and sort all kinds of things all the time. Dishes of different sizes, or uses, are placed together. We may put certain types of shoes at the back of the cupboard. We put our books in a different pile to those of our children. We organize things in a computer according to different activities. Such sorting and classification is related to our knowledge of social practices, such as eating and food preparation, and also about social roles and what these are assumed to involve (Bowker and Star, 1999). Of course, some have the power to impose their classifications upon us. This is important. When you classify your dishes and books you impose an order on the world – you are in fact constructing a world in accordance with certain purposes and values and in accordance with accepted behaviours for specific social roles. The same happens when classifications are imposed upon us by others. This happens in the case where public toilets are classified according to notions of gender. Mental illness, while complex and contested, has become classified into a number of key illnesses, which in fact are constantly up for redefinition (Szasz, 2010). Parking can be allocated according to ranking in an organization. Such classifications support and reinforce certain interests and ways of doing things.

Typical forms of data presentation

In today's visual communication we are very familiar with seeing connections being made between categories or processes at a symbolic level. We saw this in the example of the PowerPoint slide in Figure 1.3. It is not clear how the different points on the diagram are linked causally, yet the use of the design suggests 'logic' and signals 'doing something scientifically' (Ledin and Machin, 2015a). This is the kind of representation we deal with in this chapter. We will point to the affordances of typical forms of data presentation. First we deal with lists and bullet points, second with tables, line graphs and bar charts, and third with flow charts. Eventually we present the tools with which such representations can be critically analysed.

Lists and bullet points

In Figure 8.1 we see an extract from a document used in the UK to promote the use of breastfeeding (taken from Brookes et al., 2016). In their analysis Brookes et al. explain how such documents represent breastfeeding not only as better for the baby but also as an indication of good motherhood, connecting it to a sense of having more control over one's life, being aspirational, and so on. The point is that such 'health' campaigns deal not only with relative facts regarding milk or bottle feeding but a whole range of evaluations about persons and ways of life. We have chosen this particular extract for its use of a numbered bullet list, used to present the '6 Start4Life building blocks', which it is explained are 'based on the latest infant health research'.

This numbered list is presented as 'building blocks'. The thing with all bulleted lists is that they claim to be the basic components of a thing, stripped back for purpose of presentation. In a PowerPoint presentation the bulleted lists suggest the 'core points' around which the presenter will talk (Djonov and Van Leuuwen, 2014). In one sense we can think about this as regards what Kress and van Leeuwen (1996: Chapter 5) called 'technical modality'. Rather than a text describing the full details of a process or event, a bullet list presents what we

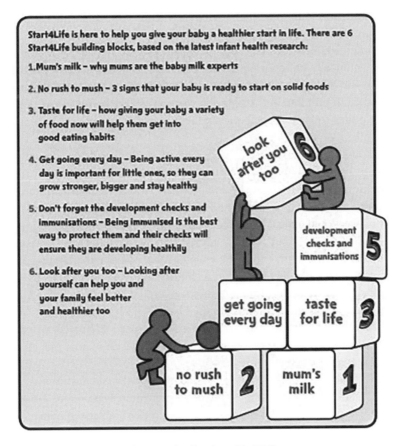

Start4Life is here to help you give your baby a healthier start in life. There are 6 Start4Life building blocks, based on the latest infant health research:

1. Mum's milk – why mums are the baby milk experts

2. No rush to mush – 3 signs that your baby is ready to start on solid foods

3. Taste for life – how giving your baby a variety of food now will help them get into good eating habits

4. Get going every day – Being active every day is important for little ones, so they can grow stronger, bigger and stay healthy

5. Don't forget the development checks and immunisations – Being immunised is the best way to protect them and their checks will ensure they are developing healthily

6. Look after you too – Looking after yourself can help you and your family feel better and healthier too

Figure 8.1 An instructional list for breastfeeding from Start4Life

might think of as the technical details. In the case of Start4Life the metaphor of building blocks directly suggests a technical construction process. It gives a sense that the presenter has full understanding of the process and has identified the important components for us.

But in this case if we look at what sits in the list we find a fairly irregular and even contradictory set of points. For example, point 2 regards not rushing to stop breastfeeding and introducing actual food ('mush'). Number 4, 'get going everyday', seems rather general. And what this numbering in fact indicates is not clear – we do not here find a list of instructions where actions are ordered chronologically. Nor do we find a numerical order of ranking of priority. But the numbering connotes logic and science.

As regards providing practical advice the list also appears rather weak. Both authors have had long periods of parent leave with small children. The advice to 'look after yourself too' can see rather banal when managing several small, energetic and needy children on a daily basis. Of course this helps the list to be feel-good. But the bulleted form allows the relationship between the parts, here caring for small children and caring for yourself, to be omitted. And the bullets allow the points to have space between them which also serves to separate them from the others.

As for language, maxims are used, typical of the kind used by self-styled 'experts' in lifestyle magazines. So we have 'mum's milk', 'no rush to mush', 'taste for life'. Here we find both rhyming ('rush'–'mush') and alliterations (where an initial 'm' is repeated in 'mum' and 'milk'). If this was a more formal type of instruction we would expect coherence coming from recurring imperatives stating actions, such as 'hold', 'put', 'give', 'remember', but here the grammatical forms vary. Instead we find a kind of poetic language that connotes something easy, fun and pleasant, as do also the drawings of children and the uneven and playful font (cf. Cook, 1994: Chapter 6). Importantly the overall coherence is provided by the technical numbering and three-dimensional boxes piled on each other, which also suggests components being used to build a whole plan. Such a set of processes would be difficult to present in a running text that tends to require that causalities and processes are presented more clearly.

Making lists is a core activity for both individuals and institutions (Ledin, 2015). List-making and the establishing of classification systems are, Bowker and Star (1999) argue, 'one of the foundational activities of advanced human society' (p. 137). The basic affordance of a list, Goody (1977) explains, is that it separates and abstracts components from each other, usually, as in Figure 8.1, by the use of spacing between units. A list gives a permanent record of a paradigm, of a certain cultural domain, with the idea of providing an inventory. So this could be a list of things that you can eat on a particular diet, or a list of cars that are economical. Such things form a paradigm, since they share properties for a particular purpose. This meaning is important for the way therefore that lists can be used to connote that the things they contain are of the same order. The individual or institution in charge of a list will have power and be in control of the knowledge involved and the uses of it. We can think of shopping lists, best-of lists, a list of all mammals in a biology book. And we get a list as the result of an Internet search. Simply, lists are made by certain actors for certain interests and therefore call for critical readings.

Lists have existed since the dawn of writing as a way to control and document people and activities (Goody, 1977). But, as Figure 8.1 shows, how we now make lists involves not just separated items of writing but the deployment of many semiotic resources. And these different resources can be used to create links across documents that each contain lists or other data and information in the kinds of more abstracted or symbolic form that interests us in this chapter. Such interlocking systems are typical of many of the audit/management systems that now control the running of organizations such as schools and hospitals. A list of learning targets may link to lists of wider institutional goals and of numerical performance indicators (Ledin and Machin, 2016c).

Figure 8.2 shows a visual list for the app and game Pokémon Go, which is a digital adaption of the Japanese fictional world of Pokémon, a trademark owned by Nintendo. Pokémon was first launched in the 1990s as a video game and has since appeared in many media, for example as a manga series and a trading card game, before being released as an app in 2016. The international impact on popular culture has been enormous during these decades, and the cute figures reappear in different media contexts.

What interests us here is that the creation of the Pokémon universe relies on making lists, or rather lists of lists. Pokémons live in different regions and come in

Figure 8.2   To the left a clickable list of the 151 first generation Pokémons in the app Pokémon Go, and to the right a list of the qualities of Pokémon #001 Bulbasaur

different generations, of which we see the first generation in the list in Figure 8.2. This generation consists of 151 species. Every region has a so-called Pokedex, which is an inventory (and list) of all species. The first generation lives in Kanto, the second in Johto, and there is also an overall Pokedex, which you can look up in the app to see how many species you have caught. As Figure 8.2 shows, every Pokémon also has a list of its own as a record of its qualities. The basic idea of the game is to fill the Pokedex with all species, to train a team of especially powerful Pokémons and to compete against other teams. In Pokémon Go each Pokémon must be caught with your phone by capturing it on your screen.

What the Pokémon case makes clear is the power inherent in connecting lists to lists. Here it affords a whole universe to be built and be launched in different media. Collecting all species is a project in a sense resembling what Carl Linnaeus did in the eighteenth century when he explored and made inventories of the environment in his book *Systema Naturae* that comprised 4,400 species of animals and 7,700 plants, and was a huge contribution to natural science. Making this kind of scientific approach to exploring and mastering a domain accessible and fun is certainly one explanation for the success of Pokémon.

The exactness rendered by combining language and numbers in the lists is important. All generations and species have a number, and the game is consequently based on different quantifications. Using your smartphone you can play it throughout the world, and here regions also matter. For example, the species Taurus is only possible to catch in the US. So due to carefully devised lists it is possible to establish a new universe inhabited by a variety of species, and controlling the lists, or the technology of the game, means controlling a world-wide business making huge profits.

As with the systems of interlocking lists that rule the running of organizations these present what appear to be 'closed' lists, as being definitive, although of course no list can be so, as Eco (2009) makes clear. Such a process is how bureaucracy and the building of states and nations have been carried out. If you want to create and impose a universe of meaning with clear boundaries, you connect lists to lists. In contemporary society this is increasingly done through technology. In the case of Pokémon Go, like the breastfeeding design, we find the defining of paradigms and also the use of spatialization. So species of Pokémon appear as the same size, as positioned in equal space with the same categories of information. Clicking on one of them, a new list will appear with more data and information. This will happen in the same way for each species.

We might find the same thing on a database of learning targets in a pre-school software package used to implement a system of checks and measures as regards quality and learning targets. Each outcome may appear as a set of options defined as regards a paradigm and through spatialization. One of the authors was once in teacher–parent meeting for his pre-school daughter. He recalls a cynical kinder-garten teacher talking with some irony about his child using such terminology, for which he had an extensive database. The author's child was present at the time and was sitting with two other children in a woodland behind the pre-school, throwing dry leaves into the air. In the times of technologization even such activities must be codified, placed into lists, measured and represented through forms of charts and tables.

Tables, line graphs and bar charts

Another feature we now find in documents presenting and structuring information is the table. Like the list the table has specific affordances (Ledin, 2015). The main affordance of a table is that it makes detailed and often numerical comparisons possible. It does so by combining several lists into a composition in columns and rows. Each column consists of a list belonging to a certain paradigm or defined domain. For example, we might find a table to compare new models of cars. The comparison would be based on different paradigms where all units are supposed to be of the same order, such as 'fuel consumption', 'cost' or 'crash test results'. These paradigms would mostly be rendered in numbers, meaning that the paradigms are based on some kind of fixed measurement, and they are materialized side by side as columns. To the left, as the point of departure, the cars involved would be listed. The rows of the table would come out as syntagms, as combinations of units from the different paradigms (cf. Barthes, 1964 on paradigms and syntagms). The comparisons that the table affords could in this case guide the purchase of a car.

A table typical for our time, part of an interactive web page, is shown in Figure 8.3. Here we find football statistics from the home page of the English Premier League, in this case for the number of 'touches' by players. As we see, five paradigms are combined from left to right: 'Rank', 'Player', 'Club', 'Nationality' and 'Stat', and they unfold from 'given' to 'new' information (Kress and van Leeuwen, 1996). These concepts can be used to characterize what is represented as given or established knowledge in a text or image, and what is represented as the new, or the contestable, the possible. So what we find is that rank and player to the left is the given information, and where the following columns specify the player, and the stat to the right, the number of passes, is the new information, updated as it is after each game. We can ask if these paradigms are transparent, if they rely on a culturally acknowledged domain or knowledge. In this sense we are asking how appropriate these categories are for a table (cf. Ledin and Machin, 2016c).

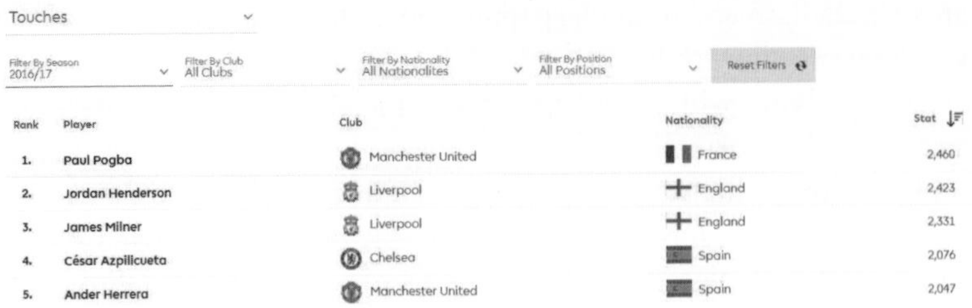
Touches
Filter By Season 2016/17 | Filter By Club All Clubs | Filter By Nationality All Nationalites | Filter By Position All Positions | Reset Filters

Rank	Player	Club	Nationality	Stat
1.	Paul Pogba	Manchester United	France	2,460
2.	Jordan Henderson	Liverpool	England	2,423
3.	James Milner	Liverpool	England	2,331
4.	César Azpilicueta	Chelsea	Spain	2,076
5.	Ander Herrera	Manchester United	Spain	2,047

Figure 8.3 Touches for players in Premier League according to the official homepage

As for the players and their affiliations this indeed is a culturally acknowledged domain, even if it takes a person interested in football to make sense of the information. The statistics are harder to assess, as is often the case with tables. It is hard to know what the difference between 2460, 2423 and 2331 (for the top three players) actually stands for. Or even what is counted as a 'touch' – does this include picking up the ball for a throw, accidently being hit by a shot, a tackle where the ball is touched but not won? Is the number one player, Paul Pogba, somehow the best in Premier League, which his first place indeed indicates? During this actual season Pogba, as a new prestige signing for a world-record £89 million by Manchester United, had in fact been criticized for not contributing to the team as much as he should. But the use of the table here draws on the affordance that elements in a column are indeed part of the same transparent paradigm.

Figure 8.3 is a good example of how we often find statistics rendered in digital tables. These have become pervasive in many social practices, including sports and leisure. What we do in different domains of life is counted and we get scores on different scales. As we see, the home page is interactive with drop-down menus. The main menu on the top allows for 23 different statistics to be chosen, besides 'Touches', including domains such as 'Hit Woodwork', 'Clearances Off Line' and 'Punches'. What is sure is that we live in an era where we are familiar with all sorts of detailed rankings of not only sports but also all kinds of public and corporate services. As with bulleted lists and flow charts with symbolized causalities, we tend not to question them.

We often find graphs, such as bar charts, pie charts and line graphs, which give a sense that they simplify the often dense information of a table (cf. Tufte, 1983). These can all be thought of as tools that visualize quantitative data, albeit in different ways. A kind of simplified table is shown in Figure 8.4 and is part of a tweet from the US President Donald Trump. It displays crime statistics and contains just two columns. The first and given one relies on a paradigm of killings. Killings are specified as to offenders and victims among white, black and police. There are no other ethnic groups, which could certainly have been possible, or other social characteristics, such as income or educational background. But it appears that the point here is to oppose these specifically chosen social groups and races.

To the right, communicated as new information, the data consists of percentages. A quick glance reveals that the blacks are the main offenders: they kill both whites and other blacks at a much higher rate than the other groups. If we continue to ponder this, we might get struck by the fact that the total percentage is not 100, which is the usual idea behind counting percentages, but in fact 200 per cent. Of these 200 per cent, blacks stand for no less than 178 per cent of the killings (81 per cent whites killed by blacks and, emphasized in bold face, 97 per cent blacks killed by blacks). We can thus suspect that this data does not come from an established or accepted source, which in this case would be official crime

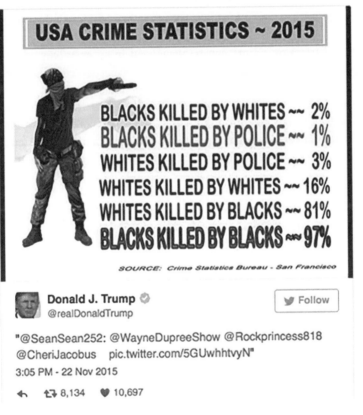

Figure 8.4 President Trump tweets crime statistics

statistics with transparent procedures for sampling data and establishing points of comparisons between entities, in this case races.

President Trump claimed that his statistics were taken from the Crime Statistics Bureau in San Francisco, but it was soon revealed that no such bureau existed. It is the FBI that are nationally responsible for these kinds of statistics, and many news agencies shared parts of these statistics in different graphs. The FBI statistics made clear that interracial homicide constituted a minor part of all homicides. Killings of blacks by whites and whites by blacks accounted for about 12 per cent of all homicides, with blacks a little bit more often being the offender. It can be noted that such statistics conceal other factors that are important in understanding crime such as poverty, unemployment and poor educational opportunities. And in fact both offenders and victims of crime tend to be those who live in relative poverty.

A type of graph often used by public media is the line graph, as in Figure 8.5. This was also used as part of the debate started by Trump. In this form of graph the point is usually to map a paradigm on a timeline, in this case homicide victims by race from 2001 until 2015. The main affordance of this kind of representation is that a trend over time can be visualized in an easy way: when the line goes upwards there is increase and downwards means decrease. The trend in this case is clear: there are no big differences between blacks and whites, even if the number of black victims has increased in 2015. Another trend is that the number of homicides does not rise during this time period. Of course it is often the case that the vertical axis can be stretched out to greatly increase the visual impact of fluctuations. We often see this in news reports that seek to emphasize 'a roller coaster situation' either for a politician or a sports club. Expanding the axis could in the case of Figure 8.5 also visually increase the difference between blacks and whites since 2009 if this were required. As we saw in Figure 8.4 images and font weight can also be used to create meaning. In television news presentation of crime statistics we may also find an image of hooded youth, or a shadowing street as a backdrop for figures on policing prostitution. In such cases we can ask what is foregrounded and what is backgrounded. What ideology of crime and law enforcement do such representations reinforce?

So the debate after Trump's tweet on crime statistics was largely carried out by using different types of charts and graphs with quantitative data as they, compared with a dense table, could visualize trends efficiently. We all recognize this from the news, where all sorts of polls and statistics on elections are continuously used. And even if the figures are taken as facts, they are often hard to assess. As in the case of tables, graphs and charts, these can be more or less true or transparent.

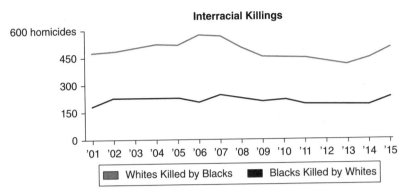

Figure 8.5 A line graph from US News showing homicide victims by race from 2001 to 2015.

In Figure 8.6 we see a bar chart that is used to represent the international success of a university. Here we are told that it is based on statistics from Web of Science with no further explanation about this. In fact, the Web of Science and its citation score is the internationally single most used indicator of research 'quality'. It presupposes that citations are equal to quality, which is clearly not the case any more than the most downloaded or sold music per definition has the highest quality. Some government studies have been highly critical of the Web of Science, concluding that it is a very poor guide to quality in research (e.g. Piro et al., 2013). Nevertheless, again given the present culture of quantification of all things, governments, who may have little understanding of what it means, continue to use it.

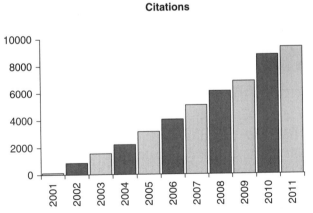

The statistics are taken from the Web of Science which uses a research database of over 10,000 leading scientific journals.

Figure 8.6 A bar chart showing increasing citations for a university

Normally the citation score is given in relative numbers and compared to a certain research field to make rankings possible. But this university chooses to sum up all research and use the absolute number of citations, which blocks out comparisons.

A bar chart, like a line graph, maps a paradigm, here citations, on a timeline, and does so in an accessible way, where the sheer size of the bars is the point. The higher the number, the higher the bar. Of note is also that the bars are separated from each other, each one being a box on its own. Yet the colour matching contributes to the design as blue and grey change (it is of course not the case that the bars in blue form a paradigm of their own). In this way technicality disappears and we get a nice and easy picture of a world with never-ending success.

Of note in the use of this graph is that no explanations are given to the numbers. How should we interpret that there are around 6000 citations in 2008? Is that good or bad in comparison to other universities? And how is it possible to have continuous increase – it seems impossible for the same staff to go from almost 0 to more than 8000 citations in 10 years? The major answer to this question is that we are dealing with a new and small university where simply more researchers were employed. Also the university policy was to hire more staff in medical sciences, where the research journals are indexed in Web of Science, whereas research in the humanities, where very few journals are part of Web of Science, was cut down. But obviously such information would compromise the basic message of this bar chart. What we meet is growth and success as part of an indisputable logic where outputs never stop to rise as if they were part of something definitive and perfect.

What we learn here is that tables and graphs have some affordances that can compellingly communicate that a logical process of data presentation is being offered and affording exact and objective comparisons. But if we look more carefully at what is compared in paradigms and how they are presented, we may find that there are problems.

Flow charts

Visual presentations of data and information are, as we have said, ubiquitous in our culture. The flow chart is a widely circulated type of data presentation, and here a basic graphic grammar has evolved, where graphical shapes and basic templates are part of all kinds of software. We showed in Figure 2.4 how Microsoft Word comes with pre-fabricated graphical shapes sorted into groups, and flow charts is one of these groups. Word has 28 graphical flow-chart symbols, and the same symbols with verbal definitions are found in many places, such as in the tutorial to flow charts in the software SmartDraw.

Common symbols and definitions include the following.

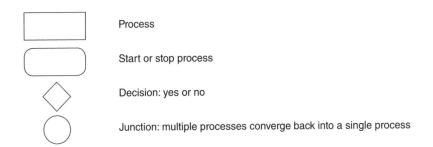

Process

Start or stop process

Decision: yes or no

Junction: multiple processes converge back into a single process

Other symbols have meanings such as 'subroutine', 'stored data' and 'loop limit', which points to computer programming as one major domain for the use of flow charts. A basic affordance of a flow chart is that it states a principled solution to a problem. In computer programming this affords to map out and monitor the data flow in a system. As seen in the symbols above, the mapping presupposes that processes and decisions are delimited and unfold over time in a predictable way. Since digital technology is built on either-or choices and loops, this can be handy for computer programming. When flow charts are used to provide solutions to human matters, things tend to become more complicated, since humans often look for practical solutions here-and-now and tend to make irrational choices.

Figure 8.7 shows a flow chart and general template which provide a solution and work routine for recruitment in HR organizations. This process over time must, when a flow chart is used, be communicated in a rational step-for-step fashion with exact start and end points and clearly defined and ordered processes and where pathways are triggered by either–or choices. The chart contains 15 processes (in light blue boxes), six decisions (in a green diamond shape), three start and stops (in darker blue and with rounded edges) and one circular junction. If this chart is functional it could from one point of view be assessed by the actual HR organization using it. But what we can say is how these kinds of diagrams abstract temporal and causal relationships and delete actors. We do so in order to promote a critical awareness of data presentations.

The flow chart as a whole is to be read from the start box to upper left to the stop box to the bottom right, taking in the possibility that the recruitment process could be ended by the stop box to the lower left. An important abstraction is that temporality and causality are intertwined, which graphically is coded by arrows. If we look at the first three processes (in the left column), the flow is that 'Define and write up job description' precedes 'Send personnel request form to HR' which is followed by 'Determine classification'. This is coded as unfolding over time and, as the arrows indicate, also as each process is both a result of the preceding

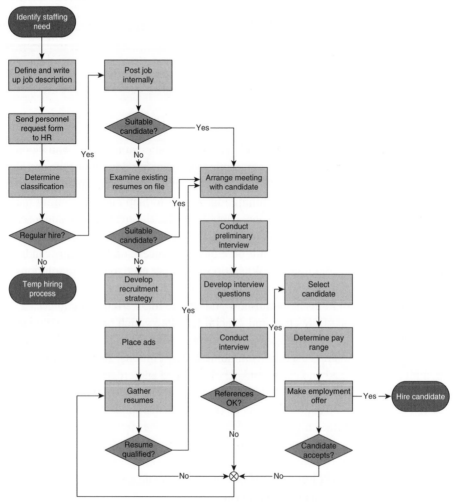

Figure 8.7 Flow chart showing hiring process in HR organizations

process and a cause for the following process. But how this actually happens in time and space is completely concealed. What does 'determine classification' mean in practice? How exactly is it based on the preceding job description – and how should that description be written in order to help classification, if that is the purpose of it? And nothing is said about how much time different processes or the flow between start and end points takes.

As for language, verbs are used, which grammatically means coding processes. This is to be contrasted with nouns, including proper names, which code people and things, as for example in the football statistics in Figure 8.3. Specifically in the HR chart we find imperatives, in this case 'Define', 'Send' and 'Determine'. Imperatives code the speech act of command and calls for action, but they do not code the subject or the one issuing the command, nor the object or the one addressed. In speech the actual situation would determine this, since we would know who is talking to whom, but in writing confusion can arise. And here it is in fact unclear who is addressed. Who shall 'define', 'send' and 'determine' – is it the same actor? It seems not, because the personnel request should be sent 'to HR', and it then seems logical that HR is that actor responsible for 'defining' the classification. We can note that the decision box in the second row, 'Suitable candidate?', codes the either-or choice typical for flow charts. The only answer possible is 'yes' or 'no' – an answer like 'perhaps', 'I don't know' or 'let's ask Linda' certainly corrupts the logic. In order words, the way flow charts delete actors and abstracts temporality and causality conceals actual work process, and it is important to be critically aware of this.

We can also ponder the 'junction', the small circle with the 'X'. What happens here is not very clear. It codes a junction where different processes converge and actually permits an infinite loop, where the process starts all over again. In actual life one might consider a different recruitment process, but here it is part of the rationale where different graphic shapes brings an allegedly exact solution to a problem.

Analysing data presentation

We have already pointed to some of the analytical tools required for describing and analysing the kinds of representations we have looked at in this chapter. Here we will present the detailed tool kit. We start with looking at how different paradigms are established and relate this to spatialization, to how they are materialized in space. The following sections account for graphic devices, temporality and causality. The tool kit aims to capture what is specific for data presentations as a semiotic material shaped as a whole. It is, depending on the kind of research question asked which we will come back to below, also possible to use many of the tools we presented for document design in Chapter 4 since borders, colour and typeface are part also of data presentations.

Paradigms

A paradigm is a set of items that we take to belong to a cultural domain (Barthes, 1964) and to be the result of classification (Bowker and Star, 1999). We can classify and make paradigms of almost anything: flowers, sports, or types of roses and free-kicks in football, different kinds of reggae music, urban restaurants, cancer types, capital cities of Asia, what we need to buy for dinner or wish for Christmas. A paradigm is a defining feature of data presentations, and paradigms are always constructed for a purpose and in someone's interest. For example, the listing of persons based on racial classification schemes was an integral part of the apartheid system in South Africa (Bowker and Star, 1999: Chapter 6).

Even if the content of paradigms is very varied, it is possible to distinguish general types if we depart from language. Paradigms can then be seen as comprising processes, people and things. Linguistically this is coded by verbs, names and nouns (cf. Ledin, 2015), and to this we add quantitative paradigms based on numbers. It is of note that culturally established paradigms are symmetrical, based on the same linguistic form. A paradigm stating what to do will normally be based on verbs, since these code activities. A paradigm of certain objects will normally use nouns, since this is the way to refer to things using language. If a paradigm would not be coded in symmetrical forms, we would not take it to be coherent or possible to generalize, but idiosyncratic. If items such as 'Anna, cinema 5.30, milk, pay electricity bill' were listed, this might be meaningful for a certain individual (as, for example, a reminder of not to forget a certain day, written on a post-it note and put on the fridge) but it would not be a coherent cultural paradigm.

Processes

Paradigms that record actions and activities will be based on verbs. We point to the use of the verb forms imperatives and infinitives.

Imperatives Imperatives code and issue a command. We can think of a parent telling a child '*clean* your room'. Imperatives are used in the flow chart in Figure 8.7 and include 'send', 'select' and 'determine' to provide the principled actions needed for recruitment. This verb form does not say who is commanding whom, just that someone should carry out these actions. If a list is about recording actions to be carried out, infinitives are certainly functional, as in the listing of actions in a recipe or to-do list. But the implied actor must be clear, which is not the case in the flow chart. As a result, this data presentation is confusing, since we do not know who does or has responsibility for what, who is sending, selecting and determining in the recruiting process.

Infinitives   Infinitives are the root form of verbs and code general processes without actors or addressing anyone. They simply evoke a process. If someone asks what you like to do in holidays, you might answer '*take* a bath in the sea', '*go* to a nice restaurant', thus pointing to these general activities. In the case of the strategic diagram in Figure 4.6 we meet infinitives pointing to such general activities as the way to state the objectives of the university: '*grow* our academic reputation', '*internationalize* our work'. There are four such objectives coding what everyone at the university must strive for. These activities and objectives are enforced as a kind of law by the management, and here the list form enables them to come out as an exhaustive and allegedly objective inventory. Even if many employees would value other goals, these objectives will be connected to performance indicators and constitute the base for measuring outcomes and 'quality'. Once again we see the power inherent in controlling lists and their use.

People

When referring to people we can treat them as groups or as individuals. In lists common linguistic forms include collective nouns and proper names.

Collective nouns   Paradigms and lists can comprise different groups of people, and then collective nouns are a congruent linguistic form. The actual classification often relies on the comparison of groups established by given criteria, such as race and gender. In Figures 8.4 and 8.5 we see how 'blacks' and 'whites' are compared, and Figure 8.8 is based on 'men' and 'women', which are all collective nouns. Of course we must be critically aware that such classifications take for granted that these groups are separated and should be treated as such. What lies behind the gathering processes and any kind of classification, such as on an ethnic monitoring form for a job application, is deeply ideological. So, for example, a person born in Britain, whose father and mother were born in Britain, may nevertheless classify themselves as British Asian due to their skin colour. Such a classification is rooted in colonialism and nineteenth-century notions of the nation. In cases of collectivization we can ask what kinds of groupings are created and why. In Figure 8.4, for example, we see more clearly the intentions with a diagram that has only three classifications of persons: black, white and police. Such a system encourages one to simplify types of person and types of social relations and to ignore other types of social groupings, such as socio-economic ones, which in fact provide actual indicators of patterns of perpetrators and victims.

Proper names People can be coded as individuals. Here proper names are important. Institutional activities rely on some kind of participant list. A teacher would have such a list, as would the person responsible for a leisure activity, and of course the citizens of a nation are listed by name in different registers, enabling taxation, selling and purchasing of properties, and so on. The neutral form for doing this would be using both first and last name. This is the case in Figure 8.3 where the Premier League top three football players ranked as for 'touches' are identified as Paul Pogba, Jordan Henderson and James Milner. We could think of contexts where the first name would be enough. When arranging a birthday party for your child you might a list and make a record of the guests in this informal way in order not to forget who is coming. In the case of Pokémon in Figure 8.2 proper names are used to depict species, and the names encourage users to develop a personal relationship with the different species. Individualization can also be used to anchor sequences in a flow of stages represented in a table or a chart. In software for pre-school, a stage may be exemplified in a use guide by photos of a named child and named teacher. Such a strategy binds the process which is otherwise highly abstracted to what appears to be a real situation.

Things

As humans we have a drive to classify and make lists of all sorts of things, objects and entities. Here once again it is important to refer to nouns and proper names. Also language makes it possible to convert processes to things by using nominalizations, and to use acronyms to construe matters in technical language and as relying on expertise.

Nouns and proper names As people, things – which can be very different natural and cultural phenomena – are rendered in nouns, which is the simplest way to code them and make them countable. This is what we use if we make a shopping list for groceries or clothes. But classifications can also come out as elaborate taxonomies, as when Linnaeus in this *Systema Naturae* sorted flowers into different classes and stamen. There were 24 classes, all named in Latin, with different numbers of stamen which in turn were subdivided. Things are often given proper names by humans, which in itself points to them being important for us, as we all know from school subjects such as geography and biology. In the football statistics in Figure 8.3 both the names of clubs (Manchester United, Liverpool) and countries (France, England) are paradigms used for comparisons.

Nominalizations   As we have seen, data presentations are about abstracting actual processes and causalities and point to the core components of something. Linguistically this means that nominalizations, turning verbs into nouns and consequently processes into things are handy, since they omit actors and erase time and space (Ledin and Machin, 2016a). We might read 'achievements' as the label of a paradigm, which means that the verb and clause 'X achieved Y', in which actors and time must be made explicit, are abstracted. In our examples, Figure 4.6 stands out as relying on nominalizations, since it wants to abstract all work processes at a university in order to monitor them and assess outputs. So we get phrases such as '*research* and *innovation* in *teaching* and *learning*', containing four nominalizations. What is concealed is who is researching/innovating/teaching/learning what, but the layout of the diagram makes explicit that this is about reaching the objective 'grow our academic reputation'. Many people, including us, would say that research and teaching is more about education and fostering a critical citizenship, but these kinds of diagrams have branding and reputation as their rationale. Of note is that the nominalizations also are coordinated with 'and'. Research is treated as separated from innovation, and teaching from learning. This is certainly not how university work unfolds in practice, where such processes overlap and are intertwined.

Acronyms   Another major way of creating a specialized language is to use acronyms (cf. Ledin and Machin, 2016c), which is an abbreviation based on some letters (often the first) of an expression. A computer word like 'modem' is also an acronym, derived from '*mo*dulator/*dem*odulator'. And social scientists conceive of class in terms of SEI, or 'socio-economic index'. Acronyms can be used to construe technical and scientific-like paradigms. This is certainly the case in Figure 2.2 which, as we saw, lays out the teaching process 'constructive alignment' as being based on such a paradigm. This teaching model seems, due to the acronyms, to be based on scientific expertise. It includes 'CLOs', 'ILOs', 'ATs' and 'LAs'. If the transparent 'learning activities' and not the opaque 'LAs' had been used, the connotations of logic and science would partly have been lost.

Quantifications

Data presentation is very much about giving quantitative information. It is beyond the scope of this book to go into statistical details, but still important to be aware of the drive to assess and rank people and activities by using quantifications. Simple ways to quantify are to use absolute numbers or percentages. Figure 8.3, 8.5 and 8.6

all use absolute numbers for football touches, homicide victims and citations, respectively, whereas 8.4 with the tweet from President Trump shows percentages (of a strange kind, as we noted). Another common quantification using relative numbers is to combine variables following the principle 'how many Ys are there in average for an X'. For example: How many TVs are there in an average household? How many children does a woman give birth to on average? This is the principle followed in Figure 8.8, taken from a dating site, where the idea is 'how many men are chasing a woman'.

Important when reflecting on quantitative paradigms is to scrutinize how and why comparisons are made between certain paradigms. In Figure 8.8 the paradigms that get different scores are 'women', 'women who go out twice a week' and 'hot babe', where the score of the 'hot babe' is 4. Needless to say, both the classification and the scores are easy to criticize. What exactly are such numbers based on? Presumably here this is based on classifications set up in the digital system used to manage accounts and contacts between members of the site. So the behaviour pattern presented as 'data' are generated in part through the nature of the classifications in the software, much like the assessments of the development of pre-school children seen earlier. As with the cases of the pre-schoolers we can then consider other visual elements as regards how they are represented. Here from left to right competition among men gets tougher. 'Going out' here is represented by the glass of champagne. The 'hot' woman is blonde, wears a tight dress and heels. Finally we find this is presented with humour, choosing the term 'chasing' to account for the interest in meeting someone, and with the long tongues indicating something like 'desire', perhaps with a view to making use of the site seem less cold. But all of these choices of what kind of data is selected must be thought about ideologically.

Spatialization

In visual communication, paradigms are materialized as spatial forms with a certain layout. Importantly, several paradigms can co-exist as part of the same layout,

Figure 8.8 Number of men chasing a woman from the dating site Dating Metrics

which is crucial for data presentation since comparisons are then afforded. When this happens we get a syntagm, a combination of items from different paradigms. For example in Figure 8.6 we get to know the number of citations per year and can see that they are around 2000 in 2004 and around 8000, four times as many, in 2008 – an improbable rise that, as we said, is basically explained by more staff being hired, which is not made clear. As we have seen, very specific forms of data presentations have been developed to materialize paradigms and make comparisons. We point to the tools needed to draw out the exact meanings of the spatializations involved. These include spacing, vertical and horizontal orientation, and information value.

Spacing

In Chapter 4 we elaborated on the use of spacing in typography and between lines (p. 79). Levels of spacing can be smaller or larger, and meanings of 'integration' and 'openness', for example, can be communicated. In data presentations spacing tends to occur between spatial forms or 'gestalts'. Spacing is regularly used between the items in a paradigm and between connected paradigms. In both cases the point is to achieve separation, to isolate components. In Figure 8.1 the numbered points are spaced which makes each point independent of the other points. In this way a logical inventory of breastfeeding is suggested. If we look at the football table in Figure 8.2 there is space between the columns. In this way the vertical paradigms are closed-off from each other and form delimited visual groups. This makes the point of systematic comparisons clear, where the reader and user can make choices from the drop-down menus connected to each paradigm, and change, for example, clubs or nationalities to create new comparisons.

Vertical and horizontal orientation

A simple list of one paradigm usually has a vertical layout, with each item placed under the preceding one with proper spacing. This is the way we usually write a grocery list. We do not write it as a sentence, as 'now I must buy orange juice, coffee, also think about the pasta sauce, and toothpaste', even if this is what you might say to your husband. We do so as vertically separated items, preferably, if the list is to be an inventory, with the pasta sauce ingredients specified. This layout is fundamental for the separation and abstraction achieved in lists, and it is what Figure 8.1 uses.

But elements can also be separated horizontally, as Figure 8.8 shows. Here each quantified visual group of men and women unfold from left to right and due to the spacing each unit is separate. This is explained by the fact that the icons are part of a linguistic sentence. It starts 'on average there are' and on the line below the three icons with scores for different groups of women are displayed. This is a way of doing more 'fun' statistics, putting forward numbers that can catch the eye on a dating site and avoiding dense columns and rows.

In comparison the bar chart is a more systematic way of rendering quantitative information since it relies on numeric scales given by a combination of what in mathematics is called a vertical 'y-axis', here numbers for citations, and a horizontal 'x-axis', for years. In this case, and typical for many data presentations, the vertical and horizontal intersect and give rise to systematic spatial areas, here the bars. The shape of the bars depends on the spacing of these axes. For example, how wide the bars are is here based on the writing of the year – each bar fits onto the numbers rendered below it. And 'vertical' is also used metaphorically to suggest quantity. A bar-chart column may use narrower columns to help emphasize 'tallness' and achievement.

The intersection of the vertical and horizontal is also the base for tables. Here paradigms are rendered in vertical columns, and these are placed side by side horizontally. As a result a table consists of cells where the values given by the horizontal and vertical intersection result in an information unit. This makes tables a powerful semiotic tool for indicating that exact comparisons are taking place, for example the exact number of 'touches' for different players, teams and nationalities as in Figure 8.3. In the line graph in Figure 8.5 the flow from left to right suggests that plotting homicides over time is unproblematic. One feature of measuring crime is the way that classifications are often shifting depending upon things like political emphasis and news focus. New categories may emerge, where pressure is put on police to take a harder stance on particular issues (Hall et al., 2013).

Information value

Many layouts employ the horizontal orientation to give elements information value (Kress and van Leeuwen, 1996: Chapter 6). What is given, the point of the departure, is placed to the left whereas the new information, what is noteworthy, is placed to the right. The football table is an example. To the left we see the ranked football players as the given information. Details about them, such as club and nationality, are specified in the following columns, and to the right we get the point of the comparison, the new information that changes after every game, the number of touches. This is both exact and easy to assess, due to the information structure. In language it would equal a syntagm of the type: 'Nr 1 Paul Pogba, playing for Manchester United and from France, has 3,460 touches.'

Even if the dating representation in Figure 8.8 is not a table it is based on the same information structure. It is the quantitative icon to the right that carries the noteworthy information, where 'hot babe' scores the top result of having four men chasing her, also indicated by the star light behind her. To the left we have the category 'woman' with the score of 1.4 functioning as the point of departure of the comparison, where we obviously could ponder the classification principle for distinguishing 'woman' from 'hot babe'. Also the bar chart in Figure 8.6 has a composition where information value is important. Here it comes from the time-line moving towards the present and consequently with increasing news value, where the present, 'latest news', is the last bar to the right.

Graphic shapes and icons

Graphics are crucial for data presentations and carry out many tasks. They are important for classification, where categories with the same graphic shape come out as part of a paradigm, for example everything in rectangles or circles. They can also represent levels and amounts, as well as different processes. Also icons are often used to make information accessible.

Shapes

This can related to simple forms where things like angularity can be used to suggest something more technical or where something circular appears more organic and movable. Although, as in Figure 8.7, these may be simply arbitrary choices programmed into the software options. We can ask whether a huge range of different shapes are used to suggest that the parts are different, that there is variation, or whether there is sameness and conformity. In Figure 1.3 in Chapter 1, we see that the diagram that represents things like 'role clarification' and 'better working environment' uses one same-sized shape. Here the suggestion is that the stages are simply points in the same process. Representing them as different shapes might suggest difference and complexity. In such cases we can also look at size of shapes, which can be used to create levels of importance. And we can look at rhyming of shapes where different things are classified as being of the same order across a design.

Icons

We have dealt with iconography in Chapter 5 on packaging which provides a set of observations that can be usefully drawn upon here (p. 106). Iconography simply means where forms are used such as those which resemble a house or a human. As an example, in the present chapter we find the case in Figure 8.1 where the drawings of small children are used to represent the way that the parts fit together to form a whole in the form of building blocks. The style, used typically to communicate about things like children's health and learning, places it within this safe family-oriented domain. We can imagine the difference were we to see a photograph of a lone parent managing in a room with actual small children. In Figure 4.6 showing the strategic diagram from Edinburgh Napier University we see that the different lists each appear under a different icon (a world map, a tree, a brick, a person), which helps to indicate that they are of the same order, which a closer look indicates that they clearly are not.

Temporality

This is where semiotic materials communicate how time is used. Graphic representation is often about development of some kind. A typical expression form is the timeline, and we see timelines in Figure 8.5 and 8.6 to pin down the development of homicides and citations (cf. Kress and van Leeuwen, 1996: Chapter 3). In data presentations, time is not, as in the case of the film clips in Chapter 7, narrative or agentative, dependent on an actor, where different characters make different actions. It is abstracted and non-agentative, rendered as a fixed unit with stable characteristics (Ledin and Machin, 2016b). The timelines in Figures 8.5 and 8.6 are divided into years as stable units and each year is given a score. In actual life a homicide or a citation would happen in actual time and space with actual people involved. In other words these fixed time units are a classification imposed, necessarily concealing how events unfold in real life. The same abstracted time can of course be used in tables. A table to assess the progress of a student in a school as regards attitudinal development may give scores for each semester. These may have been gathered in different ways and at very different times of the day, as for example when the child was tired. And the categories used may be slightly changing as policy introduced new categories and concepts.

Another expression form is arrows between elements, where these elements can be boxes with verbs coding time, as in Figure 8.7. Once again this abstracts time as each box will contain an activity with allegedly stable characteristics separated from the other activities. Time can also be merely sketched or symbolized, and here the message can be that time simply exists and that this involves progress. In Figure 8.1 we find temporality implied in the drawing of the children building. There is a sense of the kind of progress that the steps offer. In Figure 1.3 we see an example of how temporality can be included in a diagram through the use of icons, in this case wavy lines that symbolize 'flow', 'the dynamic' and 'progress'.

Causality

This is where semiotic materials are used to capture causal relations. Graphic representation often includes elements having effects on each other, and, as with temporality, such relations are abstracted. Typically causality is expressed in the form of arrows between elements as we saw in Figure 1.3. Here we can look at the kind of arrow, whether it is narrow, as in the lines in Figure 8.7 which appear to plot simple routes of connectivity, or as in Figure 1.3 where it grows in thickness to suggest the increase in quality of the working environment. Heavier arrows can suggest greater force, whereas dotted line arrows can suggest possibilities or alternatives. Causality may also be indicated by a vertical arrangement of elements in the side of a pyramid, for example, to indicate that those lower down provide the basis and conditions for those higher up (see Ledin and Machin, 2016a for examples).

The condensed and abstracted nature of causality comes from the affordance of data presentations to represent the multidirectional. It is not just about cause and effect. But an entity, such as a box containing an infinite verb, will perform the dual function of being both the effect of one activity and the cause of another activity (Ledin and Machin, 2016b: 331). This is clear in the flow chart in Figure 8.7 where the box 'Define and write up job description' precedes 'Send personnel request form to HR' which is followed by 'Determine classification'. So the activity of 'sending' is an effect of the 'defining' process, and it also causes the 'determination'. This seems like a perfect logic, but, as we said, there is no mentioning of who is to carry out the real world action. The arrows between the boxes also intertwine causality with temporality, making it impossible to figure out where and when actions take place. Another example of time and cause being fused is Figure 8.6. Here it is implied that citations and productivity have increased as part of implementing clear targets through a performance management system. As we noted, the growth was basically explained by hiring more staff.

SUGGESTIONS FOR RESEARCH QUESTIONS

Throughout this chapter we have been using these observations and tools to carry out analysis of concrete examples of data and information presentation. All the kinds of examples we have looked at give indications of the kinds of areas of research for which they can be used. In fact, these tools can be used wherever data and information are presented to us: in shopping, work, schools, sports, medicine. Here we look at how this might take the form of concrete research questions. Here are two simple examples:

(Continued)

- In what ways does the presentation of data shape how crime is represented in the news?

The literature on how the news media represent crime shows that it is generally pretty much stripped of any social context (Mayr and Machin, 2012). So issues like poverty and social deprivation which are linked to many kinds of crime are never mentioned. Other crimes that are statistically small, such as child abuse by strangers, is greatly over-reported. In contrast the statistically greater form of crime that is corporate crime gains very little coverage.

In this case such a project would find and analyse how crime figures were presented in newspapers. A sample would be collected, perhaps about a specific kind of crime, or comparing different news outlets. We may find graphics like in Figure 8.4 against a ranked list. This may use a number of icons to communicate danger and 'detective work'. There may be some kind of graphic symbolization of causality, to suggest something like 'where there are less police there is more crime', which of course misses the point. We then find the Chief of Police plan of action presented as a set of bullet points, again with another icon. Here, we just make general points, but a close analysis would be able to show exactly what gets emphasized through such data and information. What gets omitted? And therefore what kinds of understandings about society, social problems and danger to the public are being promoted? Such a project would need to be highly engaged with the literature on media and crime and sociology of crime in order to point to the ways that actual social patterns are being shaped for us.

Another simple research question could be:

- How do data and information shape understanding in a specific health campaign?

Of course, as with the previous example, this is rather broad for an actual research question. But this could be made more specific, for example by focusing on the case of breastfeeding as we saw in Figure 8.1. Here we could collect leaflets from clinics and material from websites. As Brookes et al. (2016) explain, such campaigns can carry very much class-based ideas about what is natural and good for children and families. On the other hand, some commercial baby milk powder companies take a different angle. A research project here could carry out a comparison of the two kinds of campaign. Again such a project would need to base itself in the literature on the specific area chosen and on health communication relating to such campaigns.

9

CONCLUSION

We hope that the analytical tool kits in this book can inspire you to go out and explore this fascinating visual world that we have made and that we inhabit, and to take a critical perspective on it. The book was organized into chapters that looked at specific domains. But together they provide huge possibilities to be combined in different ways. In fact many research areas will simply require this. Much of what we encounter as data for an analysis, such as an online sports equipment store, a new teaching and learning programme or a recruitment drive for a large social media corporation, will use semiotic materials that cut across chapters. The teaching programme may have forms of performance assessment using classifications. It may involve using space for forms of activities, such as instructional films or courses for teachers when implementing the programme.

In other words, we must take care to identify what it is that we need to know. What is the specific research question? The process of analysis should never simply be a thorough application of a set of tools to carry out a description. If we want to carry out research on online sports stores, we may want to know what meanings are attached to sport, for the purposes of marketing. This question may be narrowed down to how women are presented. We would have to ask where and how will we find the answer to this question. In one sense this question, like many in social semiotic research, means finding out what kinds of identities, ideas, actions and settings relate to this social practice. Simply what do the women look like, for example, when they are doing fitness? Are they giggling and sharing time with family and friends or showing concentration and stamina? The answer may also be revealed by the design features on the website, the kinds of classifications that are created. If there are short promotional clips, what takes place in these?

At the time of writing, scholars had observed that there had been a shift in how women were represented in sport and more widely in advertising, TV and movies. Scholars began to talk about the rise of the designed body which was discussed in relation to consumer society, where particularly for women there has been a trend in media images of muscular, yet also slim, women (Cohen and Colino, 2014). It was suggested that this intensified attention to body form is part of the 'body work' (Coffey, 2013) we are encouraged to do in Western consumer culture, include dieting, forms of body modification, as well as fashion and cosmetics, which all link into the purchasing of products and services (Klos et al., 2012: 257). The new rise in and naturalization of fitness regimes over the past 30 years could be explained not so much by a growth in interest in health per se but as part of the way that consumerism always requires the 'new', 'the latest thing', and creating a culture of reinvention (Elliot, 2013). The body here is one site for such reinvention. As Elliot argues: 'ours is the age of body reshaping, recontouring, upgrading and updating' (p. 12).

And such a body and the act of engaging in fitness regimes can be placed within a broader culture of 'self-improvement' (Scott, 2011: 242). It becomes part of the kinds of self-management programmes that we have seen throughout this book as regards the representation of domestic and work space, as regards food and health and management documents. Here we would want to know much more about the way that sports products and activities become loaded with meanings. As we have shown through the chapters a more systematic analysis can throw up insights providing we are asking clear questions and choosing the right tools for analysis. For example, do the textures of the sports equipment tell us anything about the associated meanings or how it is placed in space? Anyone who has used both a city centre commercial gym and a CrossFit 'Box' will know that these are very different (Ledin and Machin, 2017b). Clothing is different. In one we find moulded plastics and rows of machines. In the other we find worn metal, bare concrete walls. But what does this mean? Perhaps the notion of 'masculinity' can somehow be linked to such observations of texture (cf. Kerry, 2017)? Doing visual analysis means finding out.

What this example shows us as regards carrying out research using the tools across the chapters is that we experience the world and carry out social practices through semiotic materials. Its materiality and its look, how we look, is a part of the fabric of how we live. Hjelmslev's (1961) model of communication encourages us to see instances of visual communication, not as things that are separate from us in the world, but as based on a materiality that is interrelated with our consciousness. It is simply part of how the world is perceived and lived at any point in time. This makes the materials found on the online sports store that we encounter in the Crossfit Box, or that are used to represent women more widely in advertisements, are not simply representations. We engage with them in committed ways since they are the world as it is meaningful to us.

At any time this materiality will tend to reflect the dominant socio-political ideas and values of the time. This may not be entirely clear in every instance of communication (Foucault, 1978), but nevertheless they are infused within. This can be women and fitness, our office spaces or our organic food café. They become part of how marketing tells us that their food is healthy, that a data presentation on a PowerPoint slide is true, that a model of teaching can allow everyone to achieve better grades. And such choices in materiality and semiotic resources become interlocked with social practices at particular times. This reflects the socio-political priorities and world view that dominated in those times.

Since we experience the world through materiality this must be our entry point. The woman in the gym, developing her abdominal muscles, experiences not semiotic choices but a material world of objects and forms. And as instances of visual communication these form canons of use that themselves evolved to do specific things and are aligned with particular discourses, institutional practices and socio-political interests. And studying these canons requires an affordance lead approach. This means a form of analysis that emphasizes the idea of choices that come with associations that have been built up over time. It sees these as functional in that they have evolved due to the needs of humans to communicate specific things in specific settings using certain materials and technologies.

In each chapter of this book we have emphasized that the meaning of images, flow charts, food packaging, web page design, and so on, lies not only in the thing itself as regards what it depicts. The meaning also lies in the way that these reference other well-trodden themes and established institutionalized uses. If we want to understand the meaning carried by a photograph on a news website we must also understand something of what images are used for and by whom. We need to know something about the social practices they are a part of. We cannot in a social sense approach a news photograph and a photograph found on a food package in the same way. Whether we are dealing with photographs, the design of a café or a promotional film, we must approach them as regards the way that the choices of materials are made to accomplish specific communicative tasks. And be aware that these are communicative tasks and processes which have been established over time as canons of use which we easily recognize. In each case they are characterized by fairly typical patterns of semiotic features. And in each case these represent a particular way we have come to look at the world driven by ideology and power.

In the case of the sports website we must be aware of the clothing, the sports equipment and nutrition. The website would be much more carefully coded for meaning than we would find in an equipment catalogue of 25 years ago. Across domains of visual communication it remains to be researched exactly where this coding has most taken place. In the chapters of this book we showed that in the design of documents, space, data, promotional films, and so on, there had been increased codification of semiotic resources, what Fairclough (1992) described as technologization. This is part of a drive to take greater control over communication to fulfil political, economic and institutional aims. We saw this in Chapter 8 where we pointed to diverse processes in sport, work, crime and baby weaning being presented in abstracted categories and symbols. In other chapters we find this in less obvious places such as food packaging, space and film clips. Here we found the same kinds of control and codification. A café uses coordinated materials to communicate provenance and flexibility. Food packaging carefully uses colours, fonts, shapes, materials and textures to embed products in a range of discourses about health, gender, energy and so on. In a research project about women and fitness, what kinds of coding would we find, and what purposes would this serve? What kinds of behaviours, attitudes and social practices would this favour?

Fairclough (1992) saw these processes of codification as being closely related to other process of 'commodification' or 'marketization' which he saw as increasing in society at the time. So all things and processes become more oriented to, or aligned with, selling goods and services. This has taken the form of increased functionality. Processes and things are presented as doing a job, in an effective way, such as a bulleted list of steps to successfully wean a baby, a flow chart that explains learning processes in young children, a kitchen that is flexible for needs, an office space that fosters 'communication'. But it has also meant that semiotic materials have been increasingly coded for 'affect'. The selling of fitness equipment, clothing and nutrition becomes not only about what it can do for you, but each must engage us. Each must be loaded with semiotic resources coded to align them with specific ideas, values and identities suitable for a target market group. A bulleted list for feeding a baby uses space, colour, typeface and iconography to communicate meanings about 'building', 'working together as a family' and 'taking care of everyone'. PowerPoint presentations include templates for adding texture to the slides to engage viewers (Djonov and van Leeuwen, 2011).

What was also clear across the chapters in this book is that what is ultimately at stake is not only communication but social practices. The look of the sports equipment and nutritional products, the form of our work places, the design of our washing product packages are part of how we act and the kinds of priorities that we share each day, the kinds of social relations through which society is organized.

The tool kits in this book are not only presented to simply look at visual communication. They are designed to help facilitate research that allows students and other investigators to explore and take a stance on the use of all kinds of semiotic materials and how they shape what we do and think – how they are part of our experience of this world. The questions we ask here are only a beginning. And they are from one very narrow perspective. We have looked at visual communication from a kind of 'Western' or 'Christian' perspective, so to speak, where our examples mostly come from the UK, US and Sweden. In a sense it is driven by a social semiotic and critical analysis of globalized capitalism (cf. Fairclough, 2006). If we go to South America, Asia and Africa, to Russia, China and Egypt, and so on, other kinds of question and analysis would need to be developed to complement what we have suggested. Still, we believe that our affordance-driven and critical approach to visual communication generally holds. What is certain is that across these places visual communication is part of the shaping of how we think and what we do. It is not least a site where we can understand power relations in society.

REFERENCES

Abousnnouga, G. and Machin, D. (2013) *The Language of War Monuments*. London: Bloomsbury.

Aiello, G. and Dickinson, G. (2014) 'Beyond authenticity: A visual-material analysis of locality in the global redesign of Starbucks stores'. *Visual Communication* 13(3), 303–321.

Antaki C., Billig, M. and Edwards, D. (2003) 'Discourse analysis means doing analysis: A critique of six analytic shortcomings'. *Discourse Analysis Online*, 1, 1–22.

Barthes, R. (1964) *Elements of Semiology*. New York: Hill & Wang.

Barthes, R. (1977) *Image, Music, Text*. London: Fontana.

Barthes, R. and Duisit, L. (1975) 'An introduction to the structural analysis of narrative'. *New Literary History*, 6, 237–272.

Bateman, J. (2011) 'The decomposability of semiotic modes'. In K. O'Halloran and B. Smith (eds), *Multimodal Studies: Exploring issues and domains*, pp. 17–38. London: Routledge.

Bateman, J. (2013) 'Review of T. van Leeuwen (2009) *The Language of Colour: An Introduction*. London: Routledge'. *Linguistics and the Human Sciences* 9(1). Available at: www. equinoxpub.com/journals/index.php/LHS/article/view/20898.

Bauldry, A. and Thibault, P.J. (2006) *Multimodal Transcription and Text Analysis: A multimedia toolkit and coursebook*. London: Equinox.

Berge, K.L. (2012) 'Om forsjellene mellom systemisk-funksjonell lingvistikk og tekstvitenksap' [On the differences between systemic-functional linguistics and text research]. In S. Matre, R. Solheim and D. K. Sjøhelle (eds), *Teorier om tekst i møte med skolens lese- og skrivepraksiser* [Text theories meet reading and writing practices of schools], pp. 72–90. Oslo: Universitetsforlaget.

Berge, K.L. and Ledin, P. (2001) 'Perspektiv på genre' [Perspectives on genre]. *Rhetorica Scandinavica*, 18, 4–16.

Berger J. (1972) *Ways of Seeing*. London: Penguin Books.

Bezemer, J. and Kress, G. (2016) *Multimodality, Learning and Communication: A social semiotic framework*. London: Routledge.

Billig, M. (1995) *Banal Nationalism*. London: Sage.

Björkvall, A. and Archer, A. (2017) 'The "semiotics of value" in upcycling'. In S. Zhao, A. Björkvall, M. Boeriis and E. Djonov (eds), *Advancing Multimodal and Critical Discourse Studies: Interdisciplinary research inspired by Theo van Leeuwen's social semiotics*. London: Routledge.

Bouvier, G. (2014) 'British press photographs and the misrepresentation of the 2011 "uprising" in Libya: A content analysis'. In D. Machin (ed.), *Visual Communication*, pp. 281–299. Berlin: De Gruyter.

Bowker, G.C. and Star, S.L. (1999) *Sorting Things Out: Classification and its consequences*. Cambridge, MA: The MIT Press.

Brookes, G, Harvey, K. and Mullany, L. (2016) '"Off to the best start?" A multimodal critique of breast and formula feeding health promotional discourse'. *Gender and Language*, 10(3), 340–363.

Burgin, V. (1982) 'Looking at photographs'. In V. Burgin (ed.), *Thinking Photography*, pp. 142–153. London: Palgrave Macmillan.

Burrows, J. (2013) *Visually Communicating 'Honesty': A semiotic analysis of Dorset Cereals' packaging*. University of Leeds. Available at: http://media.leeds.ac.uk/files/2013/07/Jessica-Burrows-BACS-2013.pdf.

Caple, H. and Knox, J.S. (2015) 'A framework for the multimodal analysis of online news galleries: What makes a "good" picture gallery?', *Social Semiotics*, 25/3, 292–321.

Caple, H. and Knox, J.S. (2017) 'Genre(less) and purpose(less): Online news galleries', *Discourse, Context and Media* (available online at this time).

Coffey, J. (2013) 'Bodies, body work and gender: Exploring a Deleuzian approach'. *Journal of Gender Studies*, 22(1), 3–16.

Cohen, J. and Colino, S. (2014) *Strong is the New Skinny: How to eat, live and move to maximize your power*. New York: Harmony.

Cook, G. (1994) *The Discourse of Advertising*. London: Routledge.

Cooke, D. (1959) *The Language of Music*. Oxford: Clarendon.

Darwin, C. (1872) *The Expression of the Emotions in Man and Animals*. London: John Murray.

Depaepe, M. (2000) *Order in Progress: Everyday educational practice in primary schools, Belgium, 1880–1970*. Leuven: Leuven University Press.

Djonov, E. and van Leeuwen, T. (2011) 'The semiotics of texture: From haptic to visual'. *Visual Communication*, 10(4), 541–564.

Djonov, E. and van Leeuwen, T. (2014) 'Bullet points, new writing, and the marketization of public discourse: A critical multimodal perspective'. In E. Djonov and S. Zhao (eds), *Critical Multimodal Studies of Popular Discourse*, pp. 232–250. London: Routledge.

Eco, U. (1979) *A Theory of Semiotics*. Bloomington, IN: Indiana University Press.

Eco, U. (2009) *The Infinity of Lists*. New York: Rizzoli.

Elliot, A. (2013) *Reinvention*. Oxford: Routledge.

Fairclough, N. (1989) *Language and Power*. London: Longman.

Fairclough, N. (1992) *Discourse and Social Change*. London: Polity Press.

Fairclough, N. (1993) 'Critical discourse analysis and the marketization of public discourse: The universities'. *Discourse & Society* 4(2), 133–168.

Fairclough, N. (1995) *Media Discourse*. London: Edward Arnold.

Fairclough, N. (2006) *Language and Globalization*. Abingdon: Routledge.

Fairclough, N. and Wodak, R. (1997) 'Critical discourse analysis'. In T.A. Van Dijk (ed.), *Discourse Studies: A multidisciplinary introduction. Vol. 2: Discourse as social interaction*, pp. 258–284. London: Sage.

Fishman, M. (1980) *Manufacturing the News*. Austin, TX: University of Texas Press.

Forceville, C. (2007) 'Review of Anthony Baldry & Paul J. Thibault, *Multimodal Transcription and Text Analysis: A Multimedia Toolkit and Coursebook* (Equinox 2006)'. *Journal of Pragmatics*, 39(6), 1235–1238.

Forceville, C. (2010) 'Review of *The Routledge Handbook of Multimodal Analysis*, Carey Jewitt (ed.) London, Routledge, 2009'. *Journal of Pragmatics*, 39, 1235–1238.

Foucault, M. (1977) *Discipline and Punish: The birth of the prison.* New York: Pantheon Books.

Foucault, M. (1978) *The History of Sexuality: An introduction.* Hammonsworth: Penguin.

Fowler, R. (1990) *Language in the News: Discourse and Ideology in the Press.* London: Routledge.

Fowler, R. (1996) 'On critical linguistics'. In C.R. Caldas-Coulthard and M. Coulthard (eds), *Texts and Practices: Readings in Critical Discourse Analysis*, pp. 3–14. London: Routledge.

Fowler, R., Hodge, R., Kress, G. and Trew, T (eds) (1979) *Language and Control.* London: Routledge & Kegan Paul.

Gage, J. (1994) *Colour and Culture.* London: Wiley.

Gage, J. (1999) *Color and Meaning: Art, Science, and Symbolism.* Berkeley, CA: University of California Press.

Geertz, C. (1973) *The Interpretation of Cultures.* London: Basic Books.

Gibson, J.J. (1979) *The Ecological Approach to Visual Perception.* Boston: Houghton Mifflin.

Goffman, E. (1993) 'The Interaction Order, American Sociological Association 1982, Presidential Address'. *American Sociological Review*, 48(1), 1–17.

Goldman, R. and Beeker, G.L. (1985) 'Decoding newsphotos: An analysis of embedded ideological values'. *Humanity and Society*, 9, 351–363.

Goody, J. (1977) *The Domestication of the Savage Mind.* Cambridge: Cambridge University Press.

Graham, P.W., Keenan, T. and Dowd, A.-M. (2004) 'A call to arms at the end of history: A discourse-historical analysis of George W. Bush's declaration of war on terror'. *Discourse & Society*, 15(2–3), 199–221.

Gramsci, A. (1971) *Selections from the Prison Notebooks.* Edited by Q. Hoare and G.N. Smith. New York: International Publishers.

Grant, K.B. (2007) *Film Genre: From iconography to ideology.* New York: Wallflower.

Hall, S., Critcher, C., Jefferson, T., Clarke, J. and Roberts, B. (2013) *Policing the Crisis: Mugging, the state, and law and order.* Basingstoke: Palgrave Macmillan.

Halliday, M.A.K. (1975) *Learning How to Mean: Explorations in the development of language.* London: Edward Arnold.

Halliday, M.A.K. (1978) *Language as Social Semiotic: The social interpretation of language and meaning.* London: Edward Arnold.

Halliday, M.A.K. (2004) *An Introduction to Functional Grammar.* London: Edward Arnold.

Halliday, M.A.K. and Hasan, R. (1989) *Language, Context, and Text: Aspects of language in a social-semiotic perspective.* Oxford: Oxford University Press.

Hansen, A. (2002) 'Discourses of nature in advertising'. *Communications*, 27, 499–511.

Harvey, D. (1990) *The Condition of Postmodernity*. Oxford: Blackwell.

Hjelmslev, L. (1961) *Prolegomena to a Theory of Language*. Madison, WI: University of Wisconsin Press.

Hodge, B. and Kress, G. (1979) *Language as Ideology*. Cambridge: Polity Press.

Hodge, B. and Kress, G. (1988) *Social Semiotics*. Cambridge: Polity Press.

Hogan, P.C. (2016) 'Jesus's parables: Simulation, stories, and narrative idiolect'. *Narrative*, 24(2), 113–133.

Hopmann, S.T. (2008) 'No child, no school, no state left behind: Schooling in the age of accountability'. *Journal of Curriculum Studies*, 40(4), 417–445.

Huxford, J. (2004) 'Surveillance, witnessing and spectatorship: The news and the "war of images"'. *Proceedings of the Media Ecology Association*, 5, 1–21.

Iedema, R. (2001) 'Analysing film and television: A social semiotic account of Hospital: An unhealthy account'. In T. van Leeuwen and C. Jewitt (eds), *Handbook of Visual Analysis*, pp. 183–204. London: Sage.

Jakobson, R. (1960) 'Closing statement: Linguistics and poetics'. In T.A. Sebeok (ed.), *Style in Language*, pp. 350–377. New York: Wiley.

Jaworski, A. and Thurlow, C. (2010) 'Introducing semiotic landscapes'. In A. Jaworski and C. Thurlow, *Semiotic Landscapes: Language, Image, Space*, pp. 1–40. London & New York: Continuum.

Jewitt, C. (2013) *Multimodality and Digital Technologies in the Classroom: Multilingualism and Multimodality*, The Future of Education Research book series, pp. 141–152. Berlin: Springer.

Jewitt, C. and Jones, K. (2005) Managing time and space in the new English classroom. In M. Lawn and I. Grosvenor (eds), *Material Cultures of Schooling*, pp. 201–214. Oxford: Symposium Books.

Jewitt, C., Bezemer, J. and O'Halloran, K. (2016) *Introducing Multimodality*. London and New York: Routledge.

Karlsson, A.-M. and Ledin, P. (2000) 'Cyber, hyper och multi: några reflektioner kring IT-ålderns textbegrepp' [Cyber, hyper and multi: Reflections on the notion of text in the era of information technology]. *Human IT*, 4(2–3), 15–59.

Kerry, V.J. (2017) 'The construction of hegemonic masculinity in the Semiotic Landscape of a CrossFit "Cave"'. *Visual Communication*, 16(2), 209–238.

Klimchuk, M.R. and Krasovec, S. (2006) *Packaging Design*. Hoboken: Wiley.

Klos, L., Esser, V. and Kessler, M. (2012) 'To weigh or not to weigh: The relationship between self-weighing behavior and body image among adults'. *Body Image*, 9(4), 551–554.

Kress, G. (2005) 'Gains and losses: New forms of texts, knowledge, and learning'. *Computers and Composition*, 22(1), 5–22.

Kress, G. (2010) *Multimodality: A social semiotic approach to contemporary communication*. London: Routledge.

Kress, G. and van Leeuwen, T. (1996) *Reading Images: The grammar of visual design*. London: Routledge.

Kress, G. and van Leeuwen, T. (2001) *Multimodal Discourse: The modes and media of contemporary communication*. London: Arnold.

Kress, G. and van Leeuwen, T. (2002) 'Colour as a semiotic mode: Notes for a grammar of colour', *Visual Communication*, 1(3), 343–368.

Kress, G. and van Leeuwen, T. (2006) *Reading Images: The grammar visual design*. London: Routledge.

Krzyżanowski, M. and Wodak, R. (2008) *The Politics of Exclusion: Debating migration in Austria*. New Brunswick, NJ: Transaction.

Labov, W. (1997) 'Some further steps in narrative analysis'. *The Journal of Narrative and Life History*, 7, 395–415.

Labov, W. and Waletzky, J. (1967) 'Narrative analysis: Oral versions of personal experience'. In J. Helm (ed.), *Essays on the Verbal and Visual Arts*, pp. 12–44. Seattle, WA: University of Washington Press. Reprinted in *Journal of Narrative and Life History*, 1997, 7, 3–38.

Ledin, P. (2015) 'Listans och tabellens semiotik' [The semiotics of lists and tables]. *Sakprosa*, 7(1), 1–25.

Ledin, P. and Machin, D. (2015a) 'How lists, bullet points and tables re-contextualize social practice'. *Critical Discourse Studies*, 12(4), 463–481.

Ledin, P. and Machin, D. (2015b) 'The semiotics of modernist space in the branding of organizations'. *International Journal of Marketing Semiotics*, 3, 19–38.

Ledin, P. and Machin, D. (2016a) 'The evolution of performance management discourse in corporate strategy diagrams for public institutions'. *Discourse, Context & Media*, 13(B), 122–131.

Ledin, P. and Machin, D. (2016b) 'Strategic diagrams and the technologization of culture'. *Journal of Language and Politics*, 15(3), 321–335.

Ledin, P. and Machin, D. (2016c) 'Performance management discourse and the shift to an administrative logic of operation: A multimodal critical discourse analytical approach'. *Text & Talk*, 36(4), 445–467.

Ledin, P. and Machin, D. (2017a) 'The neoliberal definition of "elite space" in IKEA kitchens'. *Social Semiotics*, special issue on 'elite space', ed. by C. Thurlow and A. Jaworski, 27(3), 323–334.

Ledin, P. and Machin, D. (2017b) 'New codifications, new practices: The multimodal communication of CrossFit'. In S. Zhao, A. Björkvall, M. Boeriis and E. Djonov (eds), *Advancing Multimodal and Critical Discourse Studies: Interdisciplinary research inspired by Theo van Leeuwen's social semiotics*. London: Routledge.

Ledin, P. and Machin, D. (2017c) 'IKEA kitchens and the rise of a neoliberal control of domestic space'. *Visual Communication*. Forthcoming.

Ledin, P. and Machin, D. (2017d) 'Multimodal critical discourse analysis'. In J. Flowerdew and J.E. Richardson (eds), *Routledge Handbook of Critical Discourse Studies*. Abingdon: Routledge.

Lupton, D. (2010) *Thinking with Type*. New York: Princeton Architectural Press.

Lutz, A. and Collins, J.L. (1993) *Reading National Geographic*. Chicago: University of Chicago Press.

Machin, D. (2004) 'Building the world's visual language: The increasing global importance of image banks in corporate media'. *Visual Communication*, 3(3), 316–336.

Machin, D. (2007) *Introduction to Multimodal Analysis*. London: Bloomsbury.

Machin, D. (2010) *Analysing Popular Music*. London: Sage.

Machin, D. (2013) 'What is multimodal critical discourse studies?' *Critical Discourse Studies*, 10(4), 347–355.

Machin, D. (ed.) (2015) *Visual Communication*. Berlin: De Gruyter.

Machin, D. and Mayr, A. (2012) *How to Do Critical Discourse Analysis*. London: Sage.

Machin, D. and Polzer, L. (2015) *Visual Journalism*. London: Palgrave.

Margolis, E. and Pauwels, L. (eds) (2011) *The SAGE Handbook of Visual Research Methods*. Los Angeles: Sage.

Martin, J.R. and Rose, D. (2008) *Genre Relations: Mapping culture*. London: Equinox.

Mayr, A. and Machin, D. (2013) *The Language of Crime*. London: Bloomsbury.

McMurtrie, R.J. (2016) *The Semiotics of Movement and Space*. London: Routledge.

Miller, C.R. (1984) 'Genre as social action'. *Quarterly Journal of Speech*, 70, 151–167.

Miller, C.R. and Shepherd, D. (2004) 'Blogging as a social action: A genre analysis of the weblog'. *Into the Blogsphere*, 22. Available at: http://conservancy.umn.edu/bitstream/handle/11299/172818/Miller_Blogging%20as%20Social%20Action.pdf.

Newton, J.H. (2000) *The Burden of Truth: The Role of Photojournalism in Mediating Reality*. London: Routledge.

Panofsky, E. (1970) *Meaning in the Visual Arts*. Harmondsworth: Penguin.

Pauwels, L. (2012) 'An integrated conceptual framework for visual social research'. In E. Margolis and L. Pauwels (eds), *SAGE Handbook of Visual Research Methods*, pp. 3–23. London: Sage.

Peirce, C.S. (1984) *Writings of Charles S. Peirce: A chronological edition. Vol. 2, 1867–1871*. Bloomington, IN: Indiana University Press.

Piro, F.N., Aksnes, D.W. and Rørstad, K. (2013) 'A macro analysis of productivity differences across fields: Challenges in the measurement of scientific publishing'. *Journal of the American Society for Information Science and Technology*, 64(2), 307–320.

Power, M. (1999) *The Audit Society: Rituals of verification*. Milton Keynes: Open University Press.

Reavey, P. (2011) *Visual Methods in Psychology: Using and interpreting images in qualitative research*. London: Routledge.

Reynolds, E. (2012) 'Review of Sigrid Norris, *Identity in (inter)action: Introducing multimodal (inter)action analysis*. De Gruyter'. *Discourse Studies*, 14(6), 805–817.

Richardson, J. (2006) *Analysing Newspapers*. London: Palgrave.

Roderick, I. (2016) 'The politics of office design: Translating neoliberalism into furnishing'. *Journal of Language and Politics*, 15(3), 274–287.

Rose, G. (2012) *Visual Methodologies*. London: Sage.

Saussure, F. (1974) *Course in General Linguistics*. Edited by Charles Bally and Albert Sechehaye. La Salle, IL: Open Court.

Scollon, R. and Wong Scollon, S. (2003) *Discourses in Place: Language in the material world*. London: Routledge.

Scott, S. (2011) *Total Institutions and Reinvented Identities*. Basingstoke: Palgrave Macmillan.

Shugart, H. (2014) 'Food fixations: Reconfiguring class in contemporary US food discourse'. *Food, Culture and Society*, 17(2), 261–281.

Smith, M. (2008) 'Introduction, visual culture studies: History theory practice'. In M. Smith (ed.), *Visual Culture Studies*, pp. 1–6. London: Sage.

Sontag, S. (1973) *On Photography*. London: Penguin.

Sontag, S. (2004) *Regarding the Pain of Others*. London: Penguin.

Spencer, S. (2010) *Visual Research Methods in the Social Sciences: Awakening Visions*. New York: Routledge.

Szasz, T.S. (2010) *The Myth of Mental Illness: Foundations of a theory of personal conduct*. London: HarperPerennial.

Tagg, P. (1984) 'Understanding time sense: Concepts, sketches, consequences'. In *Tvärspel – 31 artiklar om musik. Festskrift till Jan Ling*. Göteborg: Skrifter från Musikvetenskapliga Institutionen. 9, 21–43.

Tagg, J. (1988) *The Burden of Representation: Essays on photographies and histories*. Basingstoke: Macmillan.

Taverniers, M. (2011) 'The syntax-semantics interface in Systemic Functional Grammar: Halliday's interpretation of the Hjelmslevian model of stratification'. *Journal of Pragmatics*, 43(4), 1100–1126.

Thurlow, C. (2013) 'Fakebook: Synthetic media, pseudo-sociality and the rhetorics of Web 2.0'. In D. Tannen and A. Trester (eds), *Discourse 2.0: Language and New Media*, pp. 225–248. Washington, DC: Georgetown University Press.

Thurlow, C. and Jaworski, A. (2012) 'Elite mobilities: The semiotic landscapes of luxury and privilege'. *Social Semiotics*, 22(5), 487–516.

Toolan, M. (1988) *Narrative: A Critical Linguistic Introduction*. London: Routledge

Triandafyllidou, A., Wodak, R. and Krzyżanowski, M. (eds) (2009) *The European Public Sphere and the Media: Europe in crisis*. Basingstoke: Palgrave Macmillan.

Tufte, E.R (1983) *The Visual Display of Quantitative Information*. Cheshire, CT: Graphics Press.

Van Dijk, T.A. (1985) *Handbook of Discourse Analysis: Discourse analysis in society*. Orlando, FL: Academic Press.

Van Dijk, T.A. (1993) 'Principles of discourse analysis'. *Discourse & Society*, 4(2), 249–283.

Van Dijk, T.A. (1998) *Ideology: A Multidisciplinary Approach*. London: Sage.

van Leeuwen, T. (1999a) 'The representation of social actors'. In C.R. Caldas-Coulthard and M. Coulthard (eds), *Texts and Practices – Readings in Critical Discourse Analysis*, pp. 32–71. London: Routledge.

van Leeuwen, T. (1999b) *Speech, Music, Sound*. Basingstoke: Macmillan.

van Leeuwen, T. (2005) *Introducing Social Semiotics*. London: Routledge.

van Leeuwen, T. (2008a) 'New forms of writing, new visual competencies'. *Visual Studies*, 23(2), 130–135.

van Leeuwen, T. (2008b) *Discourse and Practice*. London: Routledge.

van Leeuwen, T. (2016) 'A social semiotic theory of synesthesia? A discussion paper'. *Hermes*, 55, 105–119.

van Leeuwen, T. and Jewitt, C. (2001) (eds) *Handbook of Visual Analysis*. London: Sage.

van Leeuwen, T. and Wodak, R. (1999) 'Legitimizing immigration control: A discourse-historical analysis'. *Discourse Studies*, 1(1), 83–119.

Ventura, I. (2015) 'A semiotic roadmap for packaging design'. In G. Rossolatos (ed.), *Handbook of Brand Semiotics*, pp. 200–236. Kassel: Kassel University Press.

Voloshinov, V. (1973) *Marxism and the Philosophy of Language*. New York: Seminar Press.

Wagner, K. (2015) 'Reading packages: Social semiotics on the shelf', *Visual Communication,* 14(2), 193–220.

Weisser, A.S. (2006) 'Little red school house, what now? Two centuries of American public school architecture'. *Journal of Planning History*, 5(3), 196–217.

Willis, P. (1977) *Learning to Labour: How working class kids get working class jobs*. New York: Columbia University Press.

Wodak, R. and Meyer, M. (eds) (2016) *Methods of Critical Discourse Studies*. Los Angeles: Sage.

Young, K. (1982) 'Edgework: frame and boundary in the phenomenology of narrative communication'. *Semiotica*, 21, 292–310.

INDEX